IMAGES
*of America*

# OHIO COUNTY
## INDIANA

IMAGES
*of America*

# OHIO COUNTY
## INDIANA

William J. Dichtl

ARCADIA
PUBLISHING

ISBN 978-0-7385-1883-1

Published by Arcadia Publishing
Charleston, South Carolina

Printed in the United States of America

Library of Congress Catalog Card Number: 2001091375

For all general information contact Arcadia Publishing at:
Telephone 843-853-2070
Fax 843-853-0044
E-Mail sales@arcadiapublishing.com
For customer service and orders:
Toll-Free 1-888-313-2665

Visit us on the Internet at www.arcadiapublishing.com

*To my wife Julie, my children
Lauren and Zachary, and my parents
Bill and Camille*

# Contents

# INTRODUCTION

Ohio County has a rich history just like every other county in America. The different personalities and events make it our own wonderful history. The first recorded history of white Americans in the territory that would become Ohio County refers to Col. Archibald Lochery in 1781. Colonel Lochery was leading a contingent of about 100 soldiers during the Revolutionary War when he established a camp at the mouth of what would become Laughery Creek on the night of August 23. The colonel was attempting to connect with Gen. George Rogers Clark. On August 24, a group of Native Americans lead by Simon Girty and Chief Joseph Brandt caught up with the colonel and his men. A battle took place during which Colonel Lochery and 36 of his men were killed outright. All but 12 of the remaining men were taken captive.

About 17 years later, the Fulton family ventured to this area. John and his son Samuel with their families came down the Ohio River via flatboats. They liked the area and decided to stay. They were relatives of Robert Fulton, the inventor of the first steamboat.

In 1799, another colonel arrived in the area. This time Col. Benjamin Chambers came to survey the lands under a commission he received from the administration of President John Adams. Colonel Chambers fell in love with the area, purchased the land he surveyed, and built a house.

John James and his family moved west from Maryland stopping in Pittsburgh and Cincinnati. While staying with friends in Lawrenceburg, Indiana, he finally came to the place he would call Rising Sun and home. He purchased the whole survey of more than 1,000 acres from Colonel Chambers (and his house) in 1811.

On May 30, 1814, John's son Pinkney surveyed the land that would become the town of Rising Sun. How was the name of Rising Sun chosen? There are a few possibilities including that there was a tavern sign at the ferry landing below First Street that read "the Rising Sun Ferry." More likely was that John James enjoyed the rising sun each morning over the hills of Kentucky and therefore established the name.

At this time Rising Sun was part of Dearborn County. Local citizen Col. Abel C. Pepper, who oversaw the removal of the Native Americans from Indiana in 1837, was instrumental in creating Ohio County. After years of pursuing the matter it became official on January 4, 1844. The citizens of Rising Sun supported Lawrenceburg as the county seat of Dearborn County after the county seat was taken from Lawrenceburg and moved to Wilmington. By so doing, Lawrenceburg supported the creation of Ohio County as a county. It is the smallest county in the United States, measuring only 87 square miles.

The photographs used in the book are from the collection of the Ohio County Historical Society. I would like to express my appreciation to the board of directors of the historical society in allowing me to put this book together. I must thank Mary Anne and Dillion Dorrell, both board members, for verifying the historical accuracy of the text. A special thank you goes to my wife, Julie, for proofreading the text and supporting me in this endeavor.

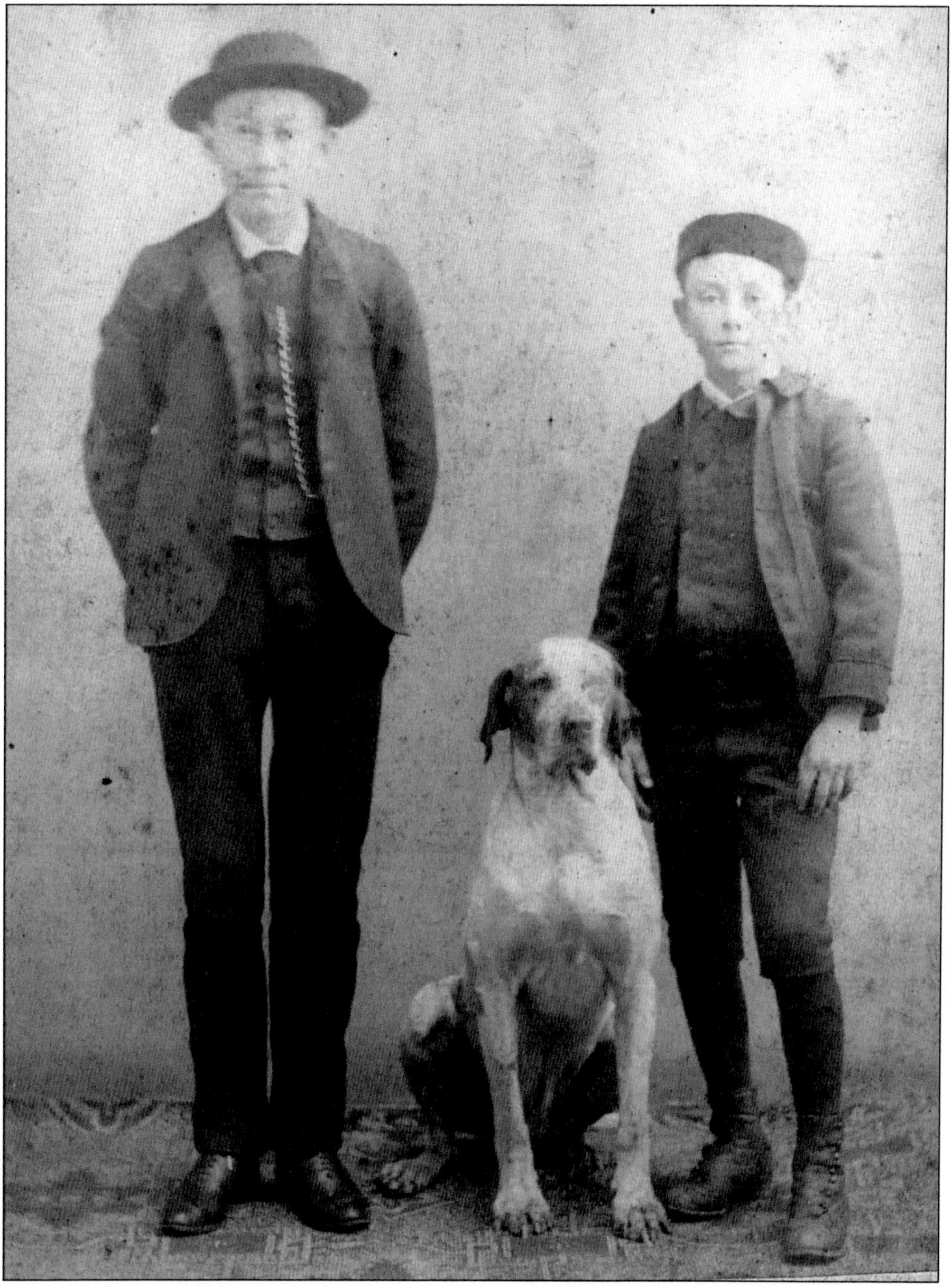

**Row and Harry Whitlock, c. 1881.** John William Whitlock (nicknamed Row) is the boy on the left with his brother Harry on the right. J.W. was born on May 2, 1871. From an early age he tinkered with mechanical things that would lead to several inventions. About 1900 he invented the Darby, the first coin-operated gaming machines. The Darby, a horse racing game, was placed on steamboats for the patrons' pleasure.

# One

# J.W. Whitlock, Chairs, Boats, and More

William Henry Whitlock's son, J.W., was born in 1871. When he was old enough, he joined the family business and learned the furniture and milling trade. At the age of 29, he opened the J.W. Whitlock and Co. on the northeast corner of Walnut and First streets. He manufactured well-crafted furniture including chairs, tables, and lamps. Eventually the company needed more space, and in 1914 purchased the vacant Clore Plow Works buildings. They were right across the street from the furniture factory, sawmill, and lumberyard.

One of the things that J.W. is best known for is his *Hoosier Boy* hydroplane. He raced these boats in Peoria, Illinois; Toledo, Ohio; Buffalo, New York; and in Cincinnati. He won many trophies and established records including a speed record from Cincinnati to Louisville and back again in just over a mile a minute. He did the 267-mile trip in 267 minutes and 49 seconds, a record that still stands today.

J.W. was an inventor and civic minded individual. He invented the first coin-operated jukebox and a coin-operated gambling game called the Darby. In the early 1900s, he organized Row's Band to play for civic events. Row was his nickname.

In 1935, J.W. Whitlock's death was a significant loss for the community. His children continued running the company, focusing on making chairs only. But by the late 1960s the company could no longer compete. In 1968, the factory that produced many quality chairs closed, and the buildings on the west side of Walnut Street were sold to the Ohio County Historical Society. The factory, sawmill, and lumberyard were razed in 1978 to make way for the senior housing center.

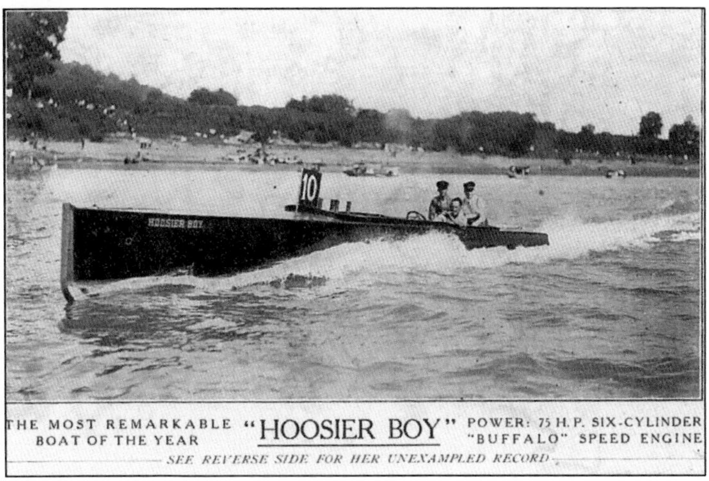


**Hoosier Boy, c. 1924.** This card advertised "Buffalo" High Speed Engines for racing boats. The *Hoosier Boy* owned and raced by J.W. Whitlock set records in several races while using the "Buffalo" engine. The back of the card claims that the remarkable performances of the *Hoosier Boy* conclusively demonstrate the efficiency of the engine for raceboats.

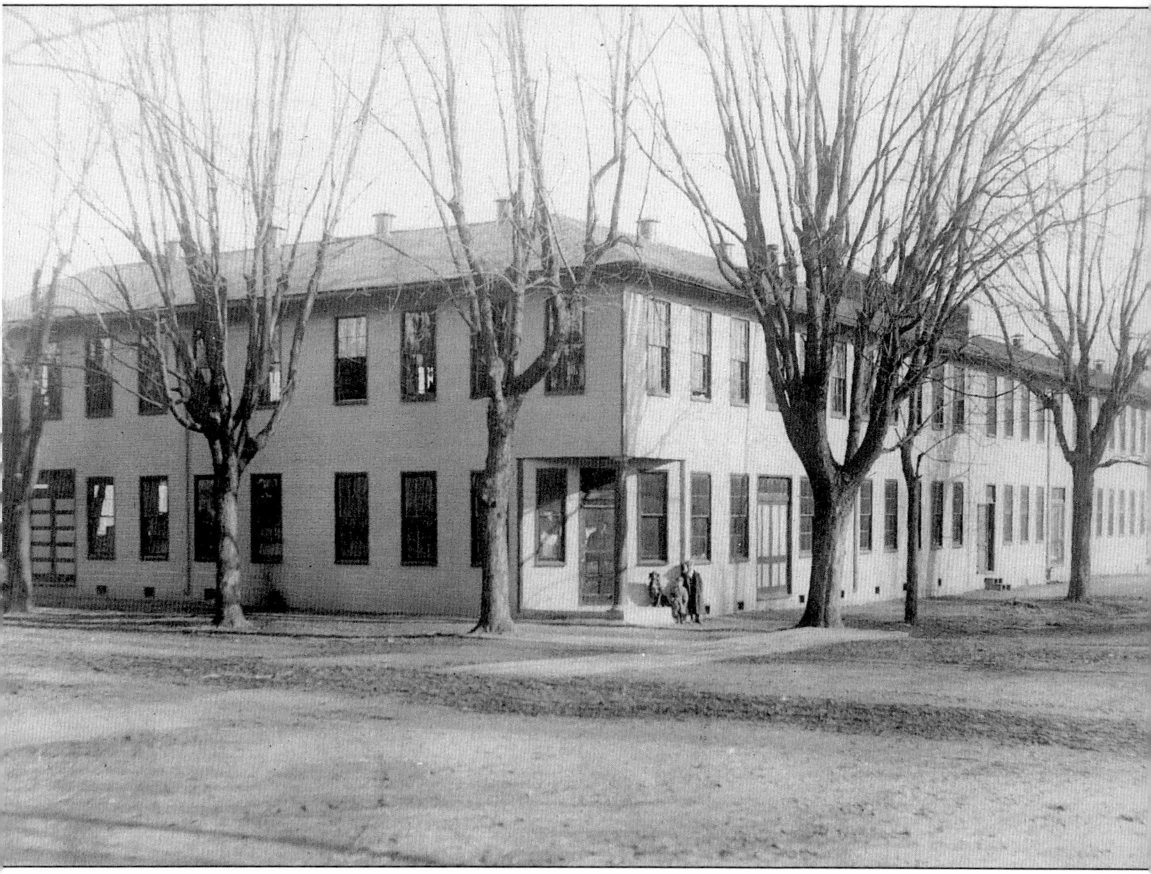

**WHITLOCK FURNITURE FACTORY, C. 1930.** From 1900 until it closed in 1967, the Whitlock Furniture Factory manufactured furniture. The furniture suited a variety of tastes from fine pieces to ordinary everyday oak dining room chairs. The furniture was shipped throughout the United States. It is said that Franklin D. Roosevelt even had Whitlock furniture.

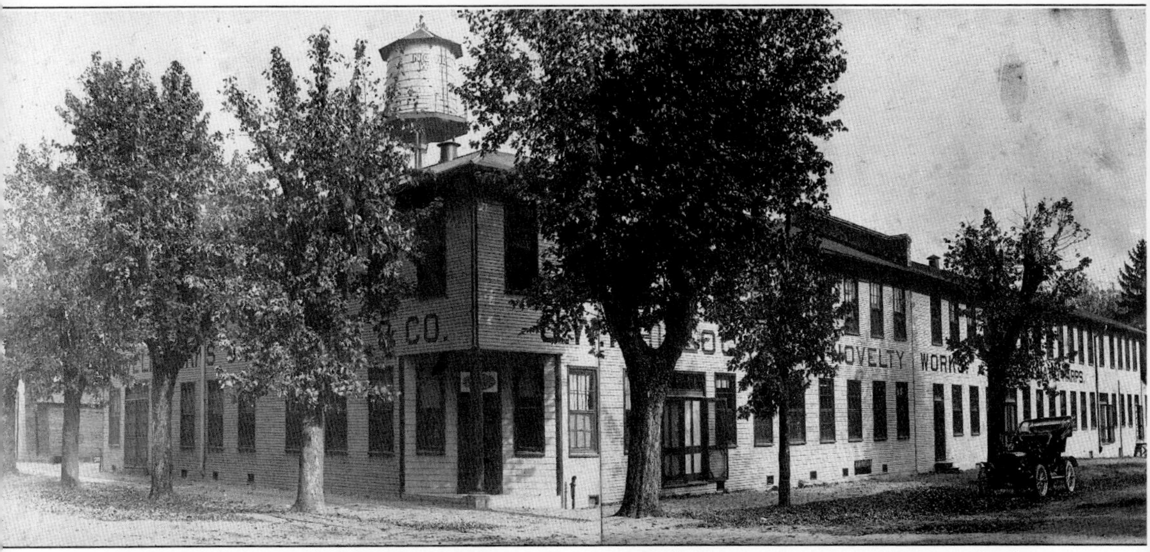


**J.W. Whitlock Chair Factory, c. 1907.** John T. Whitlock came to Rising Sun with the early settlers. He and his son, William H., started a sawmill located at First and Popular streets. Always in need of timber, William H. placed advertisements in the newspaper seeking ash, oak, hickory, and elm, for which he was willing to pay top dollar on the spot in cash. Today this is the site of the Hoosier Boy Apartments.

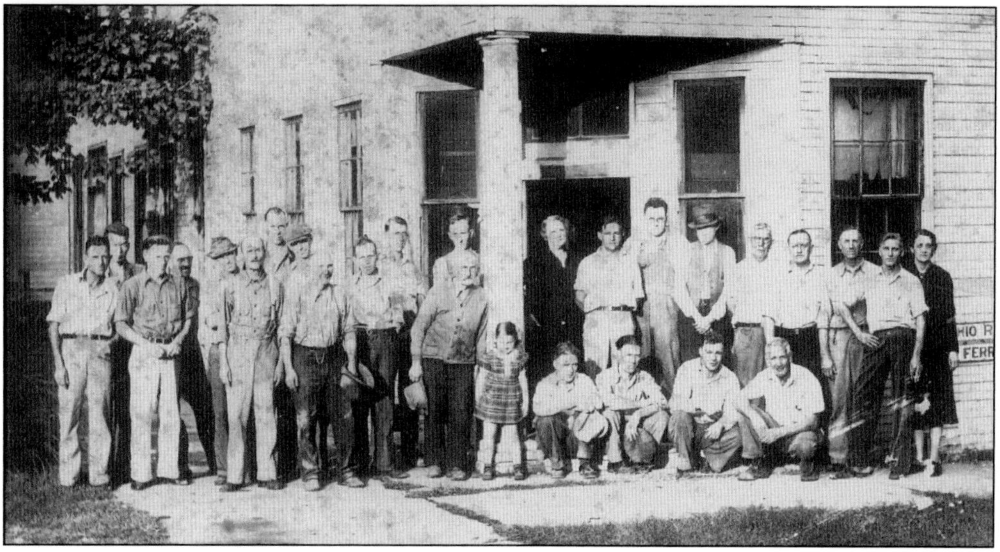

**WHITLOCK FURNITURE FACTORY, C. 1930.** The Whitlock factory survived the Depression in part because of the excellent craftsmanship of the furniture they produced. The factory played a significant role in stabilizing Rising Sun's economy. Three of his children are in the picture. In the back row, fourth from the right is Dean Whitlock; second from right is Stewart Whitlock; and to his right is Mildred Whitlock. Mildred Whitlock married Robert Neaman (seventh from the left) and for a time they ran the factory.

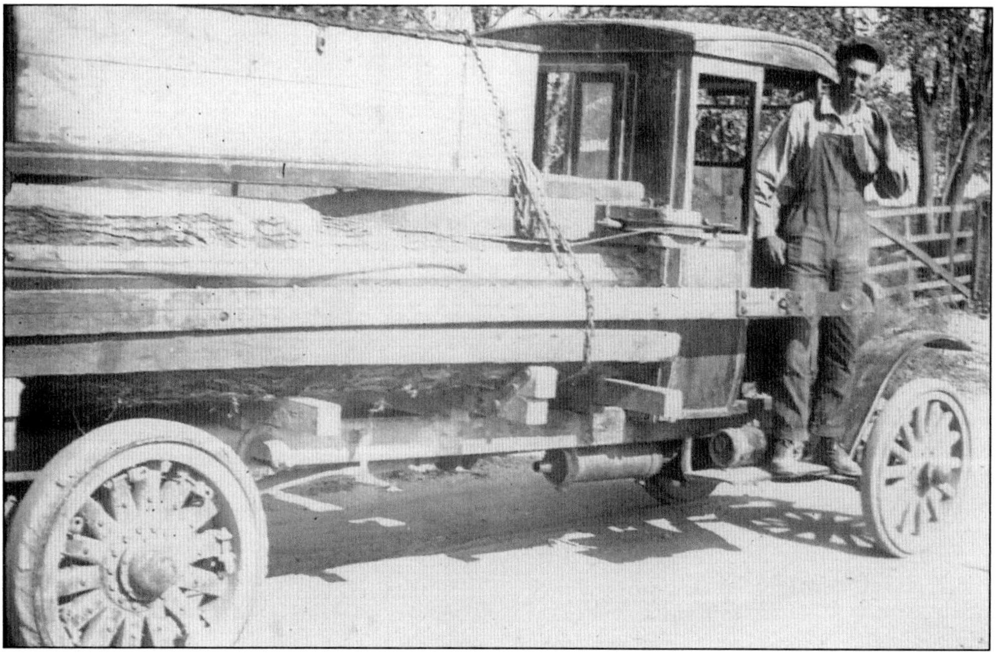

**J.W. WHITLOCK LOG TRUCK, 1920.** To continue having a supply of lumber for the furniture factory, J.W. Whitlock purchased 247 acres of land lying west of Aberdeen for $11,200. Some of the finest oak timber found in Ohio County covered approximately 100 of these acres. In the early years, a horse-drawn log cart (housed in the Historical Society Museum) hauled logs to the factory. By 1920, Harry Nieman, employed by Whitlock, drove a truck to haul the logs.

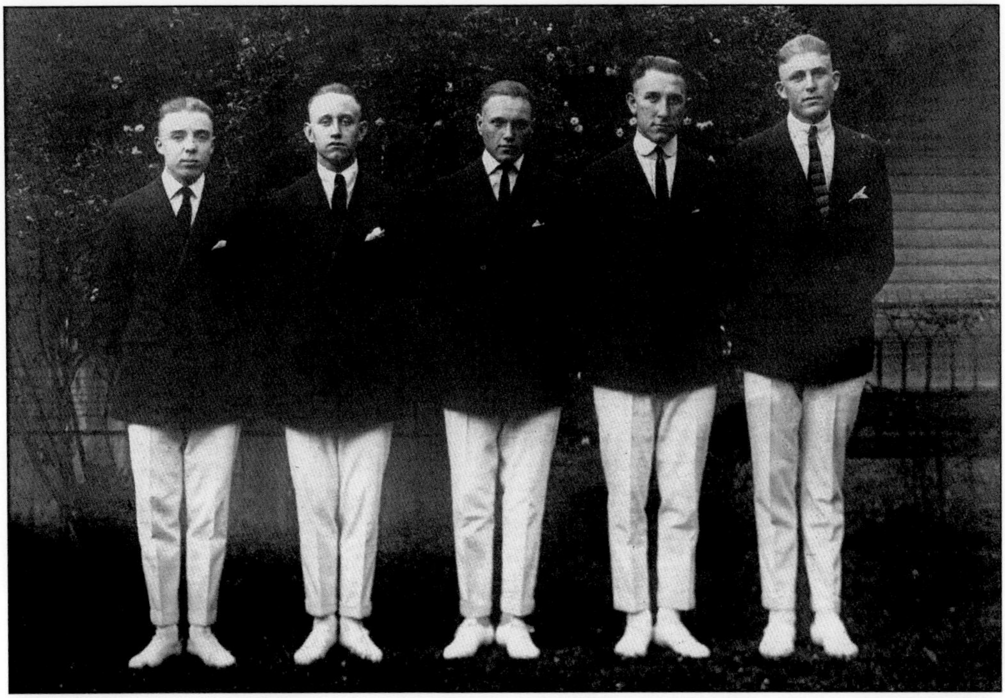

**Dean Whitlock, 1921.** These five are sharply dressed graduates of Rising Sun High School. Dean Whitlock is the young man second from the left. Dean was one of three sons of J.W. Whitlock. He later joined in the family business. Upon the death of his father in 1935, Dean headed the business until his death in 1958. Dean's brother, Stewart, assumed the presidency of the firm until his death in 1966.

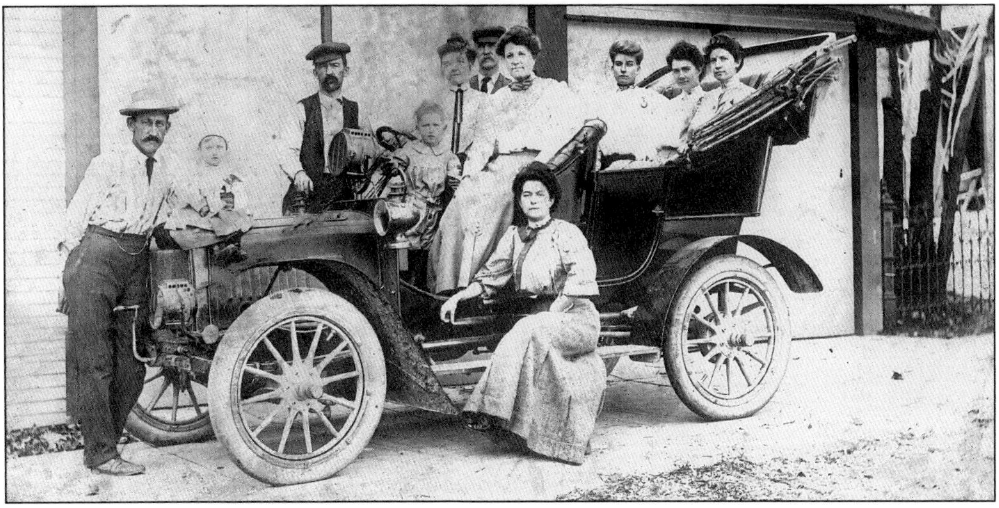

**Automobile, c. 1906.** The dapper looking gentleman to the left of the automobile is J.W. Whitlock. It looks as if he is waiting for the photographer to finish taking the picture so that he can crank up the convertible and take the crew for a tour. Also in the picture from the right of J.W. is Mildred Whitlock Neaman, Harry Hoffner, Dean Whitlock, Alice Stewart Whitlock, Percy Tumey, Kate Kelso Steele, Hattie Dugle, Jessie Miller Hannah, Lottie Scott Daly, and Susie Ernst (on the running board).

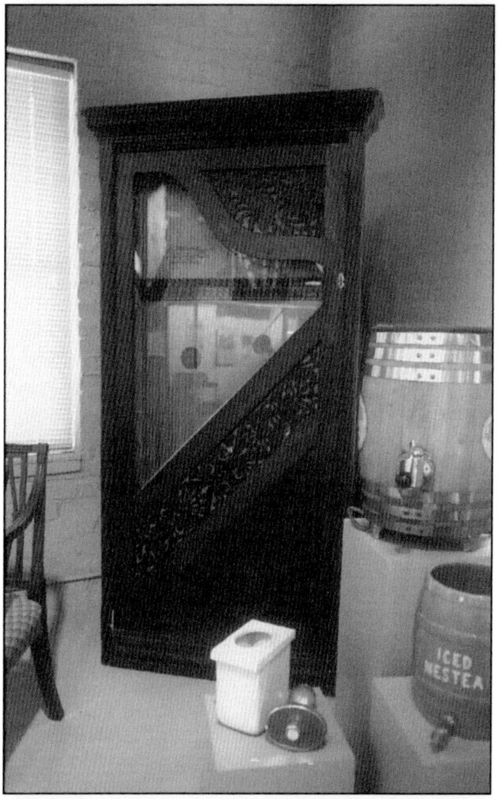


**AUTOHARP, 2001.** At the age of 28, J.W. Whitlock patented the Automatic Harp in 1899. Impressed by a demonstration of the Autoharp, Howard Wurlitzer offered a contract to J.W. to manufacture the Autoharp. The Wurlitzer name appeared on the Autoharp manufactured in Rising Sun. A separate frame building was constructed to fill the Wurlitzer initial order of 1000 harps. A Wurlitzer advertisement said the harp including one roll of music cost $750. The large music rolls were made in Rising Sun by J.W.'s wife, Alice, who operated the machine.

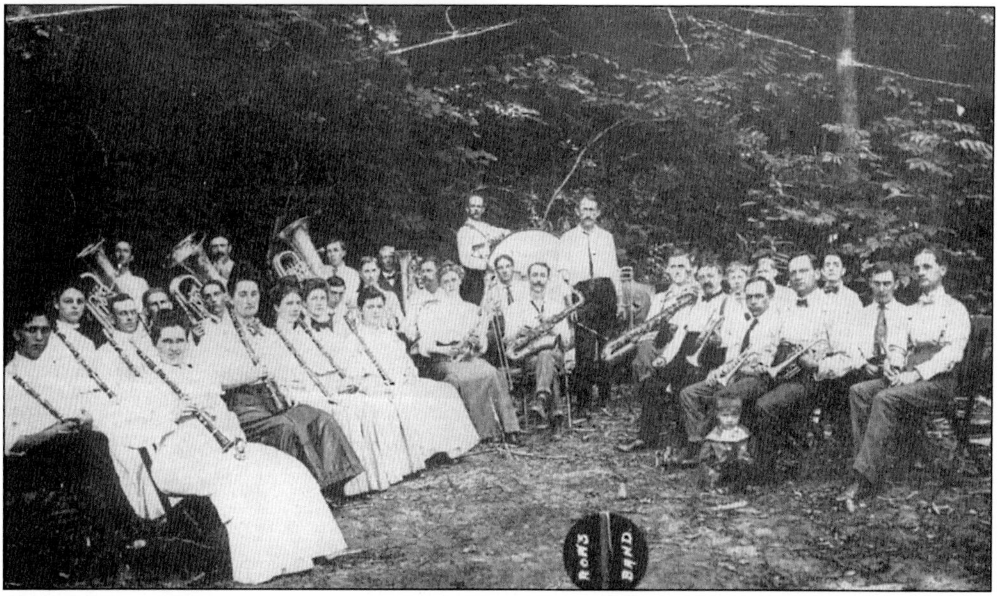


**ROW'S BAND, 1909.** While in his late 20s, J.W. "Row" Whitlock was a significant player in musical circles. He formed his own band called "Row's Band" and they performed for many civic functions. In the early years the band was relatively small, but later it grew to be a more than 30-piece band. In 1909, at least six women were part of the band lead by Whitlock (standing to the right of the drum).

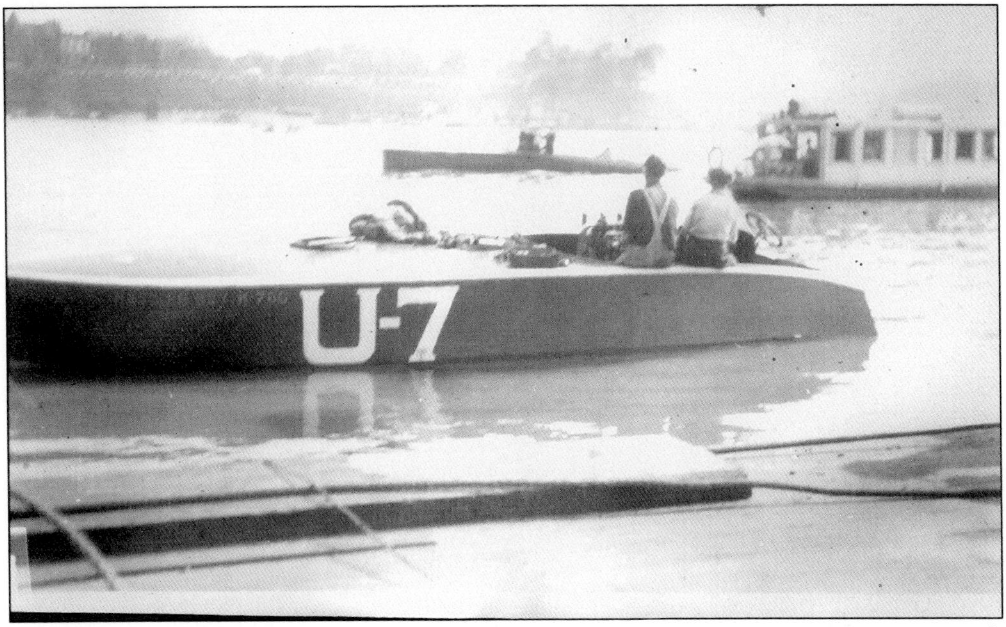


**J.W. WHITLOCK AND THE *HOOSIER BOY*, C. 1924.** Covering a nineteen-year racing career with the *Hoosier Boy* series, Whitlock lost only two races. Establishing a speed record was a goal that Whitlock achieved on October 9, 1924. On this day he raced from Cincinnati to Louisville and back again traveling 267 miles in 267 minutes and 49 seconds. Though he set a record, he was somewhat disappointed that he did not achieve a mile a minute. He once commented "If we had not run into the wake of half a dozen towboats with barges, we would have made it in 60 flat or better."

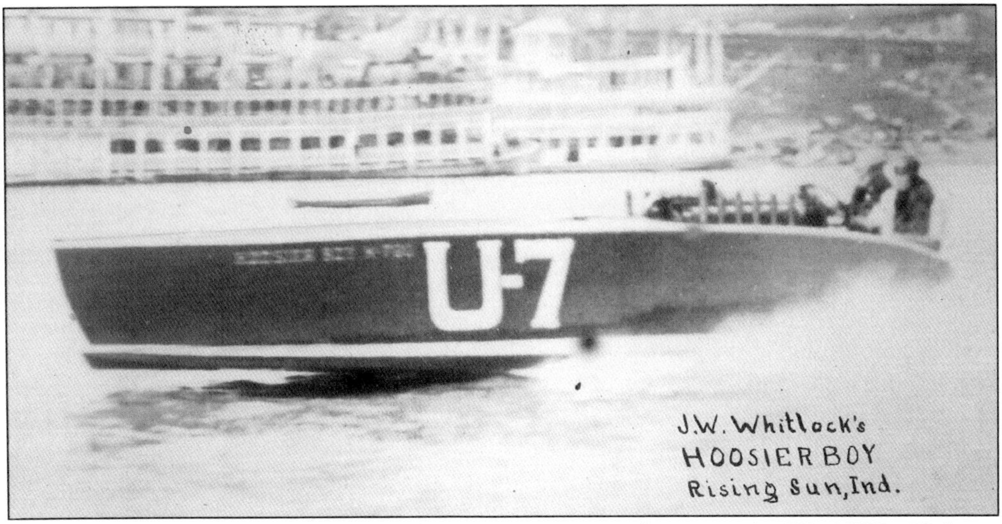


***HOOSIER BOY*, C. 1925.** The power for the *Hoosier Boy* came from a surplus World War I Liberty aircraft engine. The 12-cylinder engine had 440 horsepower. The Liberty engine did not see use only for the *Hoosier Boy*, but also in the *Big Brown Bear* necessary to transport workers through the swamps of these areas. J.W. was approached to build a swamp buggy. He developed the *Big Brown Bear* with two Liberty engines standing high in back of the 69-foot- long craft. For whatever reason the boat was never used.

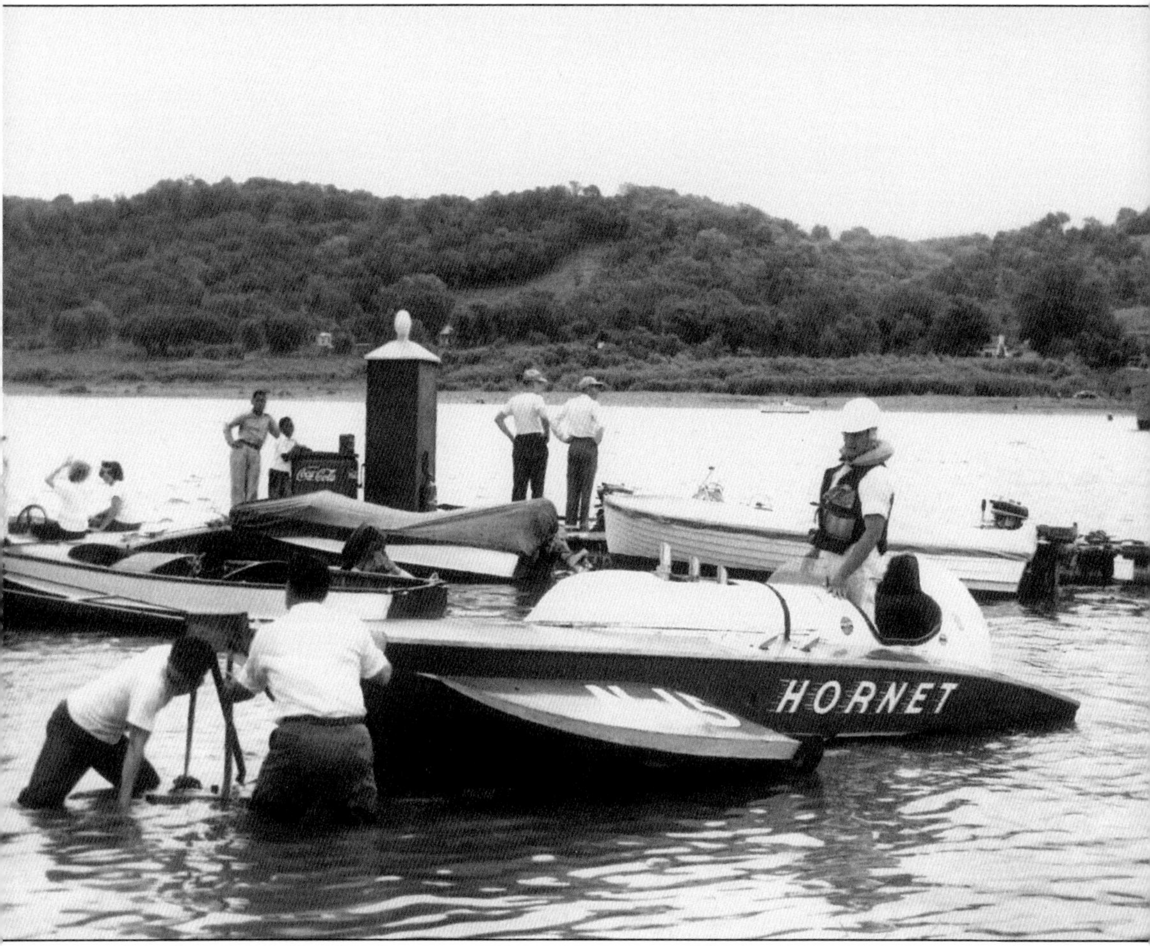


**1950 Regatta.** The first Regatta in Rising Sun was on July 4, 1925. A crowd estimated at more than 20,000 caused great excitement and the promise of another regatta the following year. Following a tragic plane crash that killed Harry Danbury and Raymond Hodges on July 4, 1927, the regatta was canceled. J.W. Whitlock, in the *Hoosier Boy*, was going to race an airplane, when the plane crash killed the two Rising Sun youths and put the pilot in the hospital for a long time. In 1948, the regatta returned to Rising Sun. It was held until 1950 and again briefly in the early 1980s. Since 1998, the Community Heritage Promotions, Inc. have organized the Rising Sun Regatta held in September. The regatta features hydroplane racing similar to the regattas Mr. Whitlock competed in during the 1920s.

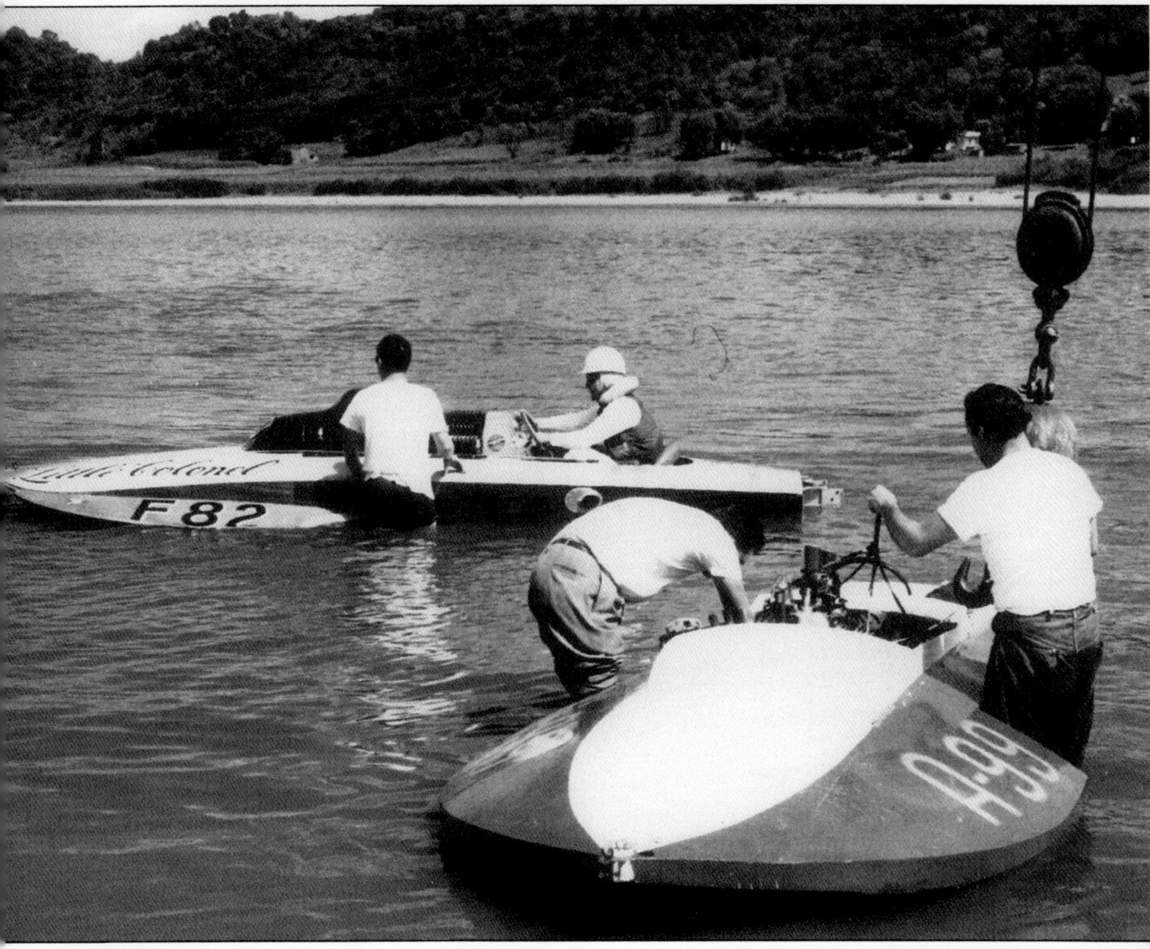


**1950 Regatta.** The 1950 Regatta held on Sunday, August 20, featured race boats primarily from the Midwest. Some came as far away as Kansas and California. The boat in the background is the *Little Colonel* driven by Bob Smith of Cincinnati, Ohio. The *Little Colonel* was one of 11 in the division 1-225 cubic inch motor category.

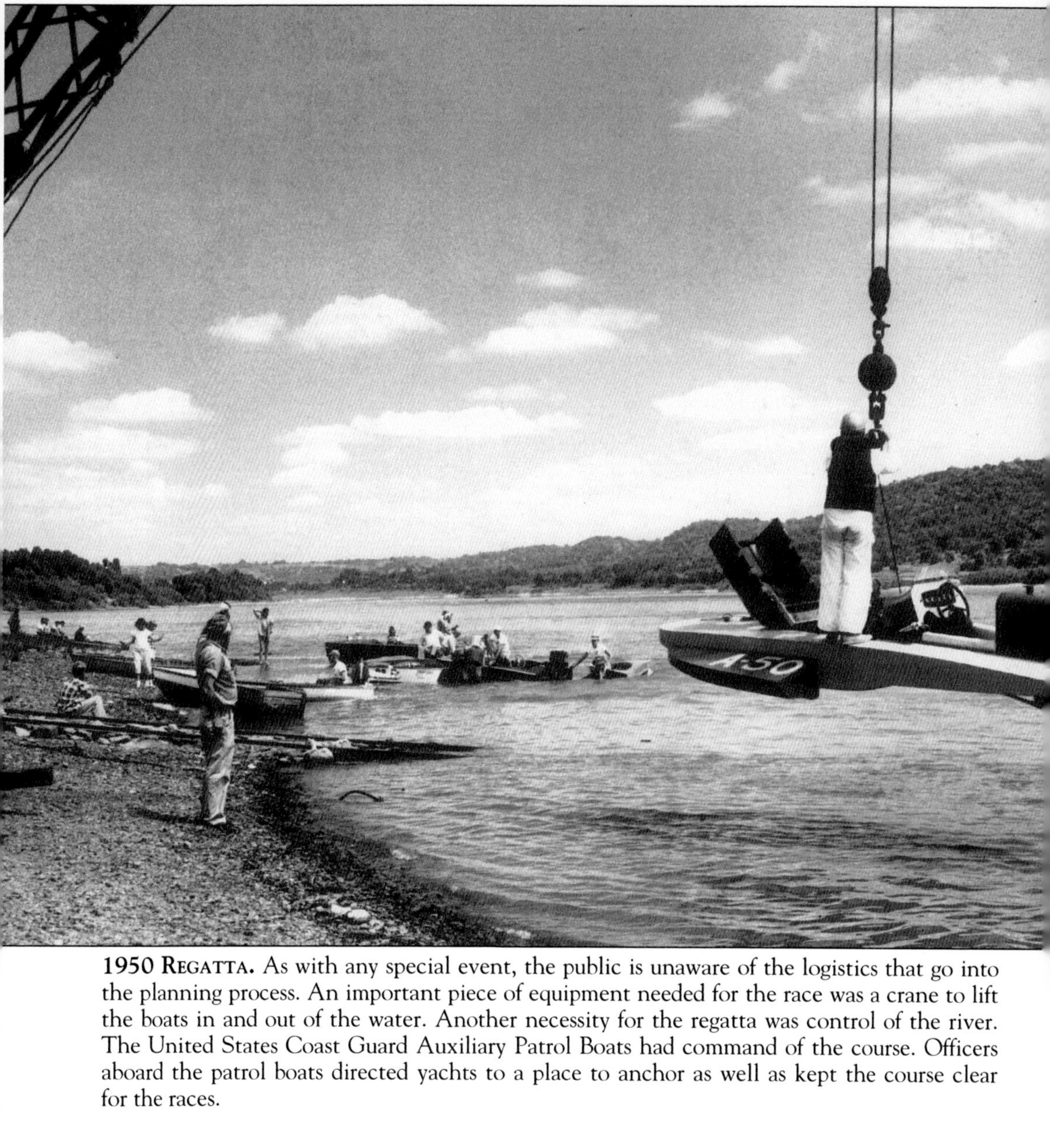


**1950 Regatta.** As with any special event, the public is unaware of the logistics that go into the planning process. An important piece of equipment needed for the race was a crane to lift the boats in and out of the water. Another necessity for the regatta was control of the river. The United States Coast Guard Auxiliary Patrol Boats had command of the course. Officers aboard the patrol boats directed yachts to a place to anchor as well as kept the course clear for the races.

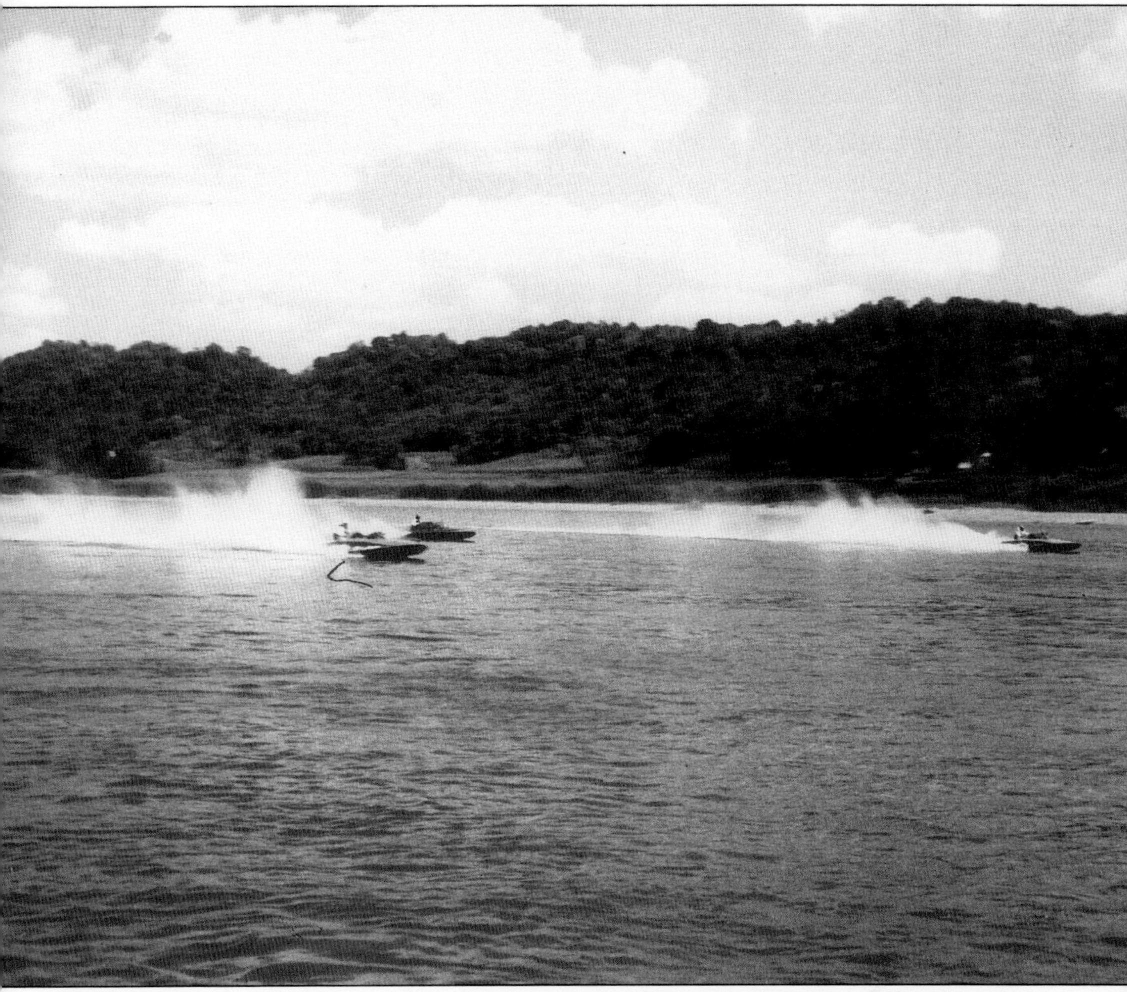

**1950 Regatta.** The 1950 Lions Club Regatta was the third annual event sanctioned by the American Power Boat Association to be held in Rising Sun. In races with two or more heats (the 1950 race had three heats), the final standings were determined by points awarded during each heat. First place received 400 points and tenth 30 points. In each heat the boats raced 5 miles.

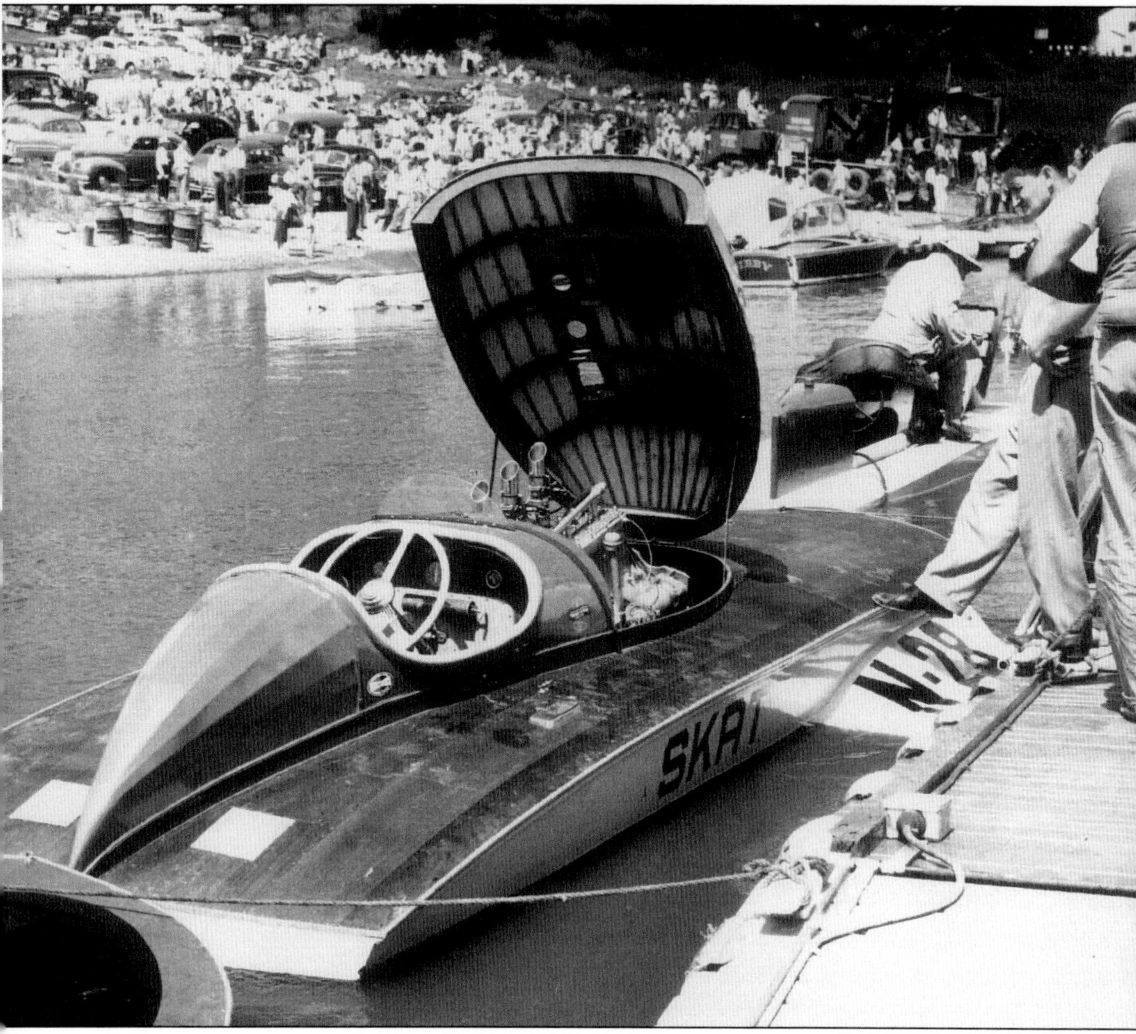


**1950 Regatta.** This photograph shows a nice view of part of the estimated crowd of 2,500 to see *Skat* which was one of approximately 20 hydroplanes entered in the regatta. Some of the other boat names included *Wild Goose*, *Skid-Do*, *Tooth & Toe Nail*, and *Gee Whiz*.

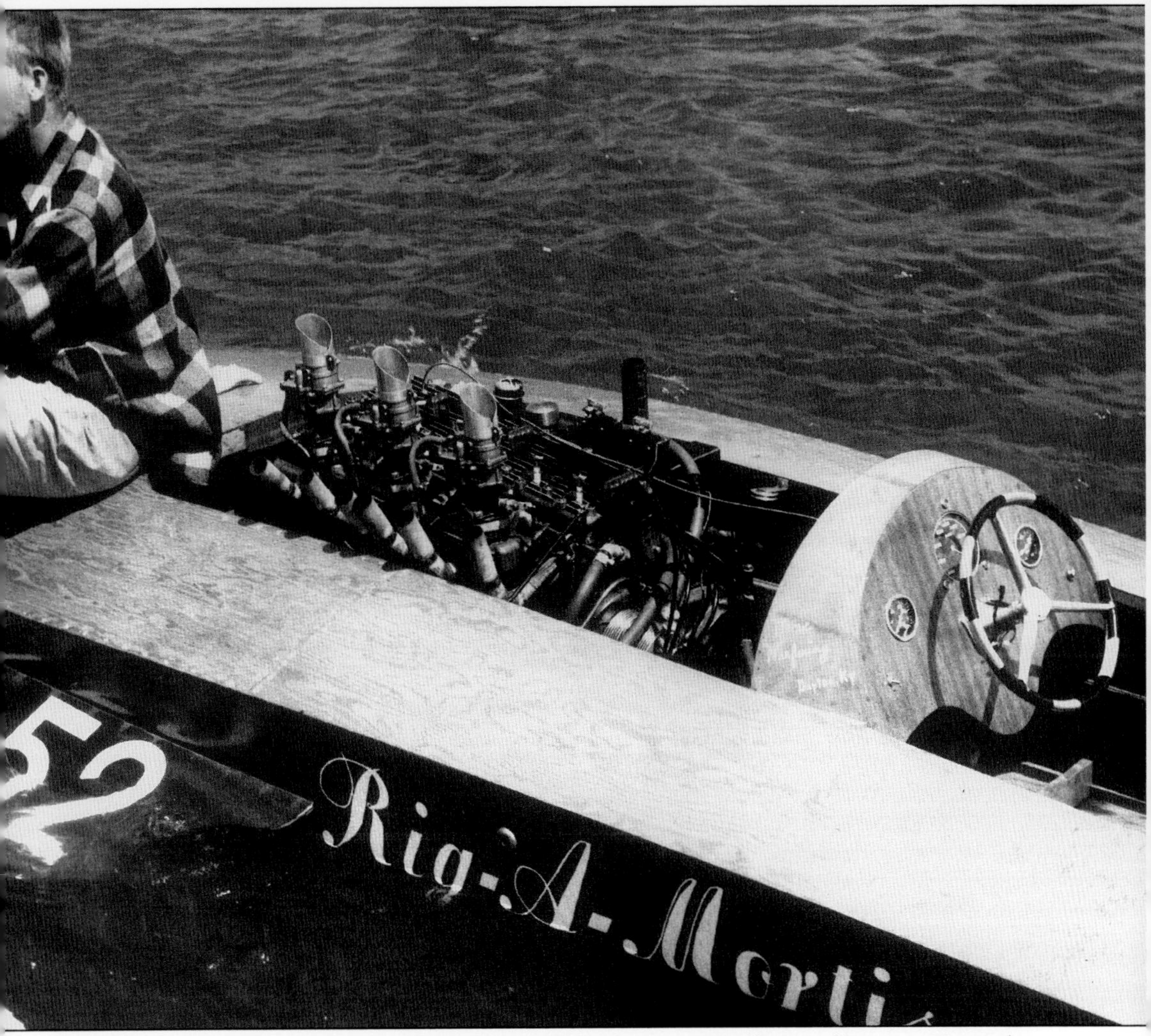


**1950 Regatta.** The hydroplane *Rig-A-Mortis* driven by Mac Wieffering of Dayton, Kentucky, finished second in the inboard free-for-all race. He accomplished this with a speed of 60.606 miles per hour for the 10-mile race. Back in 1924, J.W. Whitlock went 267 miles at a speed of just under 60 miles per hour, driving without relief.

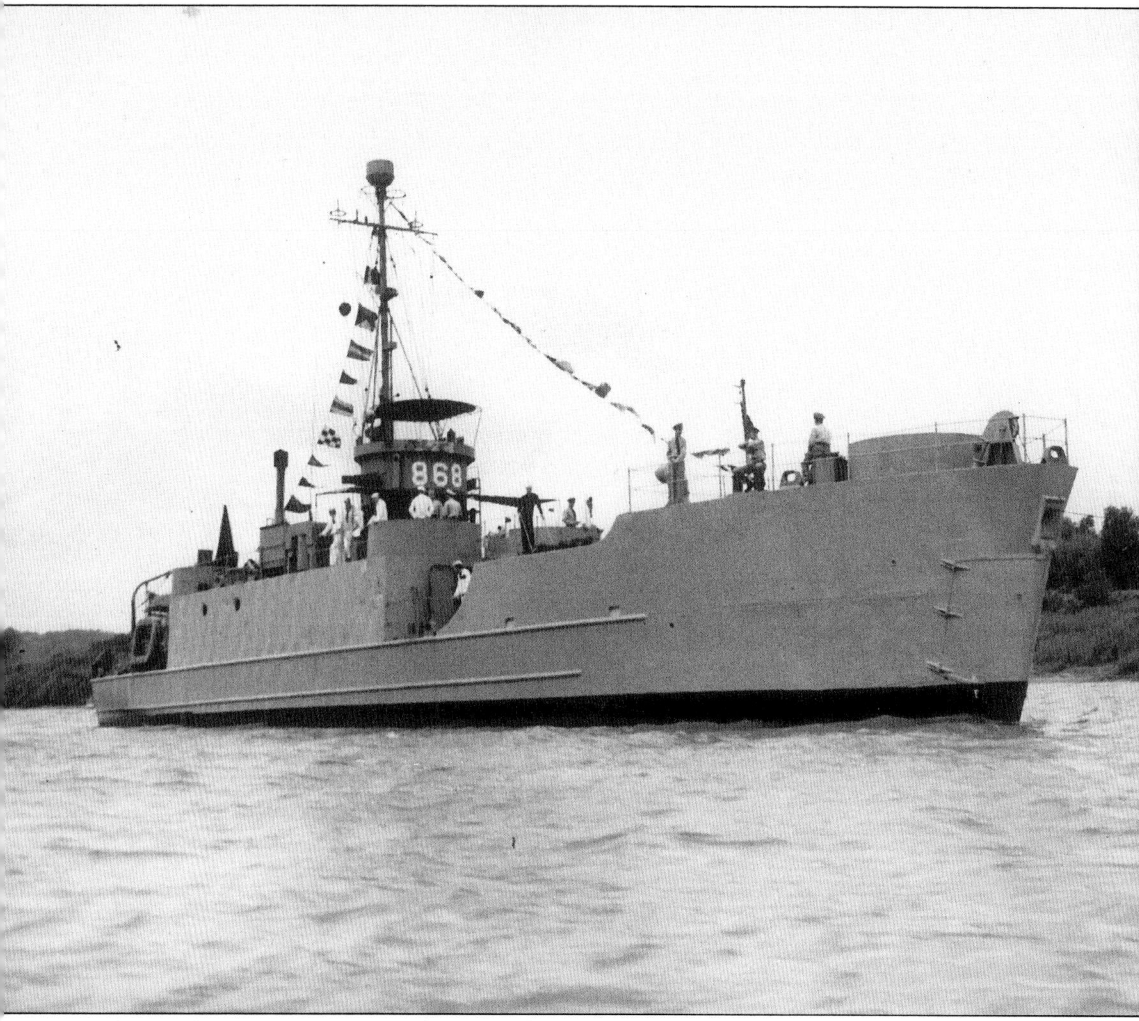

**Coast Guard Ship, 1948.** The United States Coast Guard ship sails in the Ohio River near Rising Sun. Imagine the shock the citizens of Ohio County had when they came to the river and saw the ship! The Coast Guard was here to assist with the 1948 regatta. The newspaper reported a man was pulled out of the river after his raceboat capsized. After an absence of more than 20 years since the last regatta it was again held in Rising Sun.

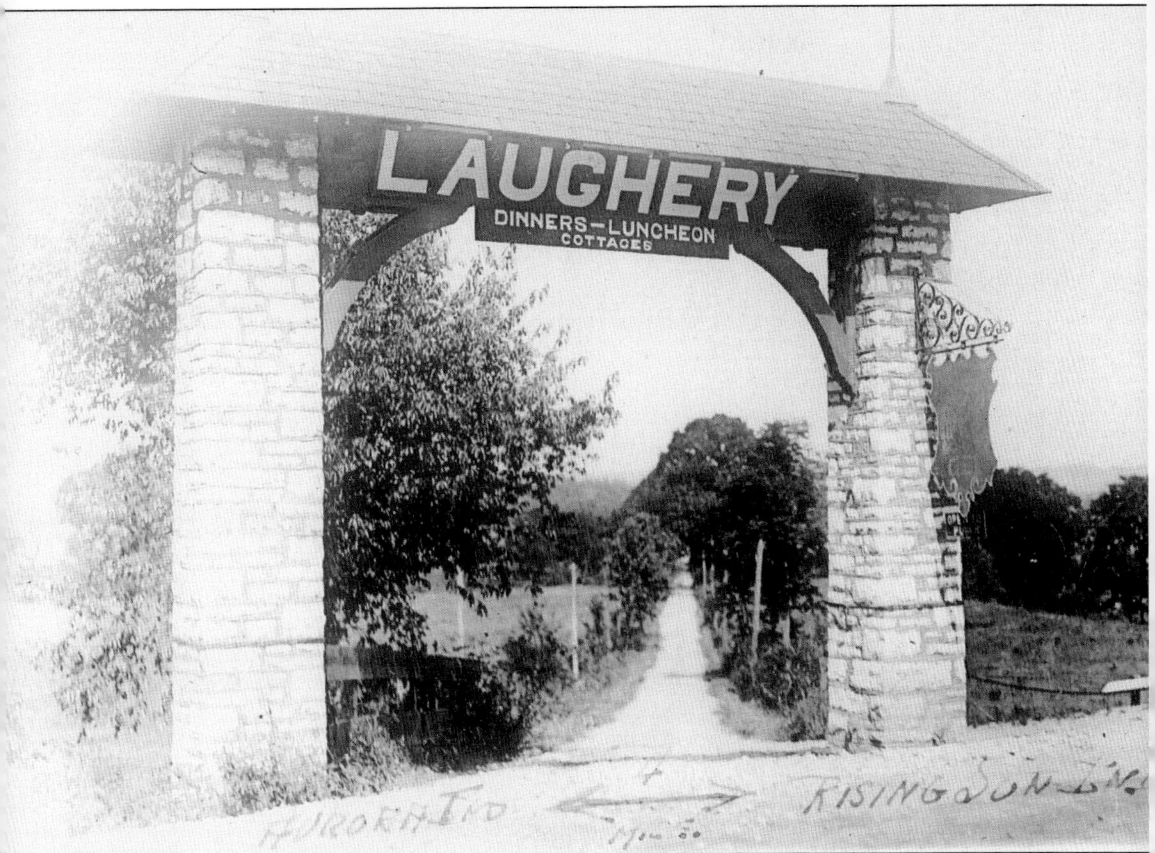


**LAUGHREY CLUB, c. 1930.** The land for the Laughrey Club, located halfway between Aurora and Rising Sun, had been purchased from O.H. Pate. George B. Cox, political boss of Cincinnati, and August Garry Herrman, owner of the Cincinnati Reds Base Ball team, owned the club. The club, built in 1900 on four acres, became famous for the large lavish parties given for members from Cincinnati, and Covington, Kentucky, and on occasion, some of the local citizenry. It was also used as a training camp for the baseball club.

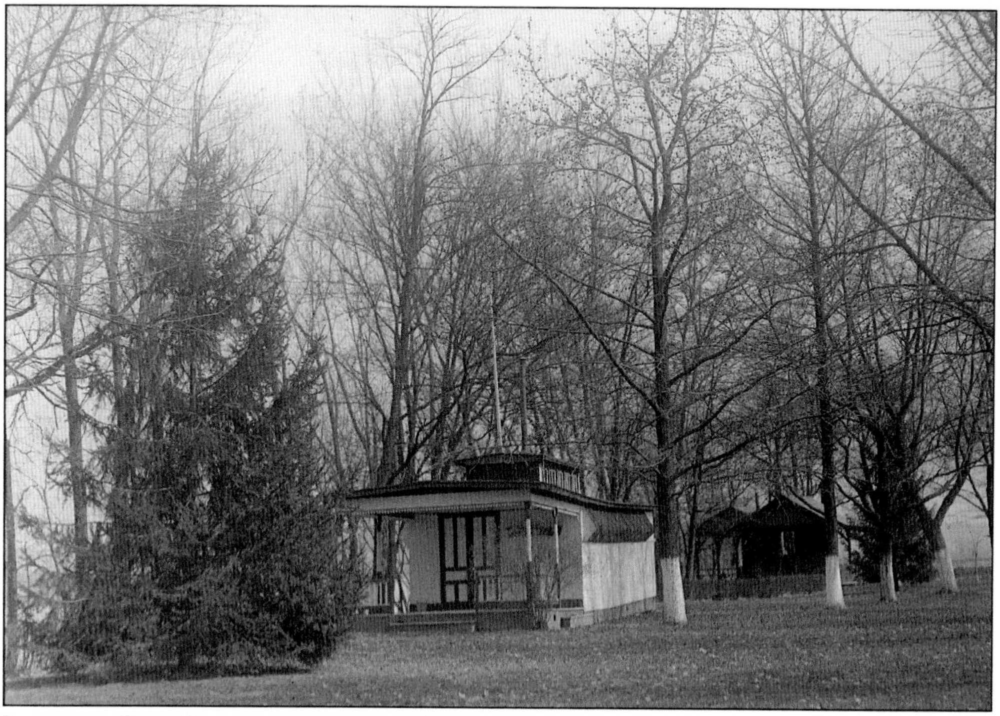

**LAUGHREY CLUB COTTAGES, C. 1930.** The club built on Laughrey Island in the Ohio River was the site of many large parties and meetings. Riverboats also stopped at the island to drop off and pick up passengers. J.W. Whitlock purchased the club in 1926 and made the club available as a public entertainment facility. In 1933, the Veterans of Foreign Wars gathered at the club for a rally. Attendance was estimated at 1,000. Whitlock provided his motor boats *Greyhound* and *Hoosier Girl* for the visitors to enjoy a ride on the Ohio River.

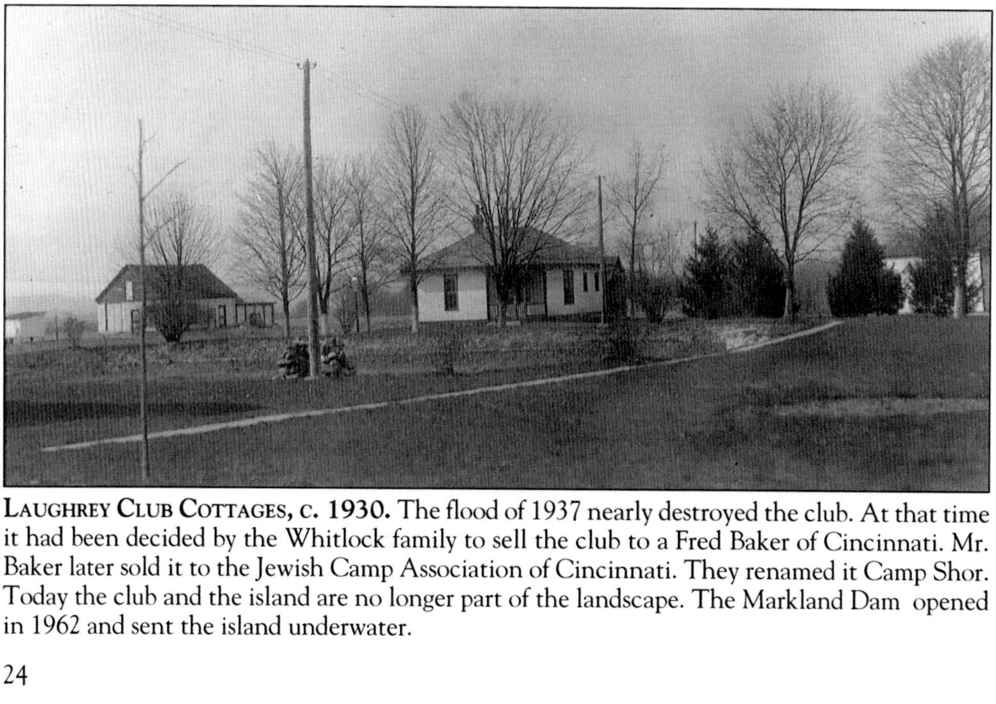

**LAUGHREY CLUB COTTAGES, C. 1930.** The flood of 1937 nearly destroyed the club. At that time it had been decided by the Whitlock family to sell the club to a Fred Baker of Cincinnati. Mr. Baker later sold it to the Jewish Camp Association of Cincinnati. They renamed it Camp Shor. Today the club and the island are no longer part of the landscape. The Markland Dam opened in 1962 and sent the island underwater.

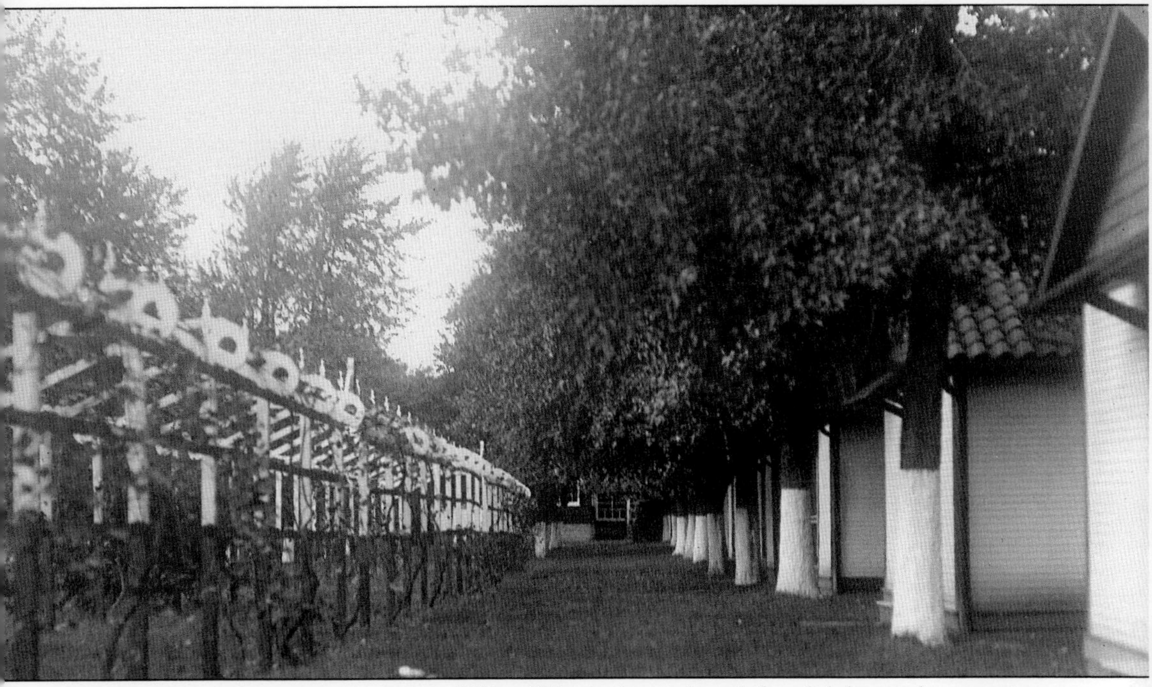

**Laughery Club Cottages, c. 1930.** When Whitlock purchased the club he made extensive renovations. The club operated successfully providing dining room services, dancing, picnicking, and rentals of cabins by the day, week, or month. This photograph shows a row of cabins with an attractive arbor out front. The Jewish Organization reconditioned the cabins and added a swimming pool after purchasing the club from Harry Baker, who did little upkeep during his ownership.

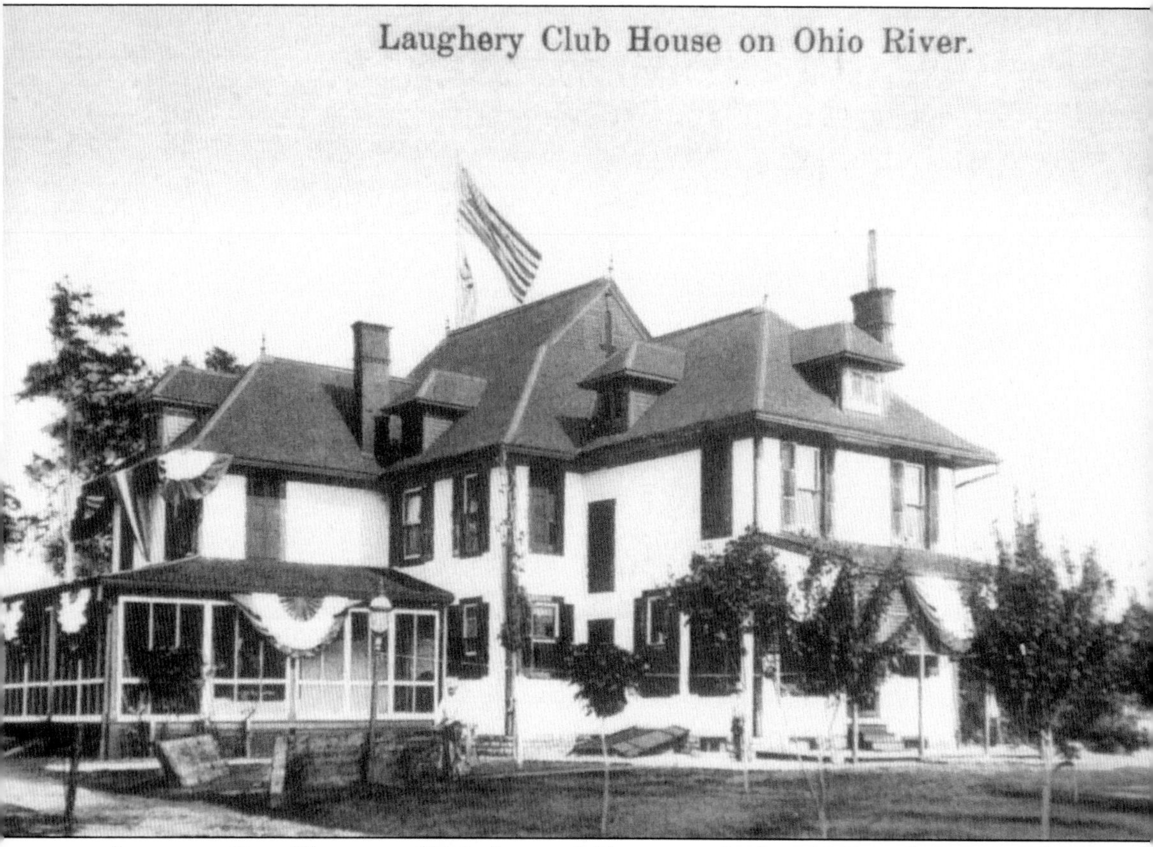


**LAUGHERY CLUB HOUSE, C. 1910.** A new clubhouse was built in 1900, and upon completion contained 32 rooms. The building had 100 acetylene gas jets in the building and five lampposts with gas jets at the front of the main building. At the time the luxury of the clubhouse was compared to the hotel in French Lick. The luxurious modern facility had running water from its own reservoir on the grounds. The reservoir supplied water for baths and toilets as well as fresh water for the kitchen. The National Baseball Commission and the joint committee of the National and American Leagues both met at the club in 1911.

# *Two*

# River Life

The people and businesses of Ohio County relied heavily on the Ohio River for business and pleasure. Those early years settlers came down the Ohio River on flatboats with all their belongings to start a new life. From that point, Rising Sun grew using the river to ship finished products like chairs from J.W. Whitlock and Company and plows and other farm implements from the Clore Plow Works. Farmers brought their produce to the steamboats and flatboats to take to eastern and southern destinations. These same steamboats and flatboats brought raw materials and different finished products here.

The river also provides enjoyment through boating and fishing. Throughout the 1900s till today, the river has been used to hold racing boat regattas. J.W. Whitlock and his *Hoosier Boy* made these regattas popular in the mid-1920s. Everyone has a different way of enjoying the river. A peaceful walk along the river trail in the early morning or evening is relaxing. Sitting on the riverbank at Rising Sun provides a picturesque view of Rabbit Hash, Kentucky, and tree- covered hills. While sitting, one or two tow barges with loads of coal may be seen chugging along. Lucky idlers may spot the beautiful Mississippi Queen cruising by in the early dusk with all the lights aglow.

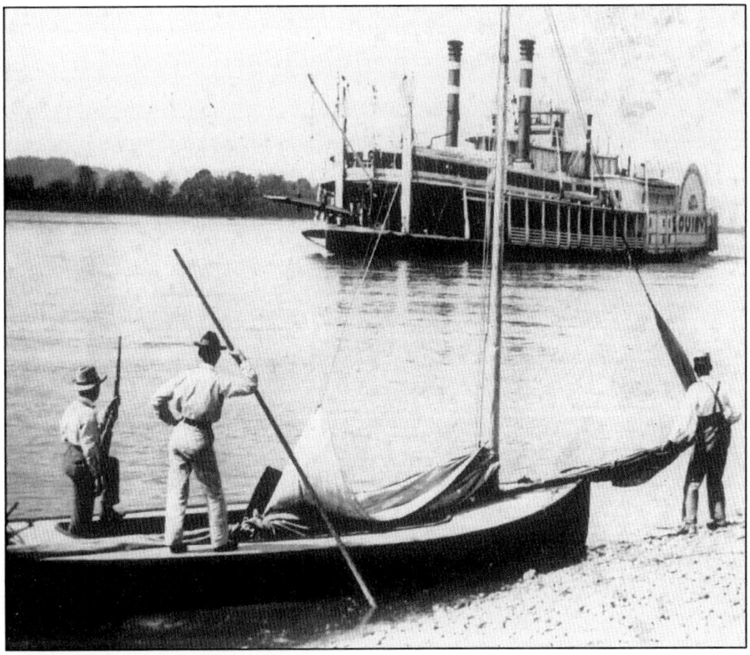

**Sailboat, c. 1915.** The three men in the photograph from left to right are as follows: William Hamburg, J.W. Whitlock, and Harry Whitlock. William Hamburg is holding a gun; it appears that the men are preparing to set sail for a hunting trip on the river. All three men are intently watching the steamer, *City of Louisville*, from the ferry landing. J.W. Whitlock probably built the sailboat.

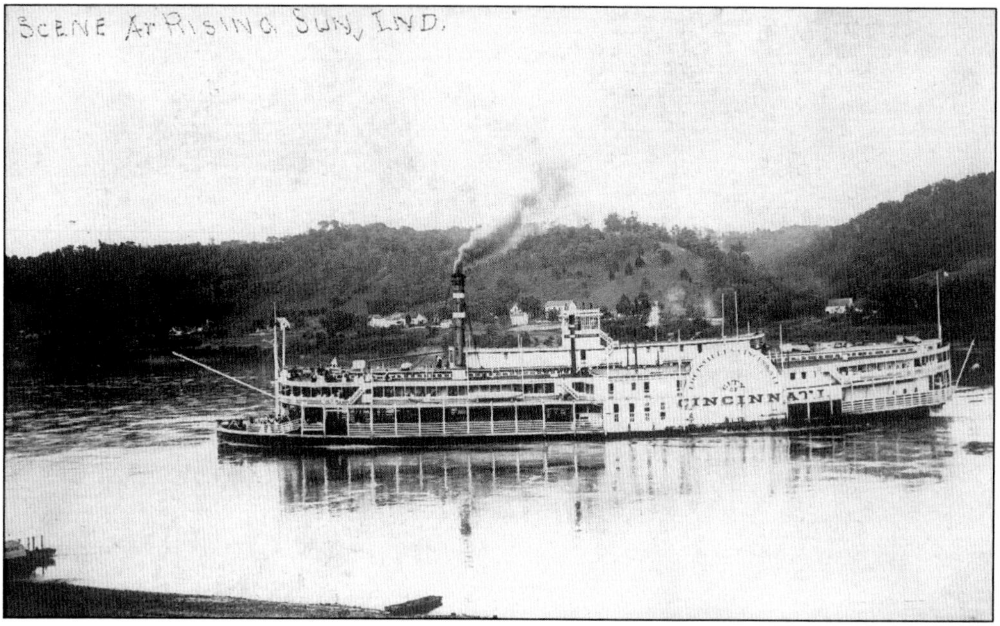


**STERNWHEELER *CITY OF CINCINNATI*, c. 1910.** The sternwheeler, *City of Cincinnati,* was built in Jeffersonville, Indiana, in 1899. The Cincinnati and Louisville Packet Company operated the *Str. City of Cincinnati* and *Str. City of Louisville*. For nearly 19 years the company scheduled a daily run of the two steamboats between Cincinnati and Louisville. The boats would stop to load and unload passengers in Rising Sun. For many years the pilot of the *Str. City of Cincinnati* was Rising Sun native, Mr. Payton.

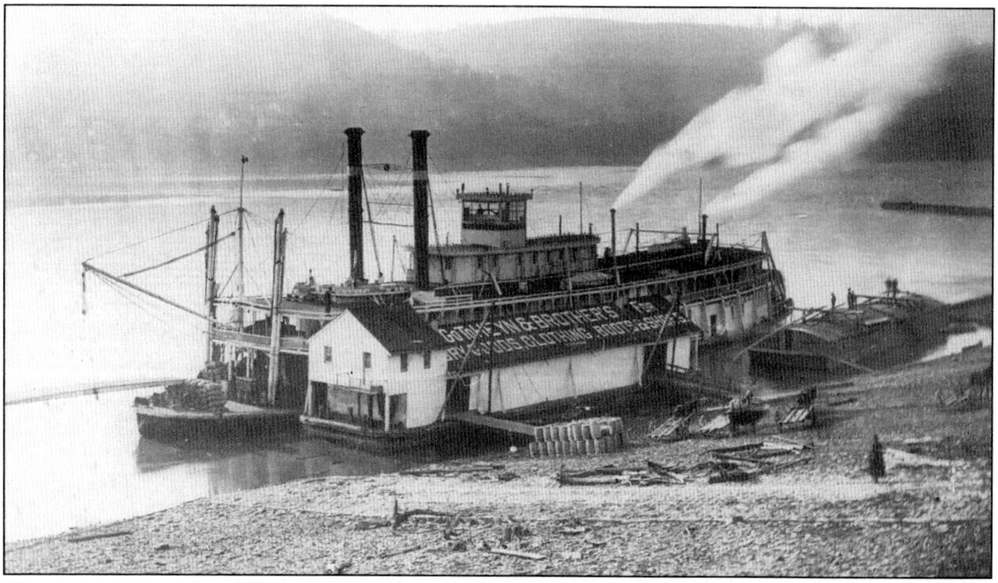

**WHARFBOAT, c. 1900.** This photograph provides a wealth of information. The wharfboat served as a floating warehouse on the river. The railroad never came to Rising Sun, although during the 1870s and 1880s surveys had been done. So, steamboats and flatboats loaded and unloaded almost all produce, hardware, livestock, and people via the wharfboat. To the right of the steamer, a flatboat can be seen with several men on top controlling the oars as it is guided into dock.

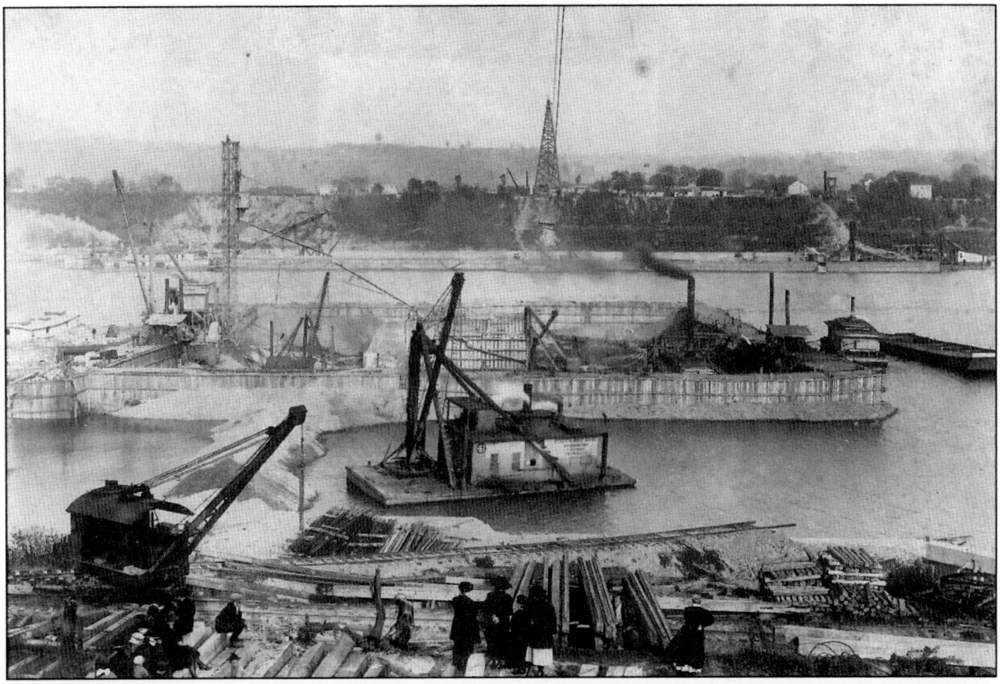

**Dam #38, 1924.** Above Rising Sun on the Ohio River, the Corps of Engineers from the Louisville district constructed Navigation Dam #38. This dam was located eight miles upriver from Rising Sun. With the completion of the Markland Dam in 1962, this dam lies under water.

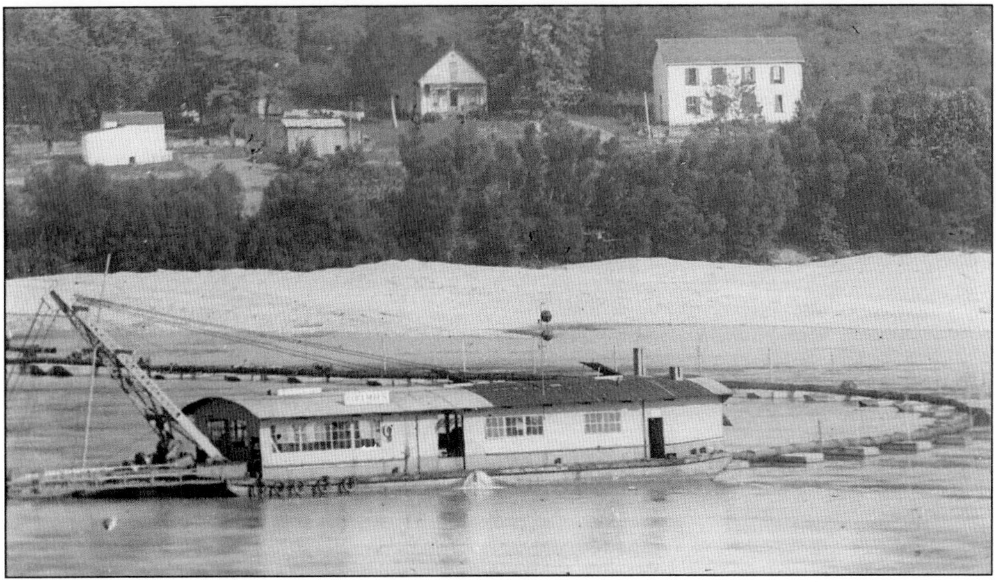

**Dredge boat, c. 1935.** The dredge boat *Columbus* used the apparatus on the front to scoop up mud, sand, rocks, and other material found on the bottom of the river. This process either deepened or cleared the channels used by the larger boats traveling the river. In the background is Rabbit Hash, Kentucky, located across the Ohio River from Rising Sun. Dredging the river was an ongoing job. According to the *Rising Sun Recorder*, in 1931 the government dredge boat *Mallory* spent several months dredging in the Rising Sun harbor.

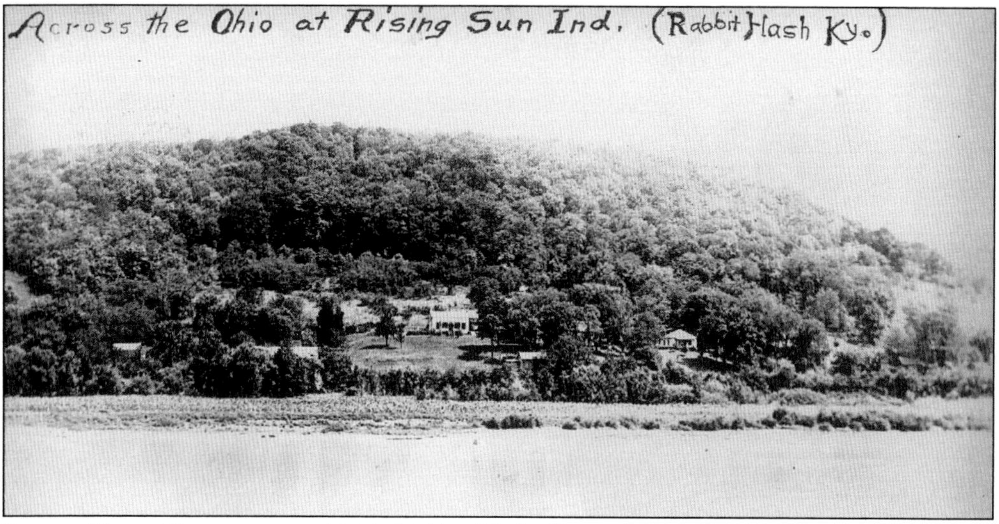


**RABBIT HASH, KENTUCKY, C. 1915.** Rabbit Hash, Kentucky, nestles in the picturesque tree-covered hillside. Rabbit Hash is the sister city to Rising Sun. At one time a ferry ran between the two towns. Some citizens of Rabbit Hash crossed the river daily to Rising Sun to go to school and to work in the canning factory.

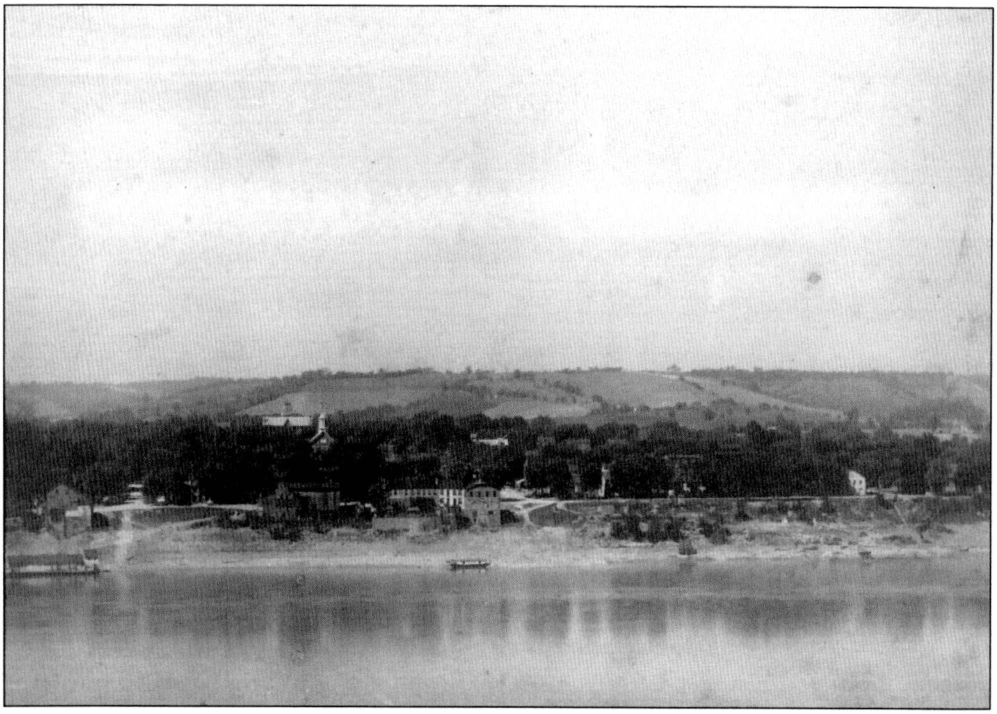

**RISING SUN-EARLY 1900S.** A great view of Rising Sun from the Kentucky town of Rabbit Hash. In the center of the picture on the river side of Front Street is Smith Riggs' (manufacturer of two electric chairs for two Illinois Penitentiaries) brick blacksmith shop. All the buildings on this side of Front Street are gone because of erosion of the riverbank. The two large structures with cupolas to the left of center, from left to right, are the Rising Sun Public School and the Methodist Church.

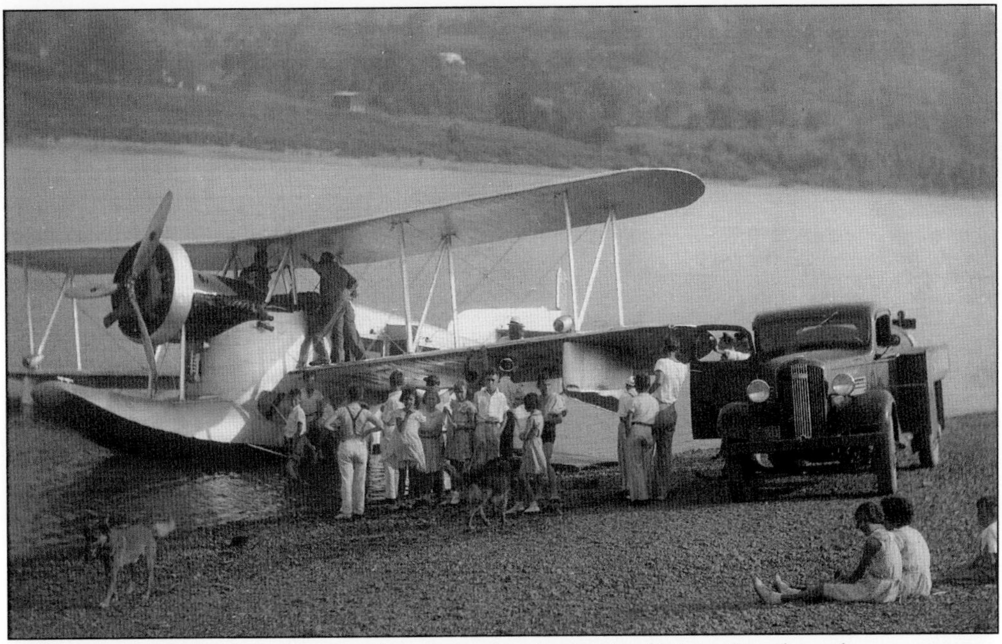

**SEAPLANE, C. 1935.** A seaplane landed along the riverbank of Rising Sun for unknown reasons. A group of boys and girls along with a couple of dogs found the event worthy of a closer look. The truck appears to be a gasoline tanker filling up the plane. Rabbit Hash, Kentucky, can be seen across the river.

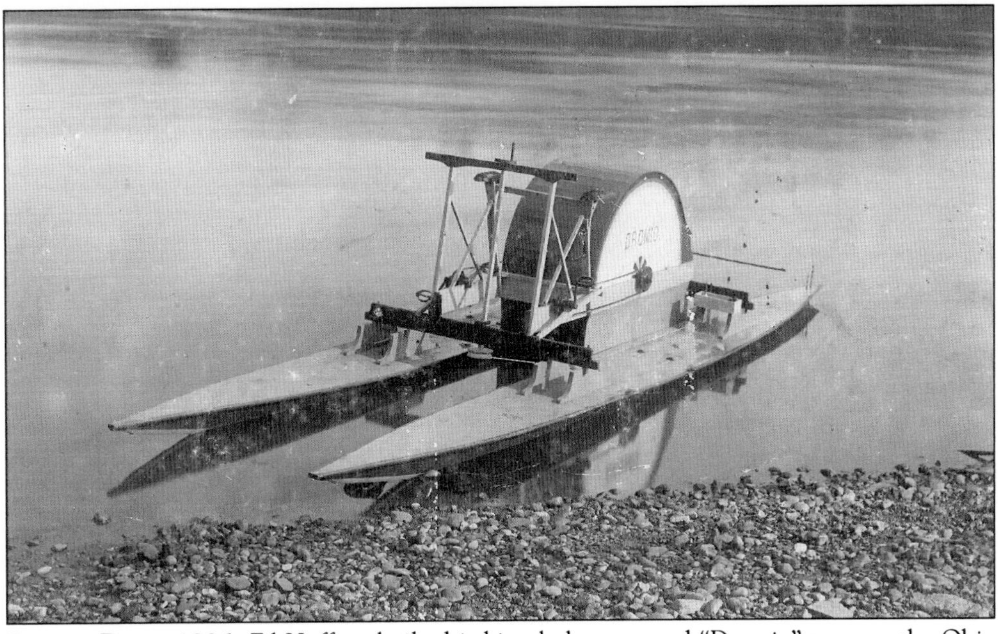

**BICYCLE BOAT, 1896.** Ed Hoffner built this bicycle boat named "Dromio" to cross the Ohio River. It could seat two people who would pedal like riding a bike. The chain attached to the large drum in back where a wheel similar to a paddle wheel boat was housed to propel the bicycle boat forward. According to a newspaper account, Mr. Hoffner took his invention down to the river and made a crossing to Rabbit Hash, Kentucky, and back.

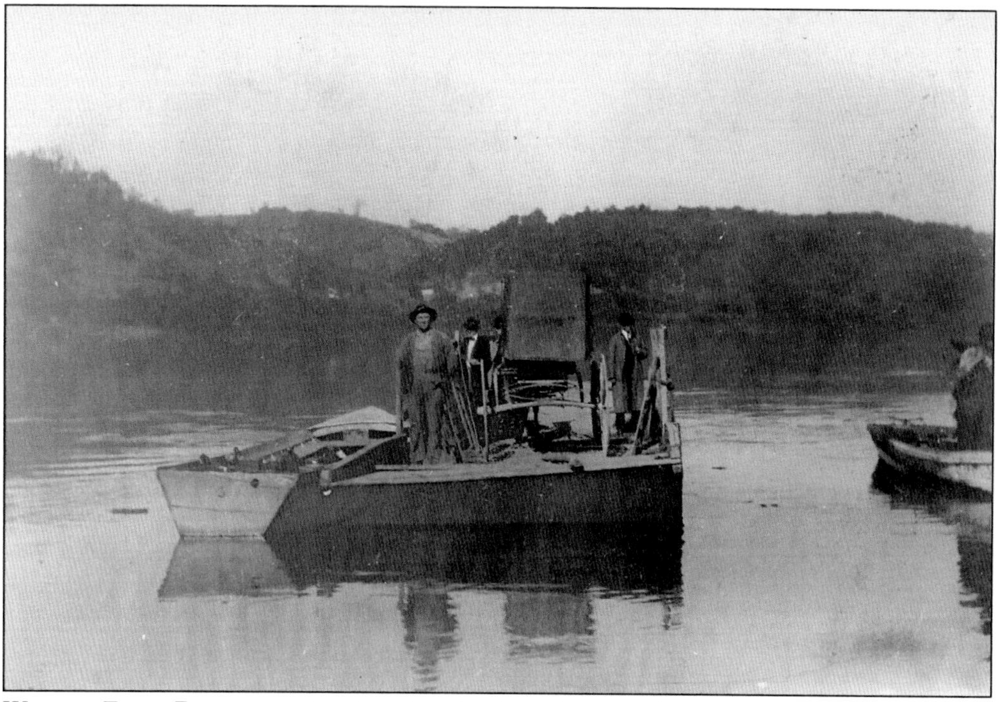

**WARSAW FERRY BOAT, C. 1915.** Crossing the Ohio River could be an adventure by the looks of Salon Irons' Warsaw ferryboat. He operated the boat from 1913–1920. Currently, there is no ferryboat to take travelers from Rising Sun to Rabbit Hash, Kentucky. For many years enterprising men offered up a conglomeration of crafts to take people, animals, and vehicles across.

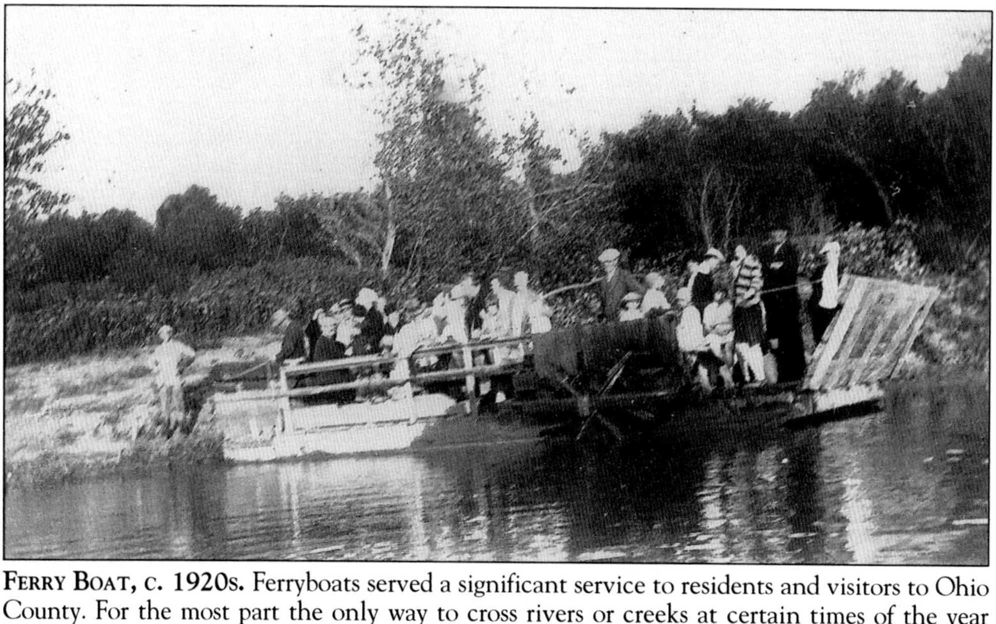

**FERRY BOAT, C. 1920S.** Ferryboats served a significant service to residents and visitors to Ohio County. For the most part the only way to cross rivers or creeks at certain times of the year was by ferry. The ferry at Hartford charged 6.25¢ per person, 25¢ per horse, 32.5¢ for a wagon and four horses, 4¢ for each head of cattle over 5, 6.25¢ for each head of cattle less than 5, and children of movers under 10 were not charged.

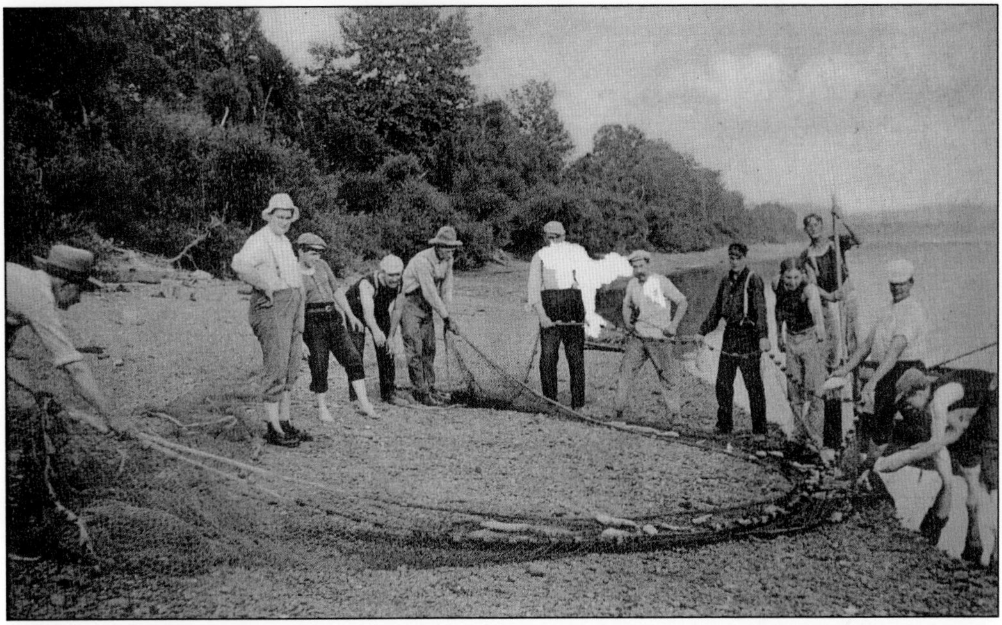

**Fishing, c. 1915.** Along any river, stream, or creek, fishermen could be found in peaceful respite. Sometimes, like in this photograph, "a good catch" was accomplished using a group of men and a large net as opposed to a fishing pole. These men were probably not out for pleasure but to catch large quantities of fish to sell in town or to a fish market.

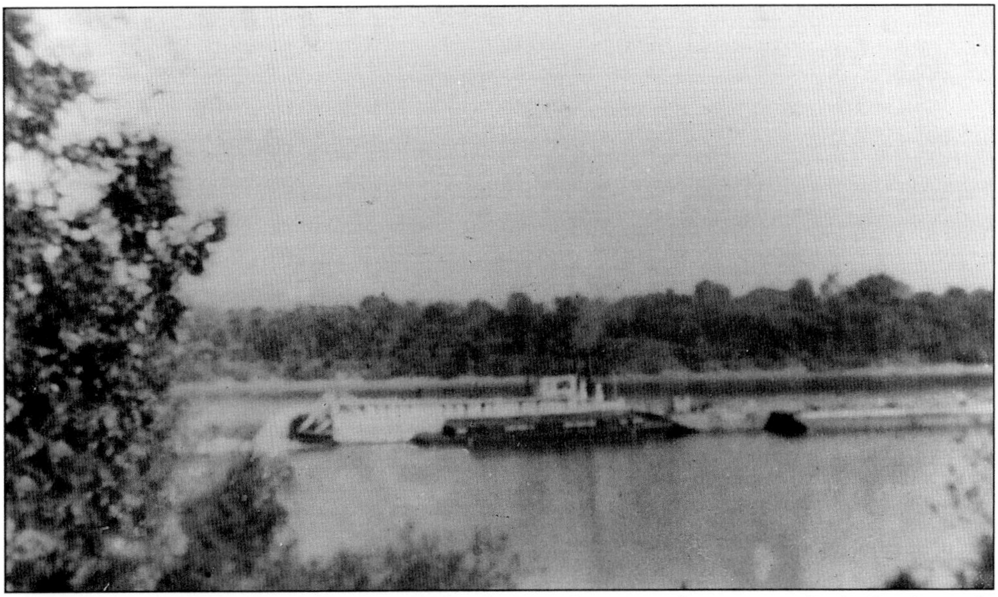

**Tow Boat, c. 1930.** The railroads brought about a change in shipping methods. By the early 1900s the steamboats were being replaced as haulers of finished products and raw material. The scene changed on the Ohio River from daily steamboats and flatboats to tow boats pushing barges of raw material up and down the river. This is still common on the river today with an occasional steamboat going past.

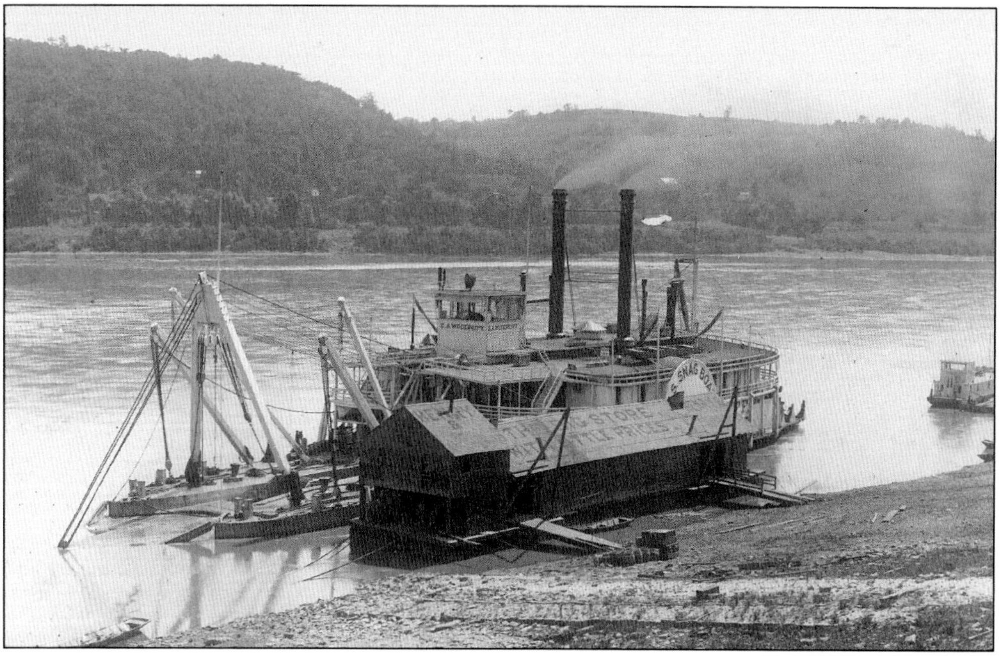

**E.A. WOODRUFF, C. 1900.** The United States snag boat *E.A. Woodruff*, docked alongside a wharf boat, saw plenty of action in the Rising Sun area. A snag is an underwater tree stump or branches dangerous to navigation. Boats like the *E.A. Woodruff* would ply the Ohio River and others locating these obstructions to gather them in the front. Then it cut the logs and let them float harmlessly away, thus clearing the river.

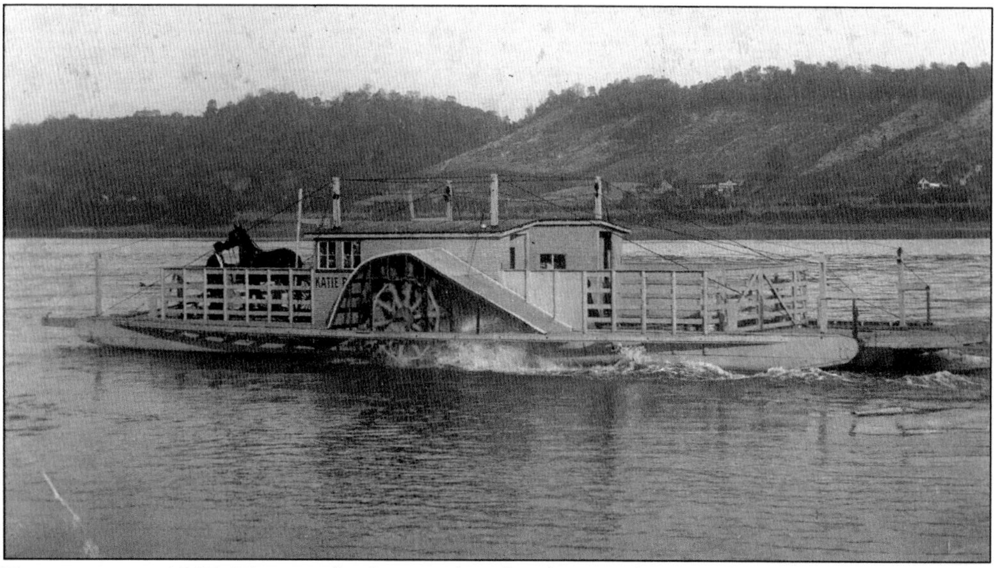

**FERRY BOAT, C. 1915.** This was the first gasoline ferryboat in the area. Gasoline powered engines were safer than the steam driven engines. The ferryboat could transport people, animals, and vehicles across to Rabbit Hash, Kentucky. The boat, like so many others, was destroyed in the Great Ice of 1918.

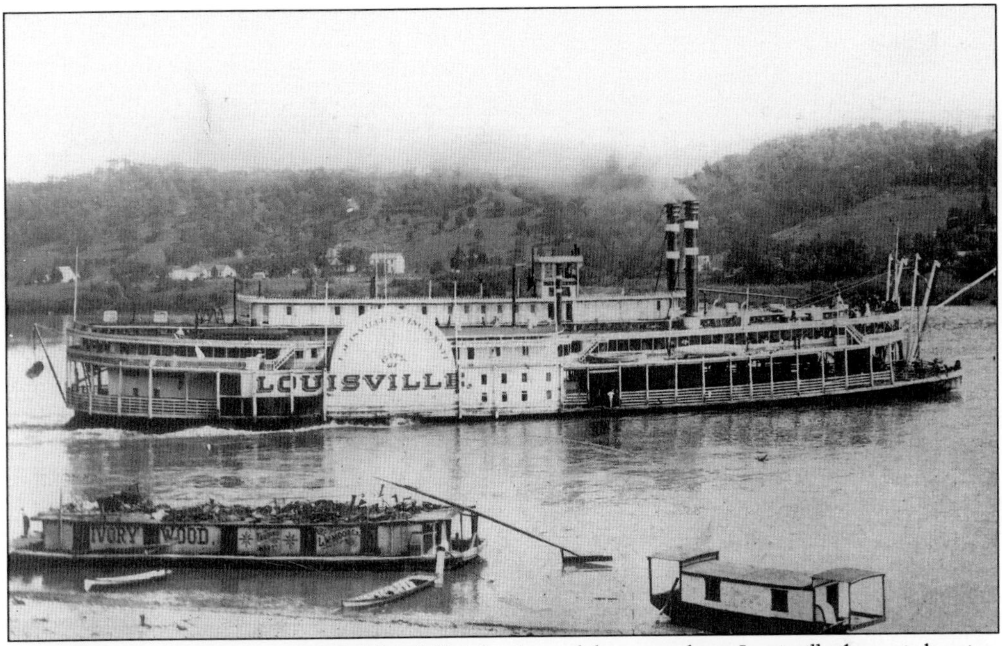


**STEAMBOAT *LOUISVILLE*, C. 1915.** This full-side view of the steamboat *Louisville* shows it leaving Rising Sun on its daily travels between Cincinnati and Louisville. The small Kentucky town of Rabbit Hash is nestled among the picturesque hills. In the foreground is L.W. Moore's trading boat. It appears Mr. Moore makes his living trading up and down the river. The watercraft in the lower right is a unique pleasure boat. This is an informative photograph showing three distinct forms of water transportation.

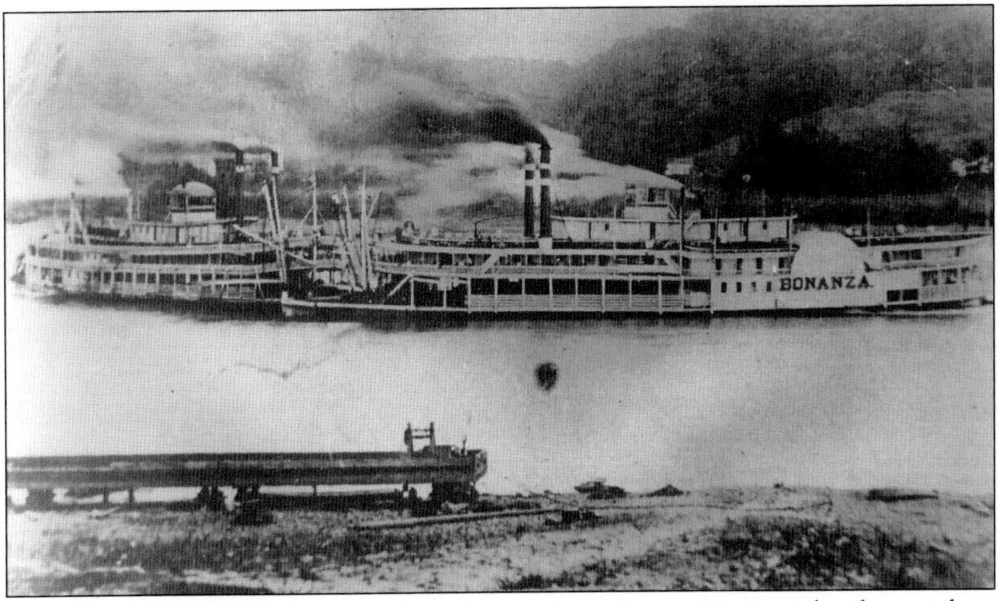


**STEAMBOATS, C. 1900.** The location of this photograph is unknown. It appears that the steamboat *Bonanza* had collided with an unidentified steamboat. In all probability the two steamboats are exchanging passengers. The steamboats *Cincinnati* and *Louisville* did that each day when they reached Vevay on their journeys up and down the Ohio River.

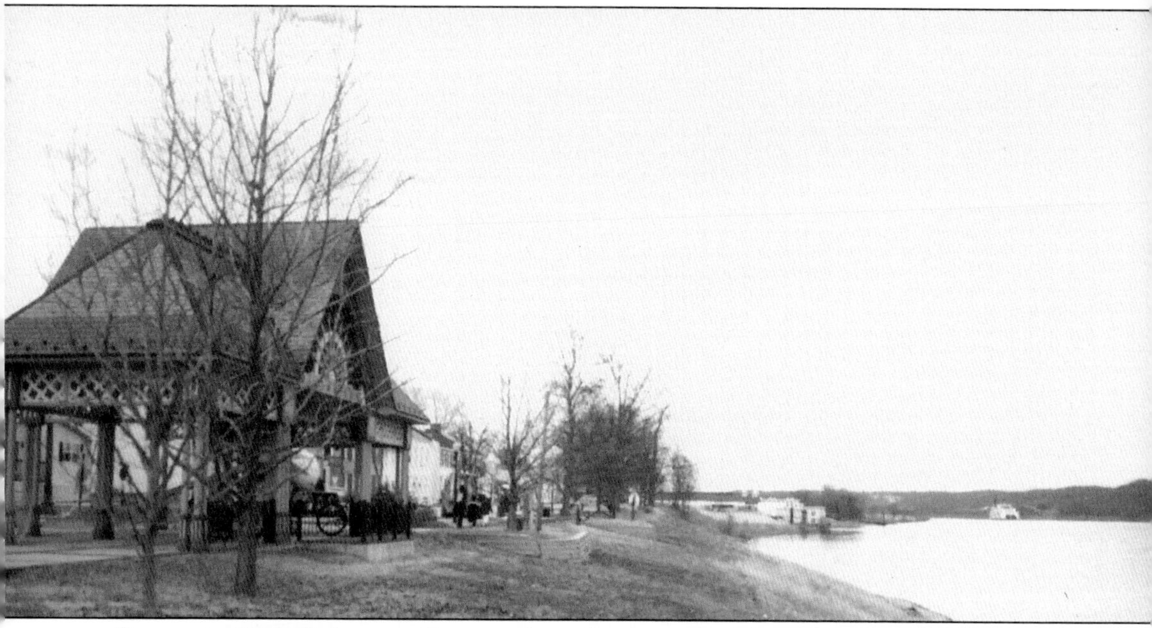

**PAVILION, 2001.** Today a pavilion stands on the riverside of Front Street at the bottom of Main Street. The pavilion is the centerpiece for many of the community's events throughout the year. Plans are in the works to create this area to be a grand entryway to the city from the water. Dock space to accommodate several riverboats at once is included. To the right in the distance is Grand Victoria's Casino boat.

# Three

# Recreation and Celebration

After a hard day or week of work or school, who does not look forward to some form of recreation? The people of Ohio County have never been different in this respect. Organized baseball teams began to take shape in the late 1800s. Music also played a part in leisure with groups like Row's Band, The Rising Sun Roarers, and the high school bands that continue that tradition today.

Recreation rejuvenates one's soul. Celebrations are an organized form of recreation. Through the years Ohio County has put on many different celebrations. In 1914, a homecoming week occurred honoring the city's founding 100 years earlier. Over 1,000 former citizens of Rising Sun returned for the event. Letters to the editor of the *Rising Sun Recorder* from other former citizens expressed sadness in not being able to attend the celebration. Fifty years later a weeklong Sesquicentennial was held, which included concerts, a parade (that attracted thousands), and a street dance. Other celebrations include the Blue Jeans Festival, Shiner Car Show, and Navy Bean Festival.

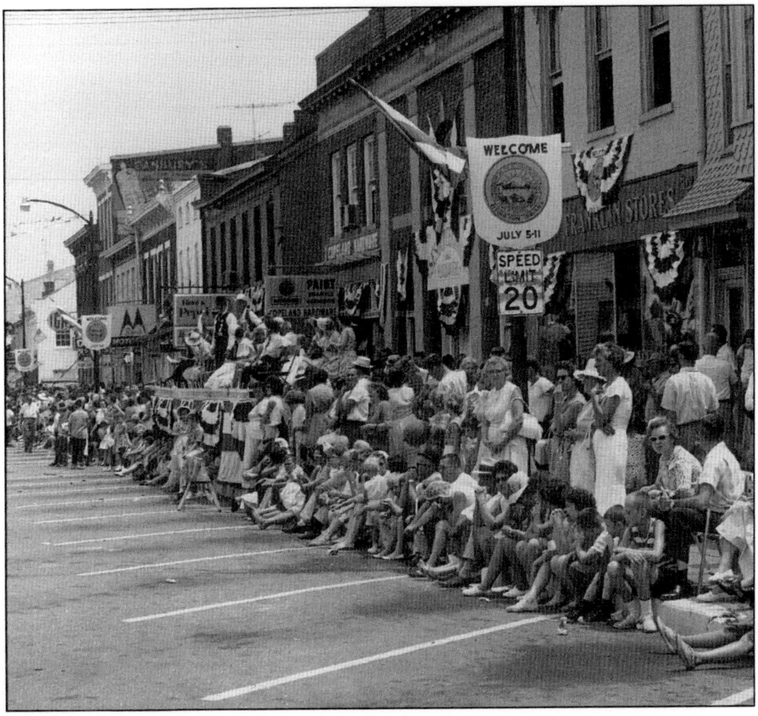


**Sesquicentennial Celebration, July 1964.** To celebrate the founding of Rising Sun in 1814 by John James, the town put on a big party that included a parade. A large crowd anticipating the parade lined both sides of Main Street. Looking down the street to the left about three-quarters of the way is the official observation stand. Note all the business signs hanging along the storefronts.

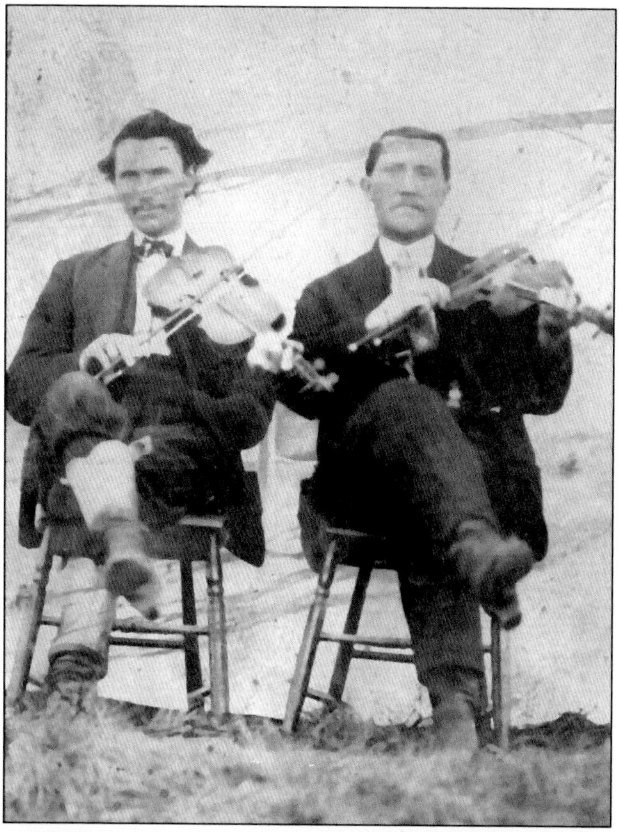

**UNIDENTIFIED MUSICIANS, C. 1890.** These two men must have been proud of their fiddles to go through the trouble of being photographed with them. An uncommon practice of the time was to have an outdoor portrait taken. A canvas backdrop was hung up along side a clapboard covered house. We can speculate why the photograph was taken, possibly that they were hired to perform for a dance. Music and dances were a common form of entertainment prior to movies and television.

**WATERMELON EATING CONTEST, C. 1924.** A popular event at many early festivals were the pie and watermelon eating contests. Here we see eight men seated at a long table involved in a watermelon-eating contest. It appears that the man fifth from the left is claiming victory by lifting his watermelon slice up for the judge (standing) to see.

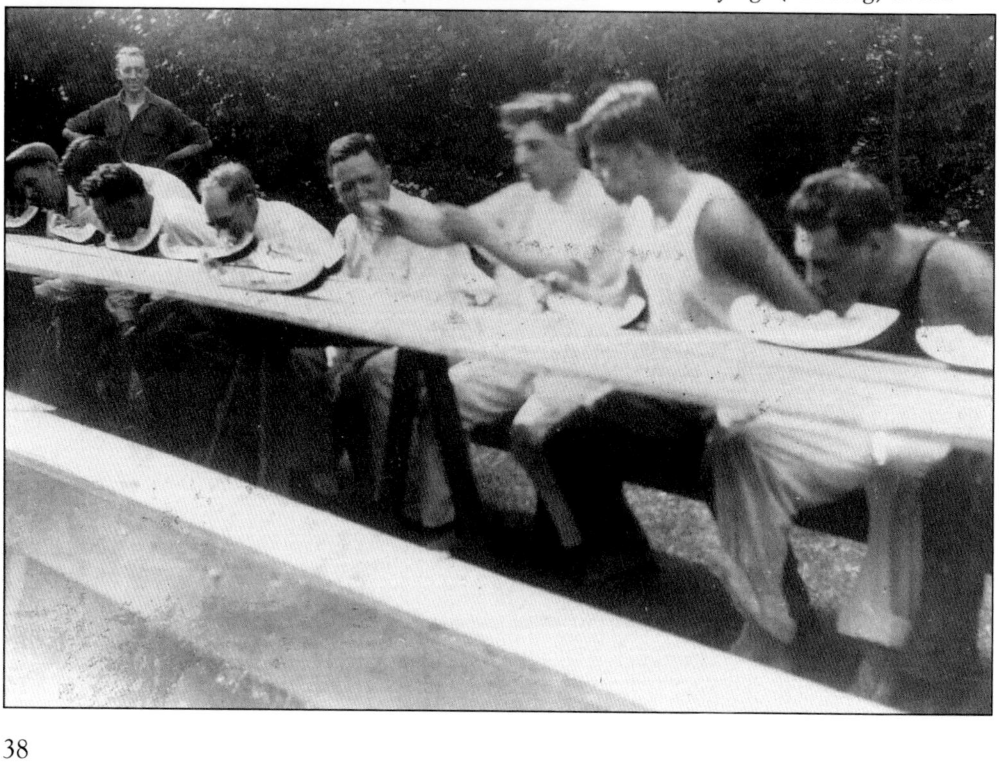

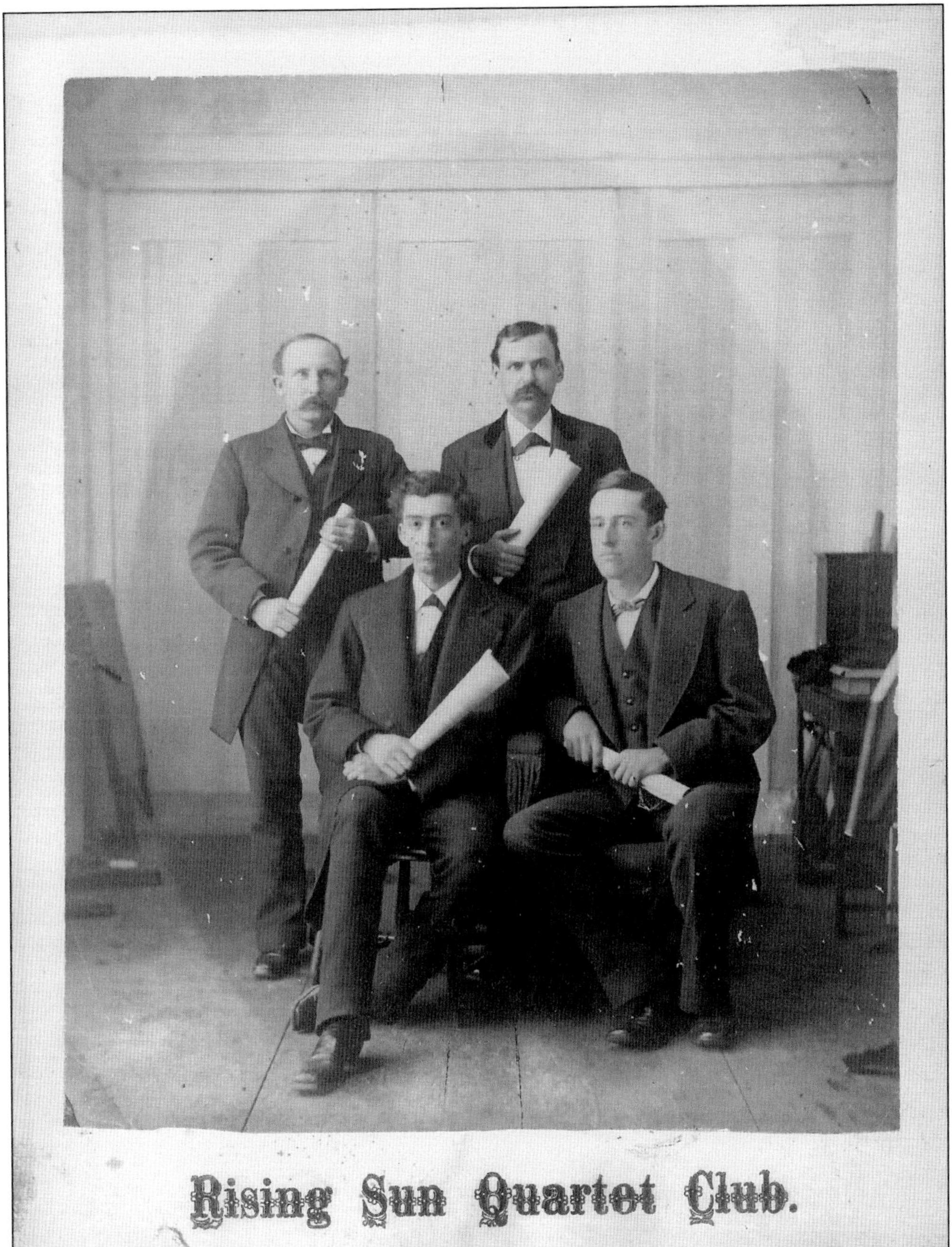


**RISING SUN QUARTET CLUB, C. 1900.** Although the population of Rising Sun and Ohio County have never been large, the area still managed to have its share of entertainment. The Rising Sun Quartet Club (unidentified) and the Rising Sun Roarers along with J.W. Whitlock's "Row's Band" produced some of the music that could be heard around town. "Row's Band" formed early in the century, consisted of 40 pieces, and performed at civic functions.

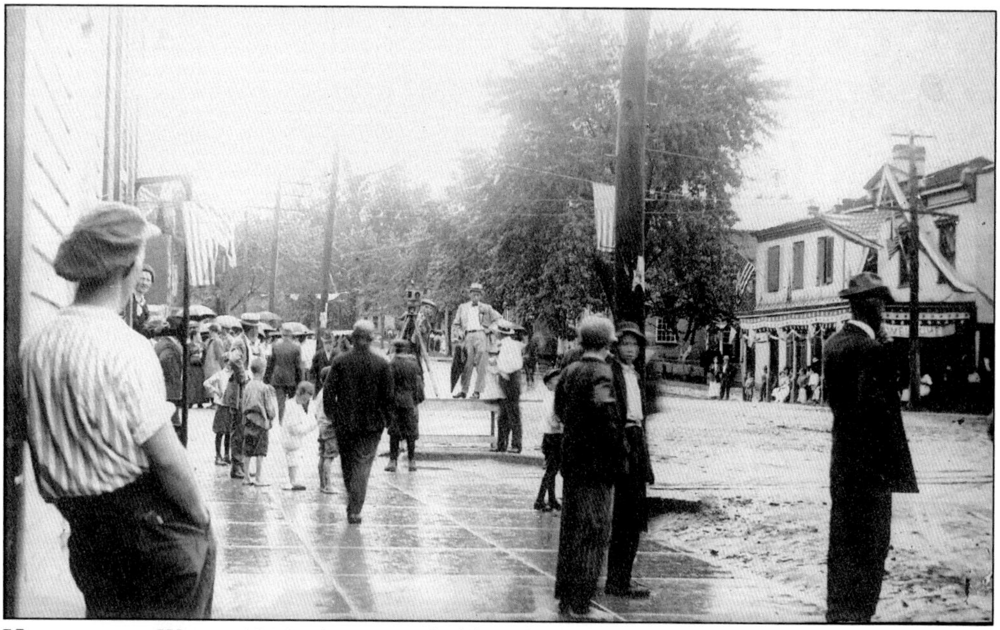

**Homecoming Week, 1914.** An event held in Rising Sun from August 10–15, 1914, was Homecoming Week. This event was a centennial celebration of the founding of Rising Sun. On this particular day it appears that the citizens are preparing to view a parade. Umbrellas are out, the sidewalk is wet, and the rain has kept some of the crowd away. In the center of the photograph on a riser are two men and a movie camera documenting this important event.

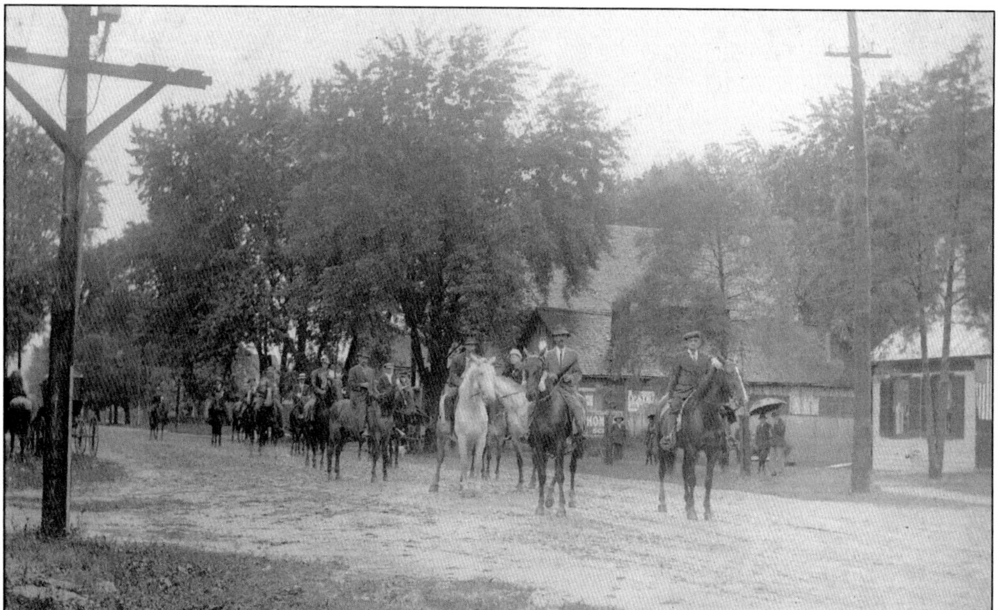

**Homecoming Week, c. 1914.** A group of unidentified men on horseback prepare to join the parade. The rain appears to have put a damper on the crowd as only a few people standing or sitting in their buggies line the street. Over 1,000 former citizens of Rising Sun came back for the celebration.

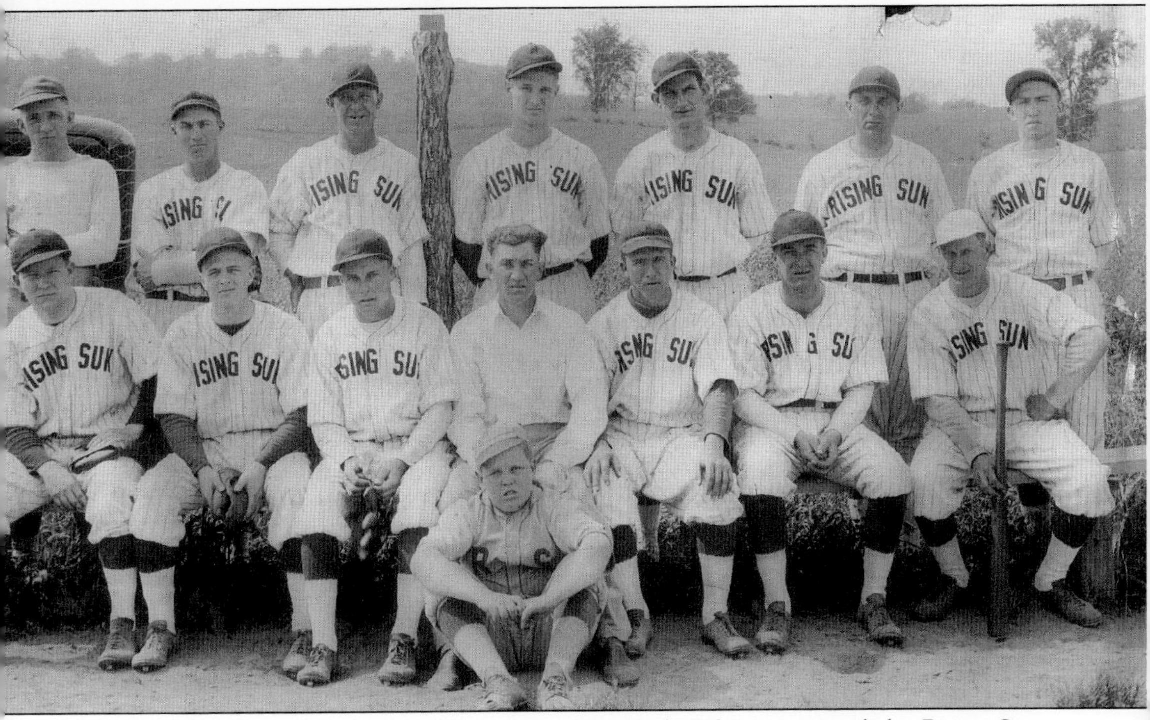

**RISING SUN BASEBALL TEAM, C. 1930S.** Grant (Grinner) Calvert managed the Rising Sun baseball until 1950, when he was forced to retire due to poor health. The 1933 baseball season began in April and finished in September. The team played games on Sunday as part of the Southern Division of the Tri-County League. They won the championship game by defeating Morris in the first game of a double header 5-0. Morris forfeited the second game.

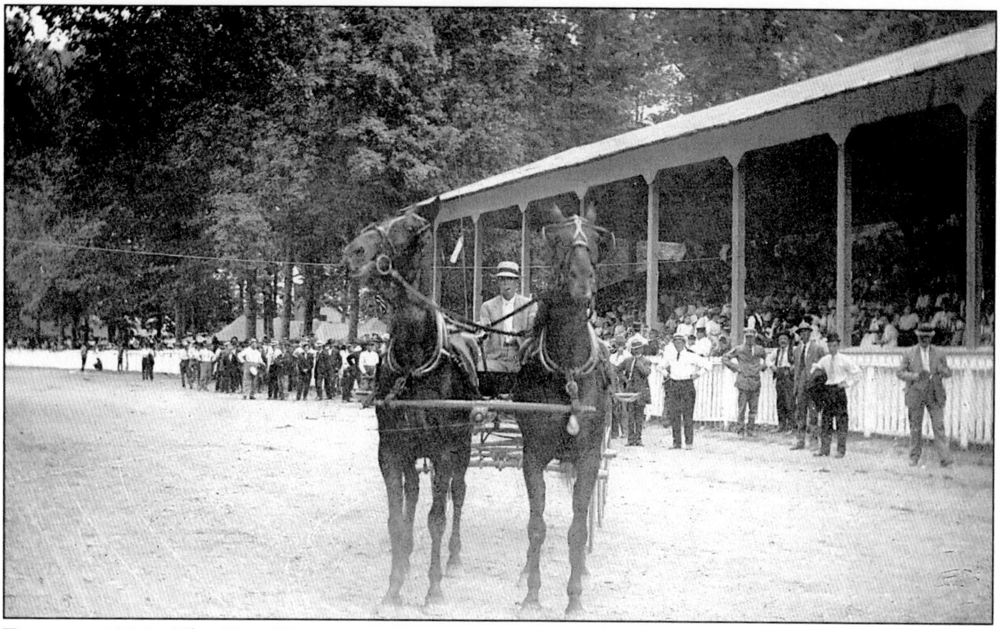

**Fair, c. 1910.** The East Enterprise Fair was an event that folks from Ohio and Switzerland counties looked forward to each year. It was a time for old friends to gather and catch up on events of the past year. There were exhibits of fruits and vegetables, displays of musical instruments, and livestock. Rides were available for the youngsters as well. The racetrack pictured featured sulky races for all ages to enjoy. The last fair was held in 1917, ending 67 years of tradition.

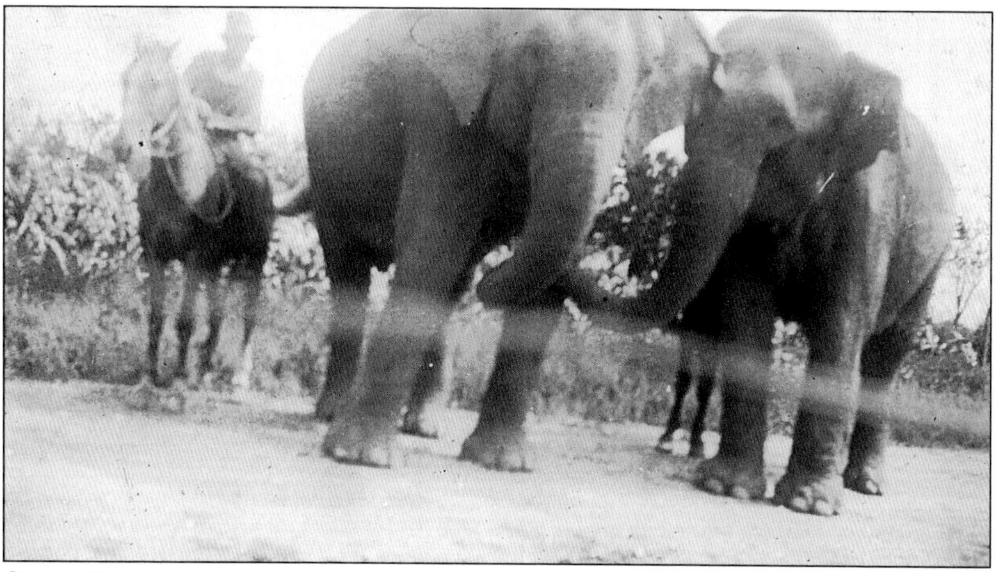

**Circus Elephants, 1922.** A much-anticipated event during the summer was the arrival of the circus. This had been a popular form of entertainment since the mid-1800s. The circus usually came via the railroad. Ohio County did not have a railroad so the only way the circus could arrive was to travel the road from Madison or Aurora. In 1922, a circus came to East Enterprise with two elephants weighing 4,890 pounds each. A circus parading through town was a great way to notify locals of their arrival.

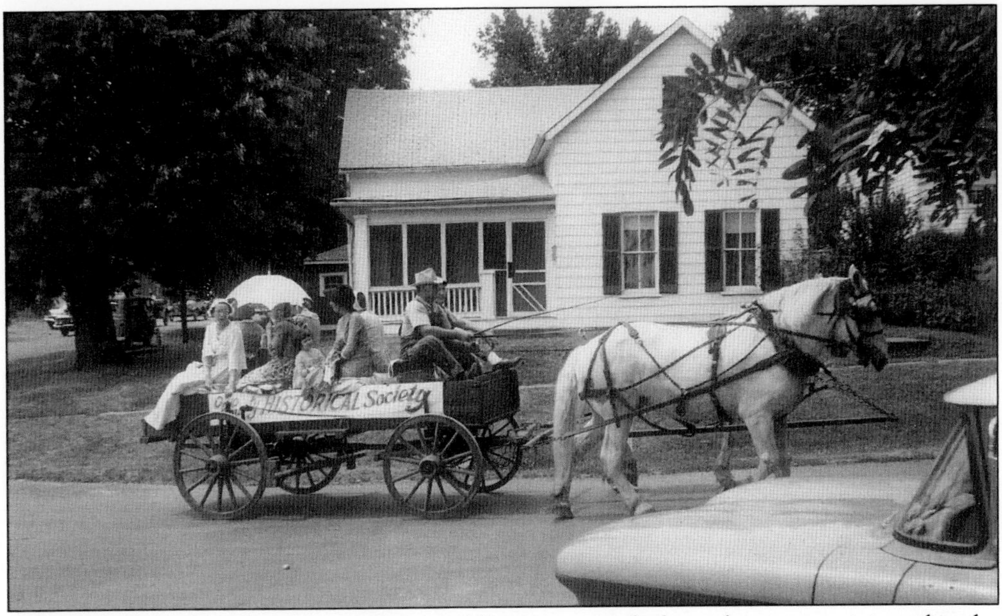


**PARADE, 1966.** The Ohio County Historical Society, a newly formed group, participated in the 1966 Blue Jeans Festival parade. The entry included two white horses pulling an old wagon with nine people. The entry won second prize.

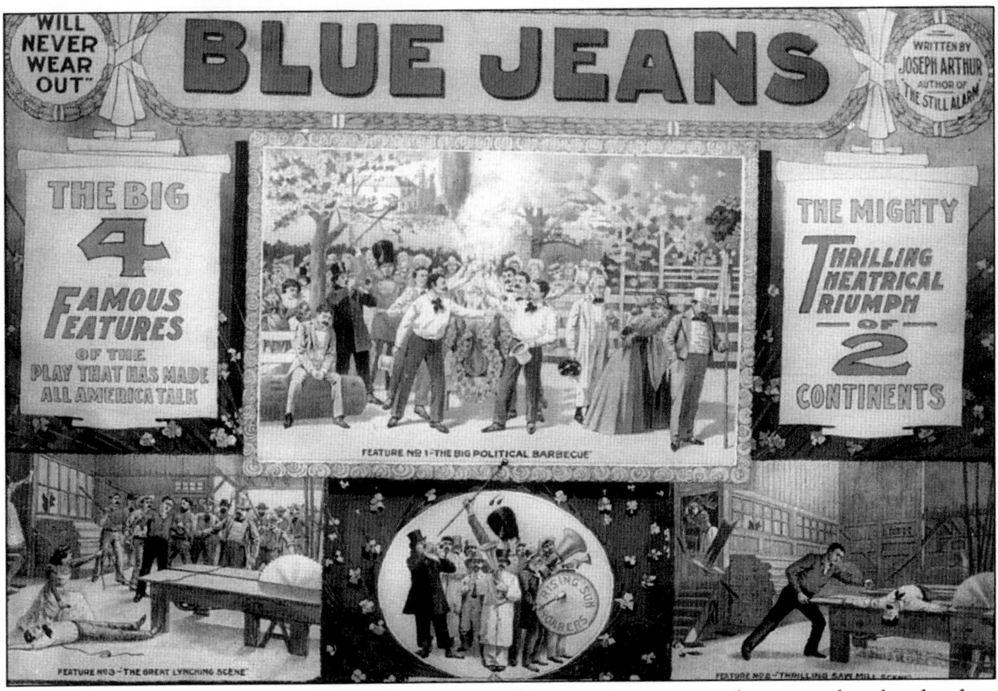


**BLUE JEANS POSTER, C. 1890.** Joseph Arthur of Rising Sun wrote what is said to be the first melodrama in 1888 titled *Blue Jeans*. The scene in which the villain prepares to do in the hero on a saw, only to be stopped by the heroine in the nick of time, has become a popular scene for many movies. The melodrama ran on Broadway in New York for several years, and in 1917 was made into a silent movie.

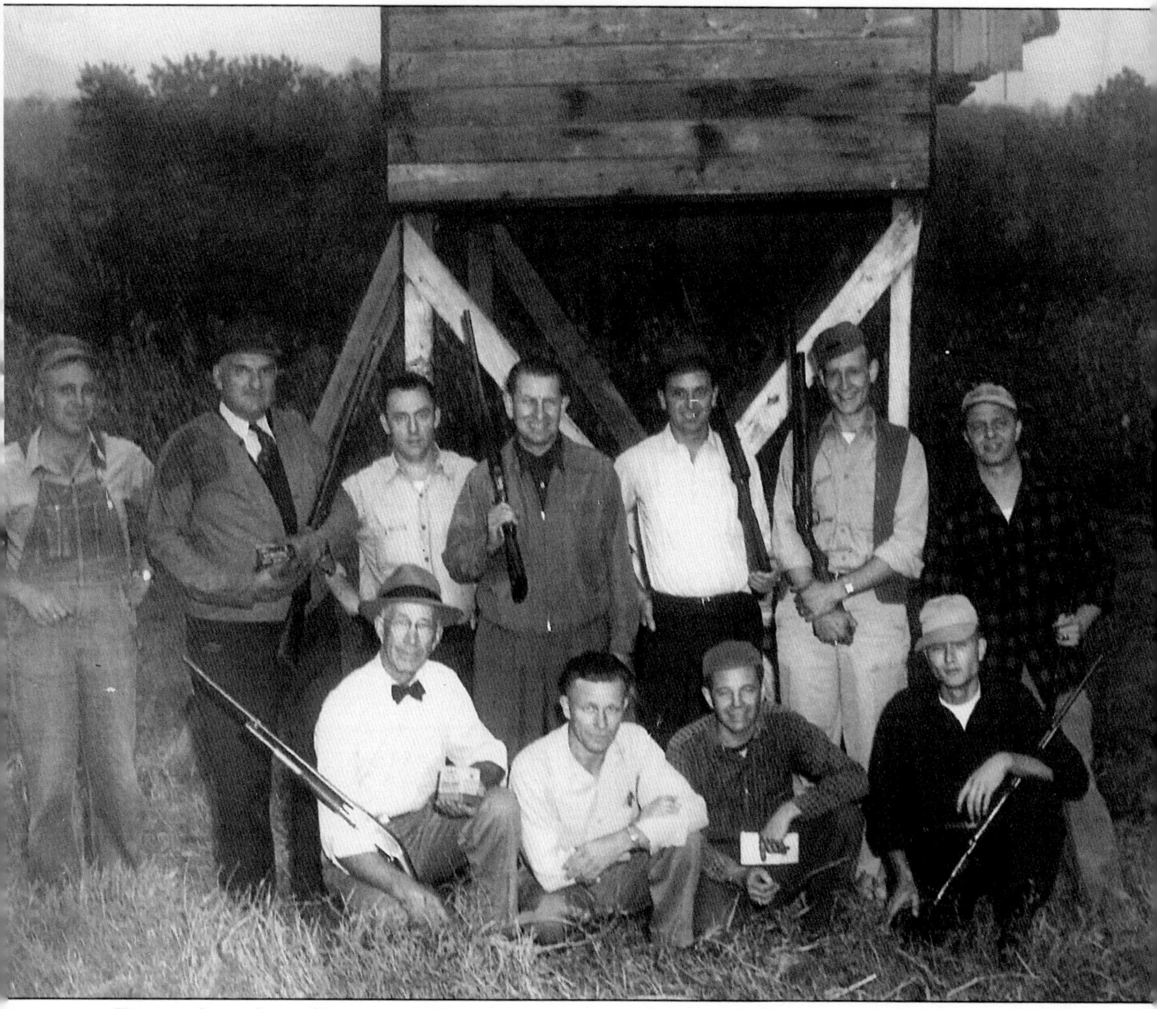

**Rising Sun Gun Club, c. 1950.** A group shot of club members near a deer blind. From left to right are as follows: (front row) H.D. Green, Paul Whithiam, Howard Dugle, and Eddie Weisickle; (back row) Bob Brown, Clarence Woods, Orville Phillips, Earl Danbury, Lowell Bliss, Martin R. Green, and Roy Gibson.

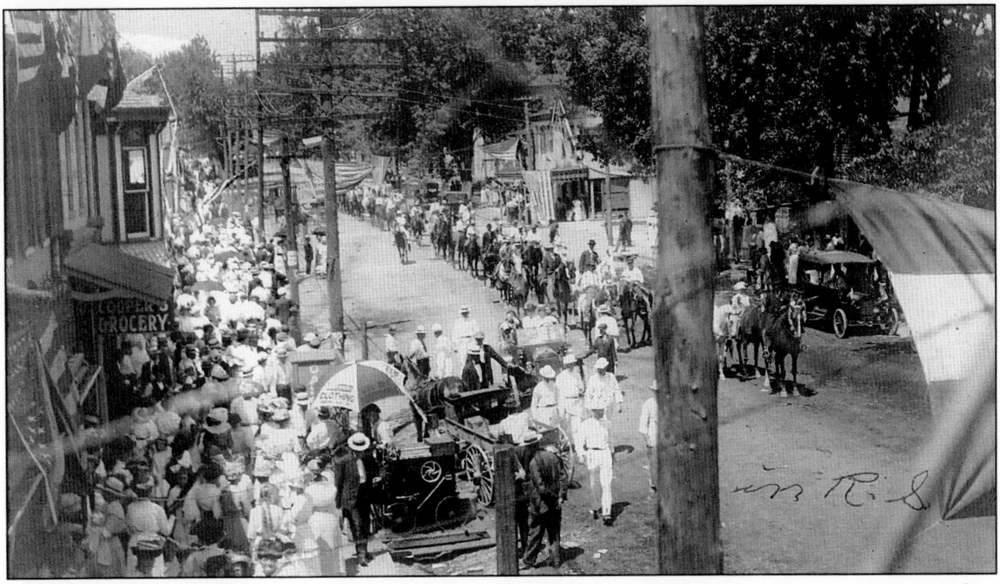


**MAIN STREET, C. 1916.** As with many towns, the citizens found many reasons to get together and have a parade or celebration. The streetscape is decked out with patriotic bunting flags. On the left side of the street can be seen a sign for Cooper's Grocery. Albert B. Cooper along with Harry G. Whitlock assumed management and ownership of Mr. Whitlock's father, J.T.'s, grocery in 1901. Sometime in 1940, the building was remodeled to house a Ben Franklin Variety Store.

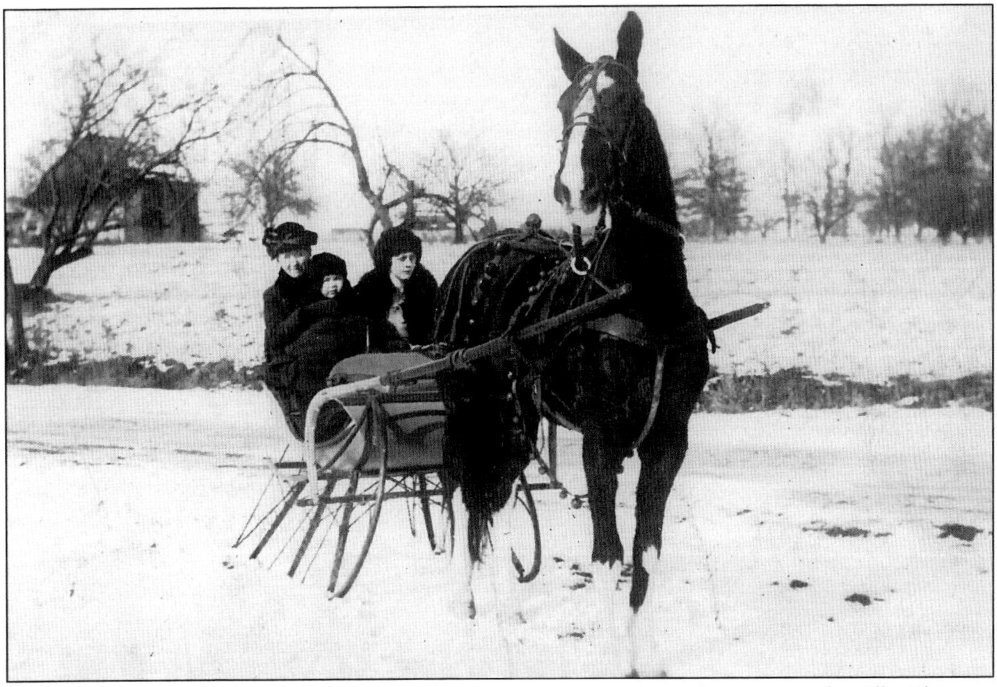

**SLEIGH RIDE, 1920.** As you look at the photograph, think about the song *Jingle Bells*. This is a one-horse open sleigh that probably dashed through the snow on more than one occasion. Note the two sets of sleigh bells around the horse. Pictured from left to right are Elizabeth Vanosdol, Nan Gibbens, and (?) Dorrell.

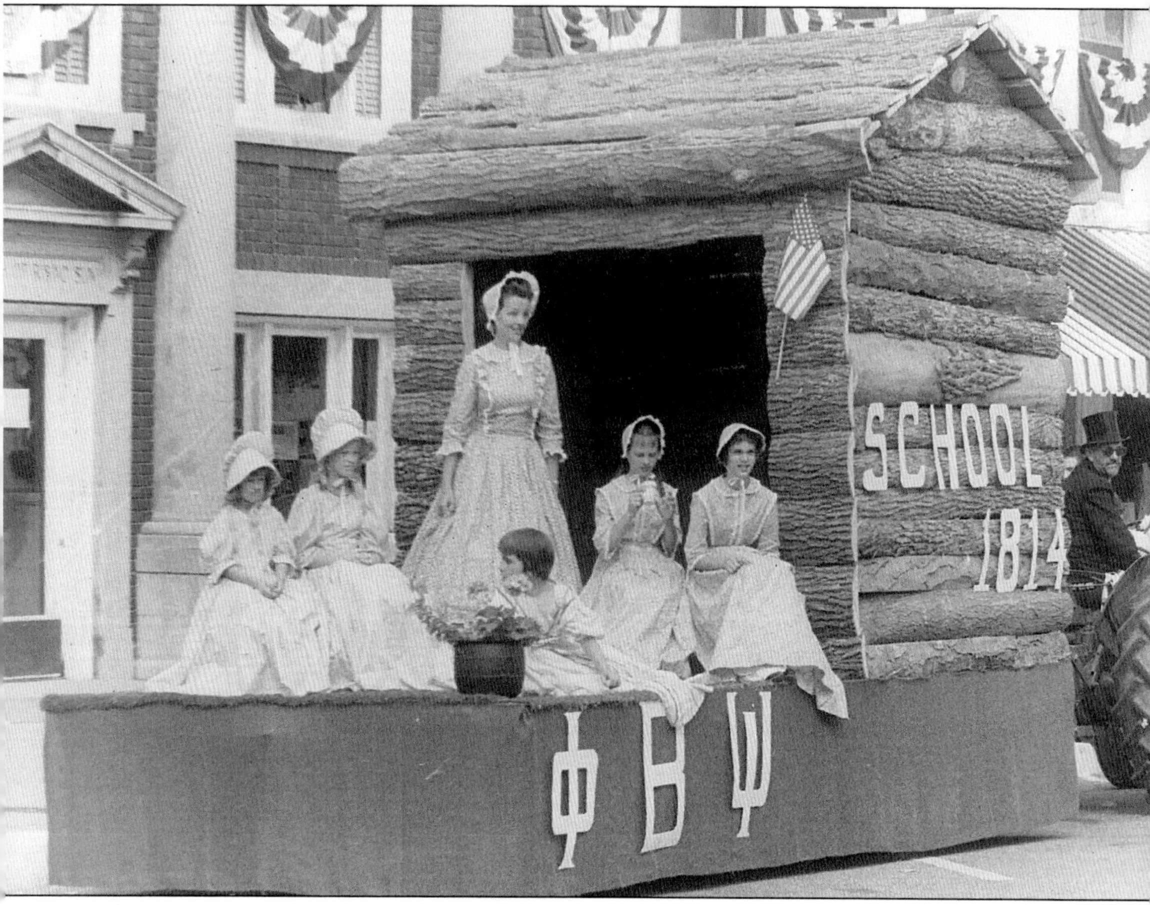


**Sesquicentennial Celebration Parade Float, July 1964.** Various clubs, organizations, and individuals participated in the parade. Some of the groups designed floats to be pulled by tractors. This float shows an early one-room log cabin school. Those on the float are portraying early settlers. The clothes they are wearing are more typical of the *Little House on the Prairie* time period with calico dresses and bonnets rather than 1814.

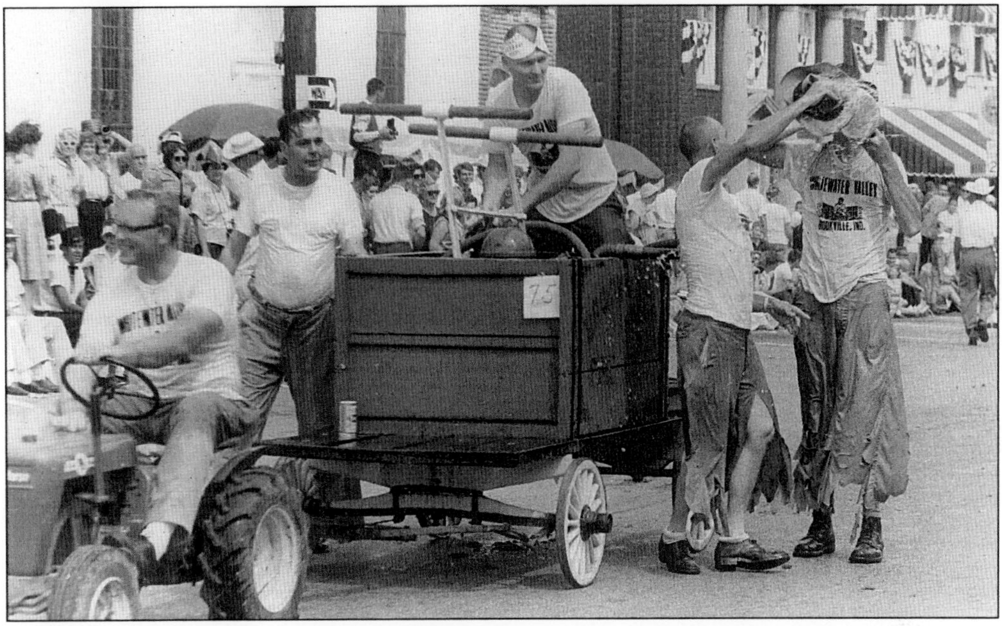

**Sesquicentennial Parade, July 11, 1964.** The parade celebrating the 150th anniversary of the founding of Rising Sun had the biggest and best parade scheduled for 1:30. Parade chairman Gerald W. Licking announced that officially 102 entries had been received and placed in position for the parade. Space for nine additional late entries needed to be determined. This photograph shows entry #75, a hand pumper from the Brookville, Indiana, fire department. The parade drew participants from Southeastern Indiana and Ohio.

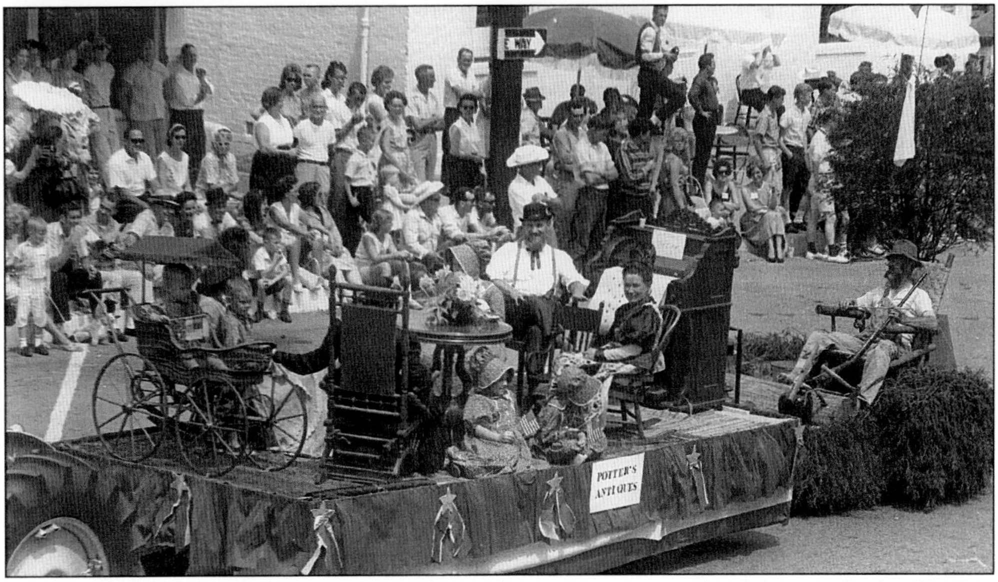

**Sesquicentennial Parade, July 11, 1964.** The Sesquicentennial celebration had eight days of activities from July 4th to July 11th. The kickoff event included the crowning of Mr. and Mrs. Rex Noble as the king and queen, and a fireworks display by the Lions Club on July 4th. July 11th was the big parade, a teen hop featuring Bob Braun from Cincinnati, and a square dance on Main Street. Other programs included an ice cream social, talent show, and a pet parade.

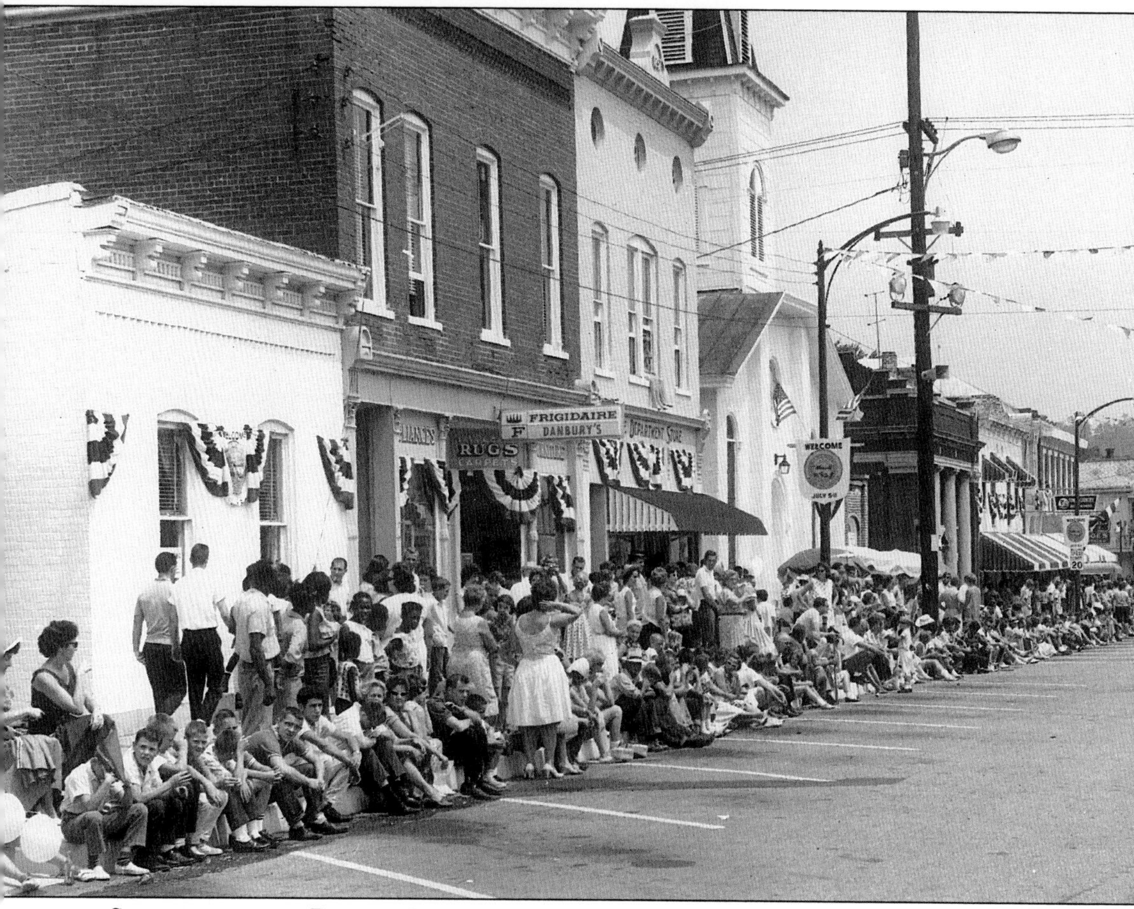


**SESQUICENTENNIAL PARADE, JULY 11, 1964.** An estimated 30,000 people attended the parade, braving hot-humid weather to watch for two hours and 15 minutes. Old automobiles, floats, high school bands, horse-drawn vehicles, and more made up the parade. Several elderly persons and a female member of a marching band succumbed to the oppressive heat. After receiving treatment from the Ohio County Life Squad, everyone recovered.

# *Four*

# AGRICULTURE

This chapter looks at images depicting the farming community of Ohio County in the late 1800s to the early 1900s. At this time in American history very few companies had created industrial farms to produce for the likes of Heinz or Del Monte. These were family farms to produce food for themselves and to make a modest living. Many of the images are of the John Dorrell farmstead near Aberdeen. Tobacco, pumpkins, and hay were a few of the crops that the Dorrells planted and harvested. Some farmers raised livestock such as pigs, cows, and sheep. In fact some of them diversified and did a little of everything, including having a dairy farm. This was a time of change. Competition with the larger farmers and companies, as well as new technology, made change a necessity. Tractors and steam threshers changed how farmers operated their farms.

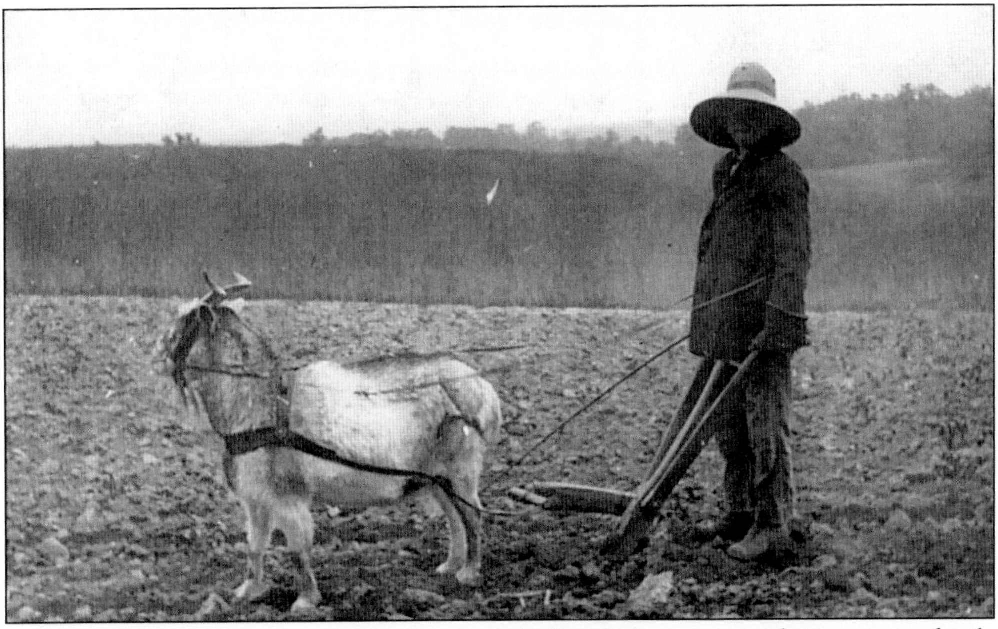

**RUSSELL DORRELL & IKE, C. 1920.** On an early farm before mass mechanism every family member participated in farming. This photograph shows Russell Dorrell and his goat Ike plowing the fields. Russell may not have been the proper size to handle horses for plowing the field. Ike's yoke is in the collection of the Historical Society. Ike also pulled a cart around the farm.

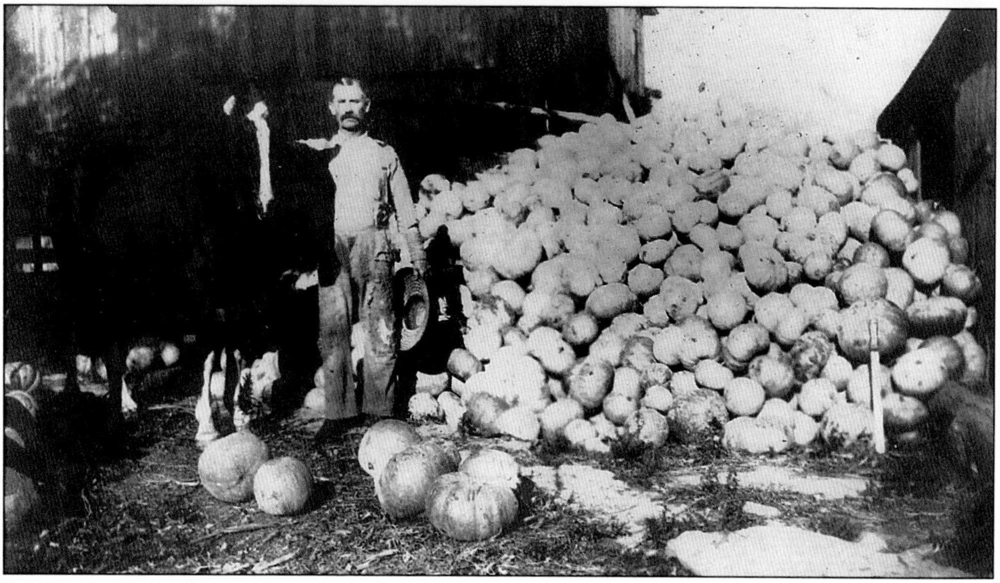

**PUMPKINS, 1921.** As was the case with many farmers, several cash crops were produced throughout the year. Pumpkins would be one to harvest in the early autumn. The pumpkin pile is located between two barns on the farm. Russell Dorrell's father, John, stands with Russell's horse.

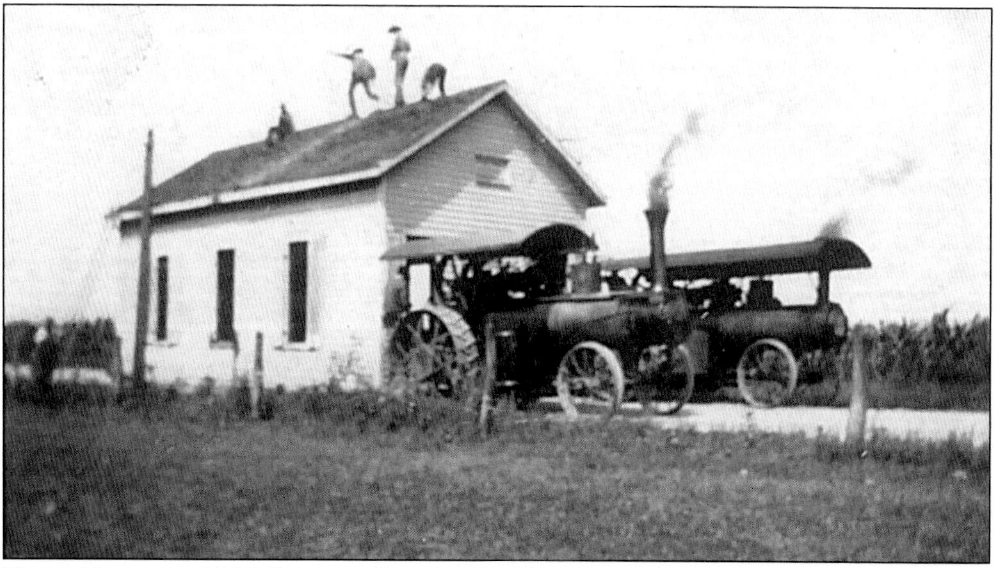

**HOUSE MOVING, C. 1910.** Occasionally today a building is moved intact from the original location to a new site. If you have ever witnessed such a move, you may have wondered how this engineering feat is accomplished. As this photograph depicts, buildings were also relocated a century ago. This unidentified building is being relocated using the steam power of two threshers.

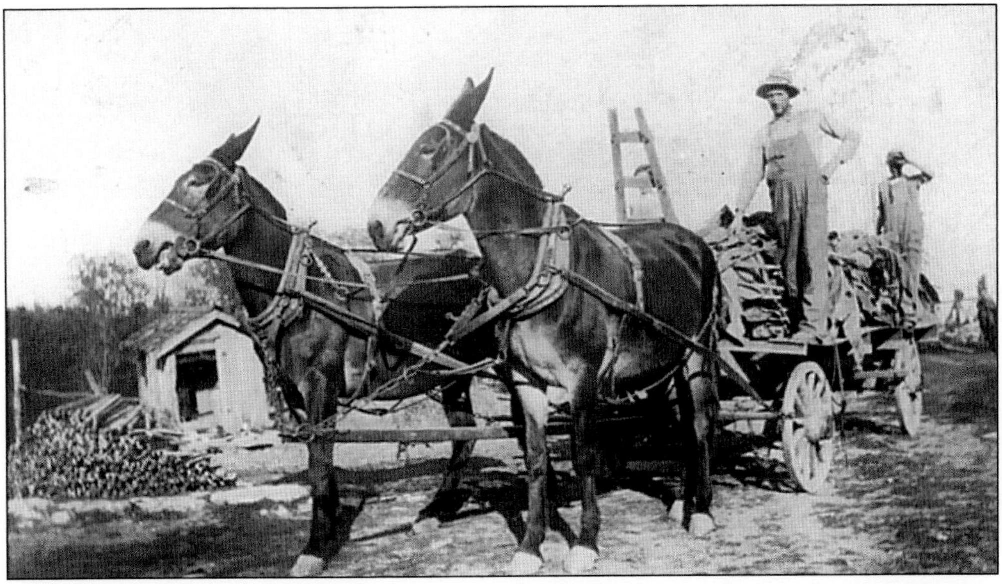

**UNIDENTIFIED FARM, C. 1930.** The location and individuals are unknown, but the event was typical in Ohio County: collecting of cut tobacco. The tobacco was hauled on a flatbed wagon pulled by two mules. Tobacco was and still is one of the important crops for area farmers.

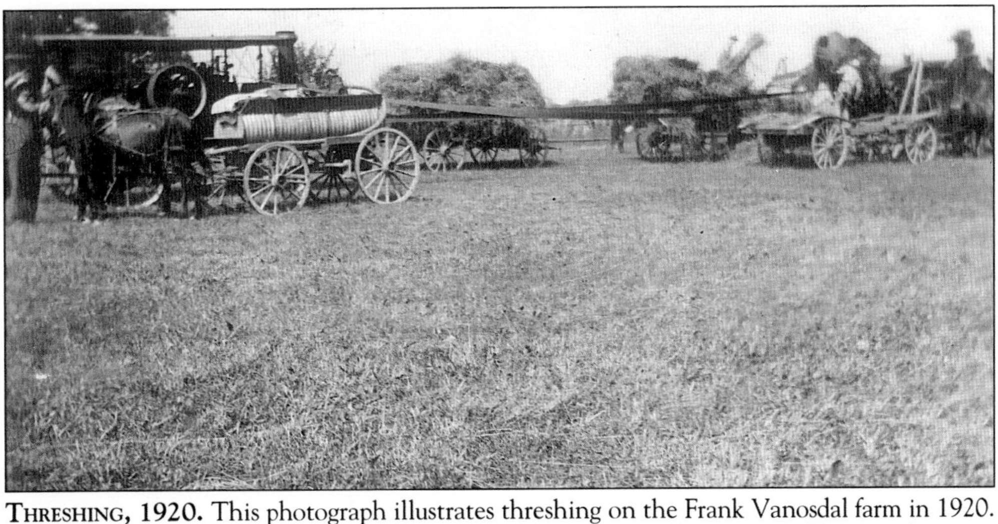

**THRESHING, 1920.** This photograph illustrates threshing on the Frank Vanosdal farm in 1920. Frank Vanosdal was the uncle of Russell Dorrell. Threshing is the process of beating the grain from the husk. Prior to the steam threshing machines, a flail was used. The steam threshers were a labor saving device.

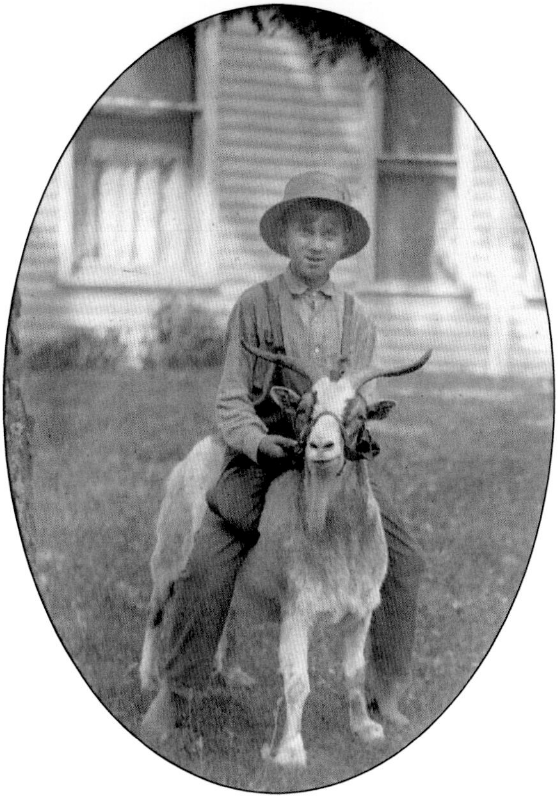

**Russell Dorrell, 1913.** Russell Dorrell, age 11, sits on his pet goat, Ike. Russell took many of the photographs in this book depicting farm scenes on his father's farm in the 1920s.

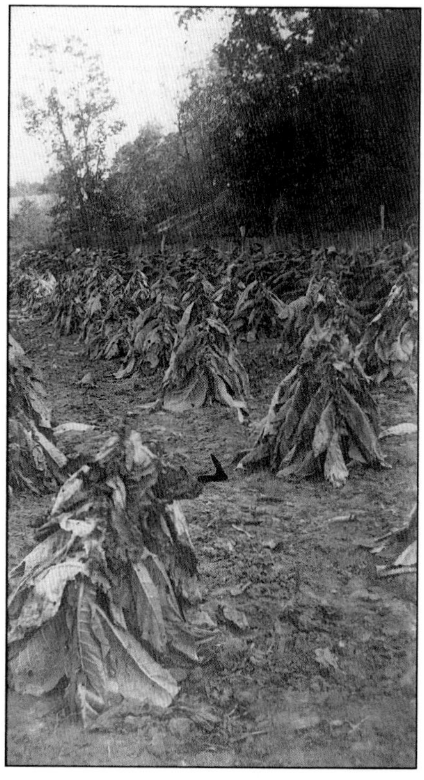

**Tobacco crop, 1919.** Tobacco was one of the crops grown on the Dorrell farm. It has been cut and stacked and is ready to be picked up and taken to the barn to dry. Tobacco is still grown in Ohio County.

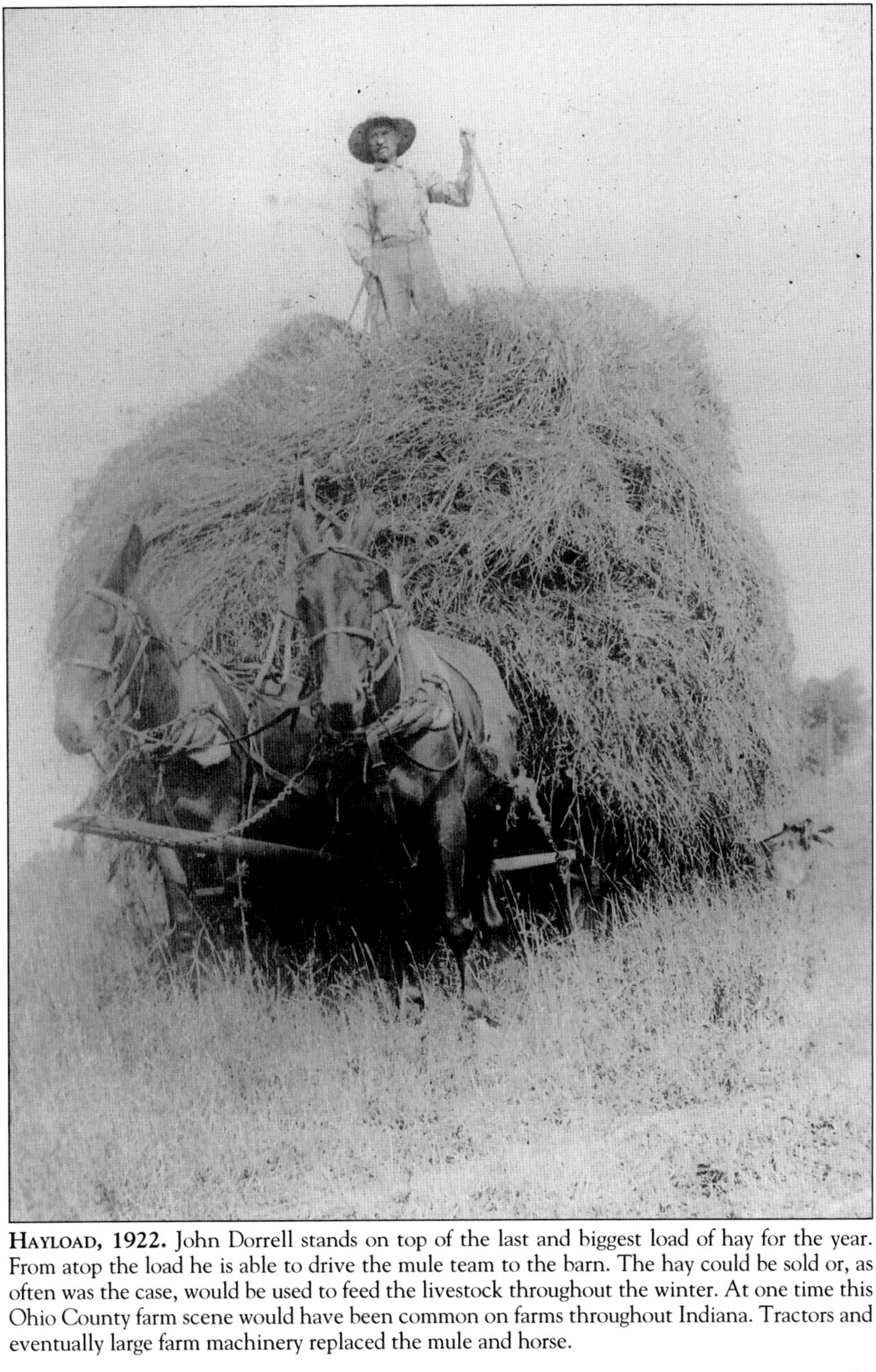

**Hayload, 1922.** John Dorrell stands on top of the last and biggest load of hay for the year. From atop the load he is able to drive the mule team to the barn. The hay could be sold or, as often was the case, would be used to feed the livestock throughout the winter. At one time this Ohio County farm scene would have been common on farms throughout Indiana. Tractors and eventually large farm machinery replaced the mule and horse.

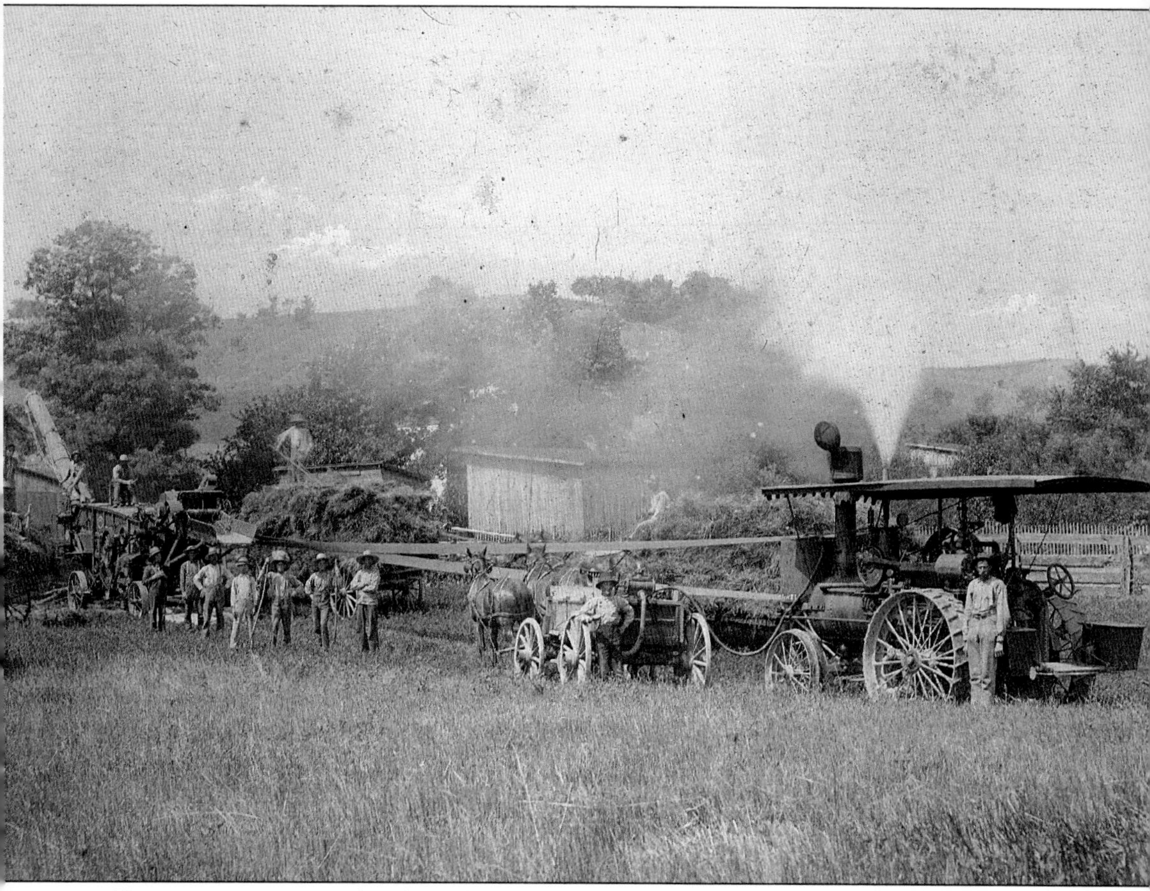

**THRESHING, C. 1910.** This photo depicts threshing on an unidentified Ohio County farm. There are 15 men at various positions to carry out the activity. Note the two large wagons of grain to be threshed. The process was dangerous because the large belts moved at high speed. The wagon in the foreground is supplying the steam engine of the thresher with water.

# *Five*

# Disasters

What area of the country has not been affected by some type of disaster whether it be a flood, tornado, or fire? Ohio County has not been spared. Floods have paid frequent visits to the county. The earliest recorded flood was in 1864 followed by others in 1884, 1913, 1937, 1945, 1955, and 1997. During these times the people of Ohio County pulled together to assist others in need. The construction of the Markland Dam in 1962 has helped control the level of the river to prevent a flood. In some cases, most recently in 1997, the continuous rain throughout the Midwest meant the dam was insufficient protection against flooding.

Fire is another disastrous event that can cause loss of life and property. The first major fire in Rising Sun occurred in 1866 on a Monday morning. Several homes and businesses on Main and Front streets suffered damage at a total loss of $22,900. The fire is believed to have been caused by foul play. The fire of July 17, 1885, left part of the business district in ashes and debris. The fire started in the saloon of Wallace P. Hall on Popular Street. Total estimated losses came to $39,100. Insurance covered half of the damages.

High winds and tornadoes can also cause serious damage. This was evident in 1915 when a tornado tore through the county destroying several buildings in town and additional ones in the surrounding area. Barns and fences were knocked down and some animals were killed. In 1948, another tornado hit Rising Sun. Again several buildings were seriously damaged, including the high school which lost its cupola and bell. School was in session when the tornado hit. Fortunately, the students had just left the room where the cupola and bell landed.

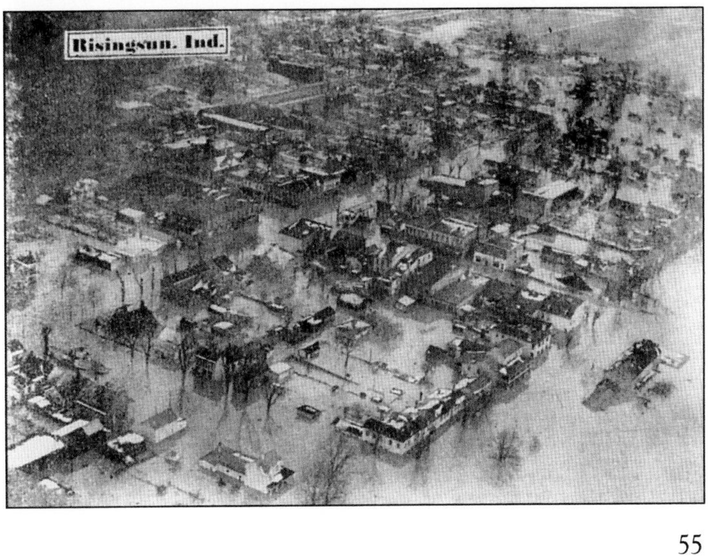


**Bird's-Eye of Rising Sun, 1937.** The flood of 1937 was recorded as the highest flood stage of the Ohio River at 496.5 feet. The United States Corps of Engineers classified the flood as a 100-year flood. Other severe floods that hit the area include the 1913 and 1945 floods classified as 25-year floods. This photograph shows how high the flood came over the bank and invaded the town.

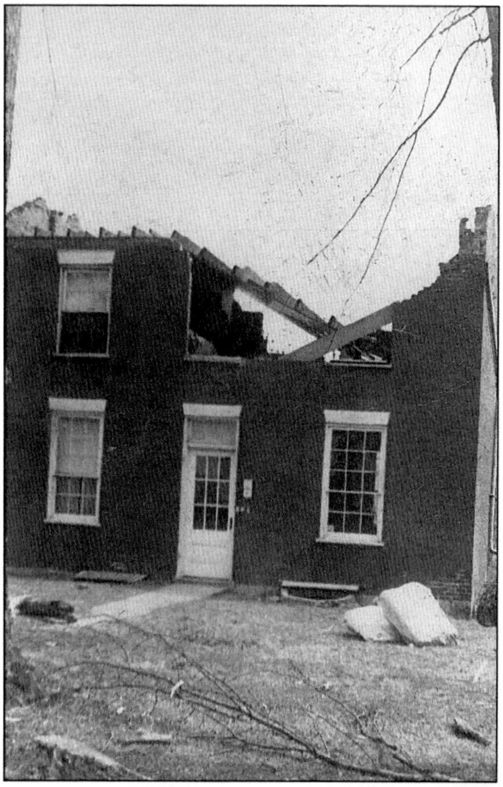

**FRED HESS HOUSE, 1915.** At 9 p.m. on July 7, 1915, a cyclone hit Ohio County causing major damage. According to the oldest residents, at the time this had been the worst storm in their recollection. A few cows and horses were killed, but no other loss of life was recorded.

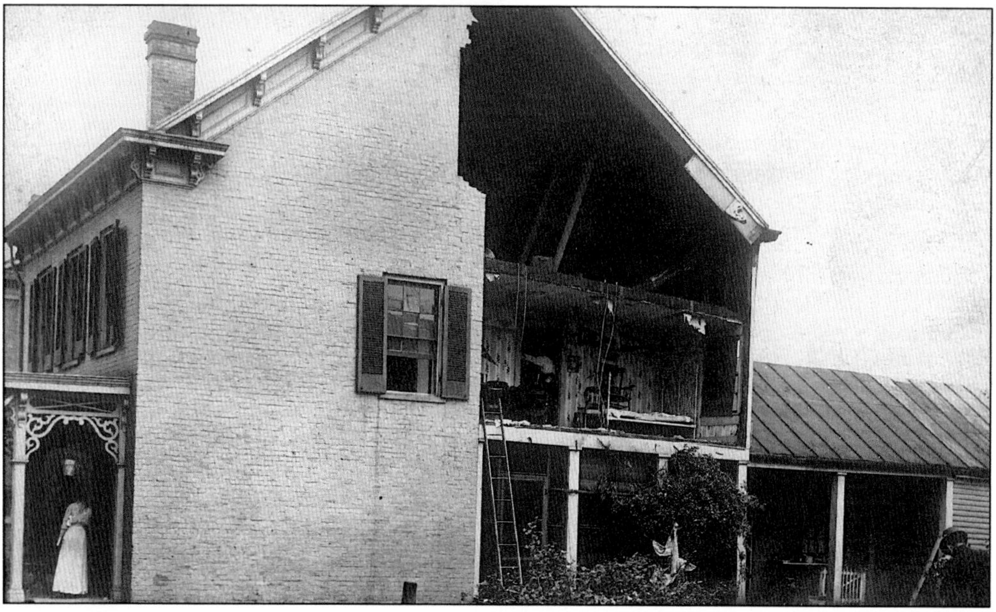

**GIBSON HOUSE, 1915.** The Harry L. Gibson residence suffered extensive damage in the 1915 tornado. The house, located on High Street, had a portion of the side cleanly ripped off, exposing the contents of the house. The Gibson family was descending the stairs when the damage occurred, fortunately with no injuries. Harry Gibson was part of the Gibson family that owned the hardware store. The warehouse of the Gibson building lost the tin roof in the storm.

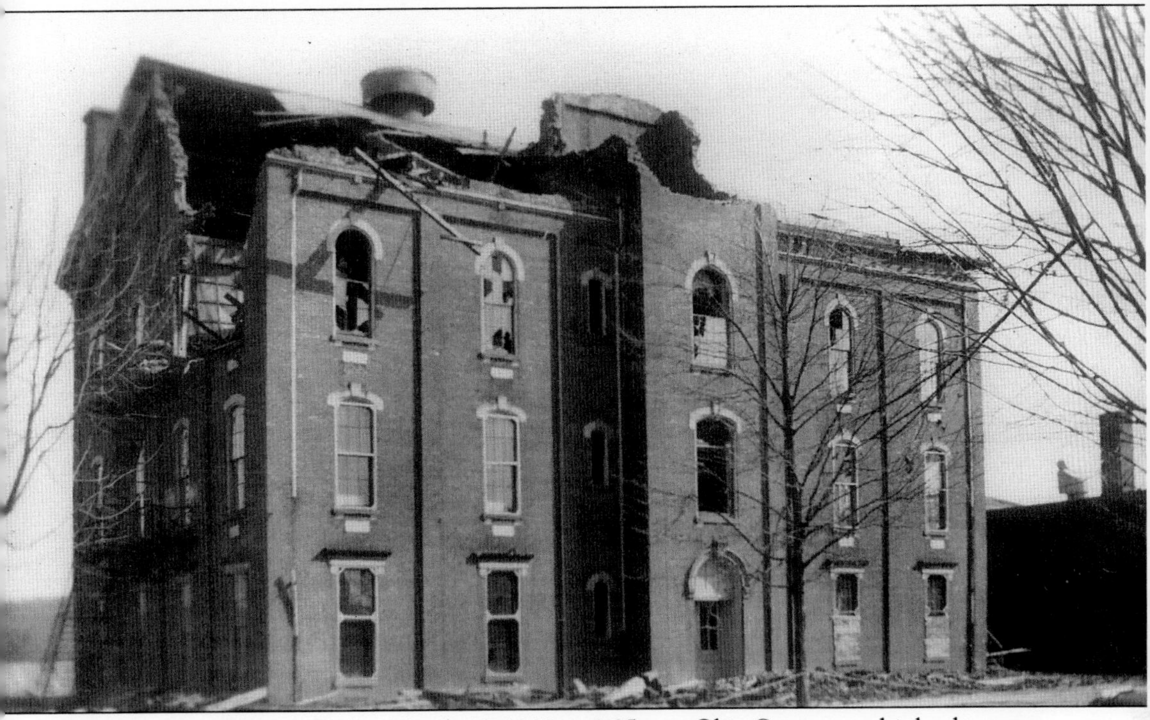

**High School, 1948.** On Friday, March 19, 1948, at 1:05 p.m. Ohio County was hit by the worst tornado in the county's history. A week after the tornado hit, the county was still accessing the damage. One of the causalities occurred when the tornado struck the old high school, sending the cupola and bell through the roof to the third floor. Fortunately a typing class had just vacated the room where the cupola and bell landed. Repairs to the building resulted in the entire third floor being removed.

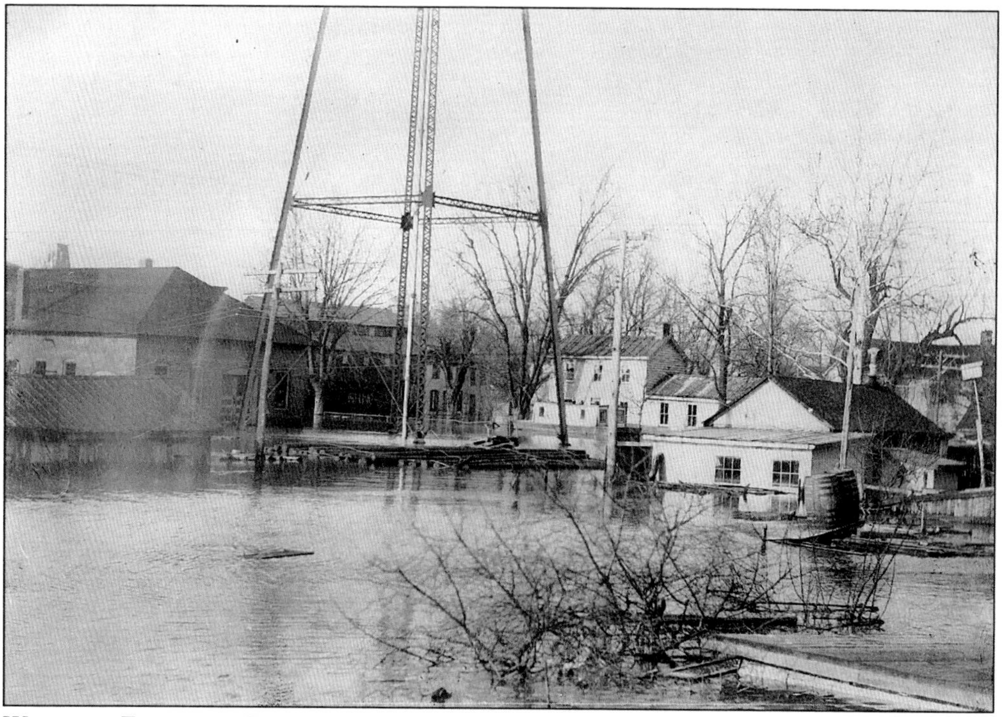

**Whitlock Furniture Factory, 1937.** Early rains in January 1937 brought the creeks out of their banks and washing out dams such as the one on Dry Branch. This view of the Whitlock Furniture Factory indicates the extent of the flood. Boy Scouts went from house to house warning citizens to boil the water before drinking and encouraged them to continue to do so for several weeks after the floodwaters receded. Some failed to listen and became ill, but no epidemic occured.

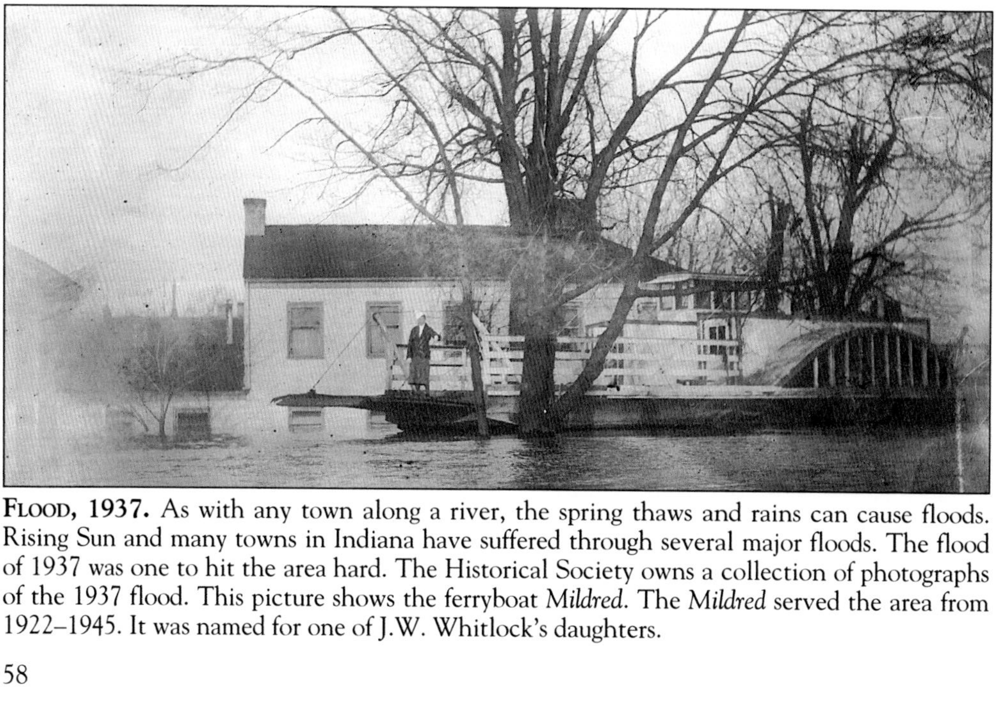

**Flood, 1937.** As with any town along a river, the spring thaws and rains can cause floods. Rising Sun and many towns in Indiana have suffered through several major floods. The flood of 1937 was one to hit the area hard. The Historical Society owns a collection of photographs of the 1937 flood. This picture shows the ferryboat *Mildred*. The *Mildred* served the area from 1922–1945. It was named for one of J.W. Whitlock's daughters.

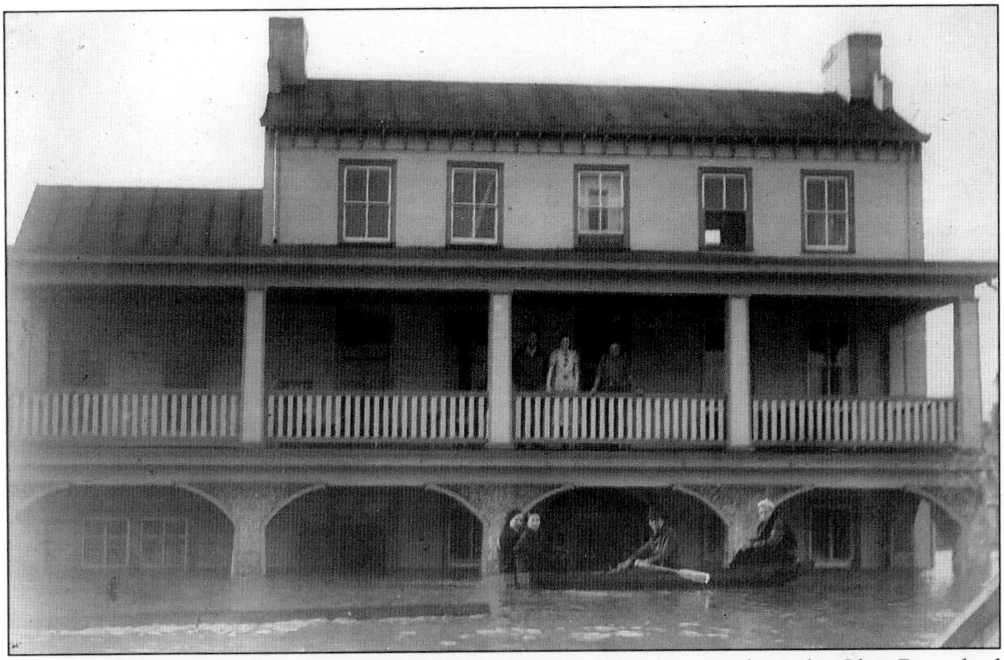

**Empire House, 1937.** Being situated on Front Street a short distance from the Ohio River had its advantages and also its disadvantages. For the Empire House in 1937, the floodwaters reached halfway up the first floor in this photograph. It had been reported that all electrical power had been lost when the water covered the electric lines. This, coupled with the high water, would not have made a stay at the Empire House very pleasant.

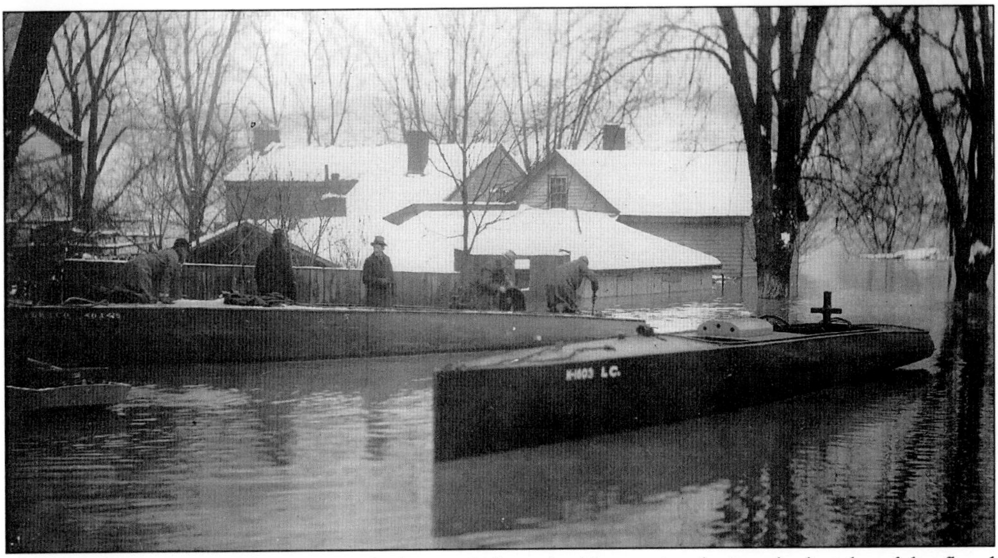

**Hoosier Girl, 1937.** The *Hoosier Girl* provided a valuable service during the height of the flood crisis. On January 26, the *Hoosier Girl* made a trip to Lawrenceburg to get supplies under the Red Cross flag. The four men who made the trip included Raymond Bedgood, Dr. W.M. Hall, Orville Hodson, and W.D. Burns. Those pictured, from left to right, are as follows: unknown, Robert McConnell, Stewart Whitlock, Clarence Bedgood, and Raymond Bedgood. These men were preparing to take food to Patriot, which was hit harder by the flood.

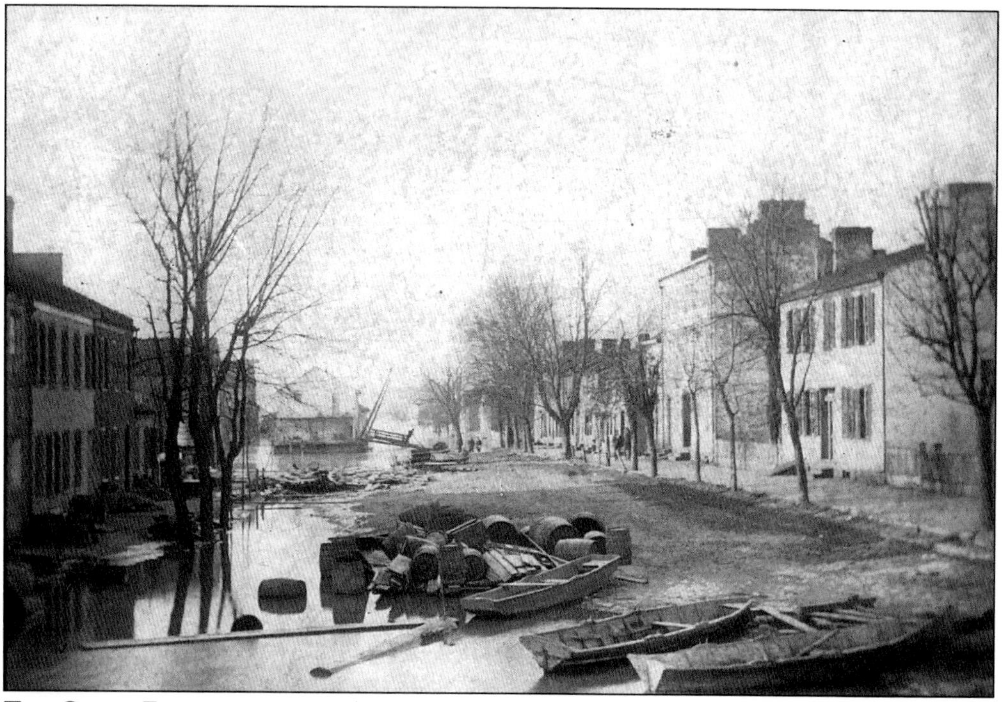

**The Great Flood of 1884.** The flood of 1884 was the first flood to be documented in photographs. This scene depicts Front Street. At the time of the flood, houses and businesses were located on the riverside of Front Street with their back doors facing the river. Over time erosion of the riverbank made it necessary for the owners to relocate. The large three-story building on the right is the Empire House minus the balcony.

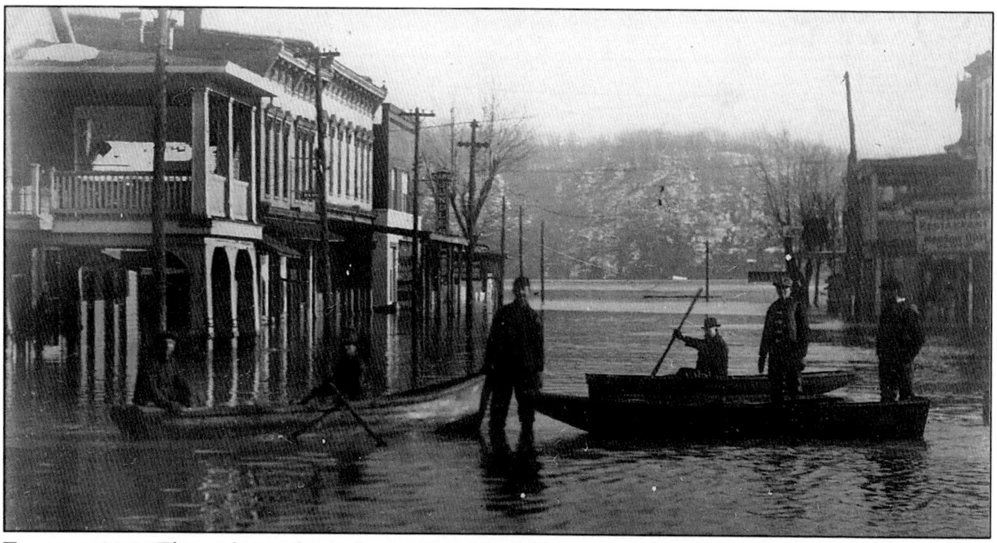

**Flood, 1937.** The only method of travel on Main Street was by boat or putting waders on and walking very slowly and carefully. To the right of the picture is John Talbott's Restaurant. A report in the paper on January 28 noted that most businesses and residences were high and dry. The water on Main Street came in on the floor of Bowman Meat Market and the G.B. Gibson's Sons store. In this photograph it appears to be more water that came later.

**FIRE ENGINE, 1937.** The flood of 1937 caused quite a bit of damage, not just along the riverbank but down Main Street as well. The flood stage reached 82 feet 2 inches. The fire truck provided a valuable service during the flood. Here two fire men pump water off of Mr. Uhlmansiek's building.

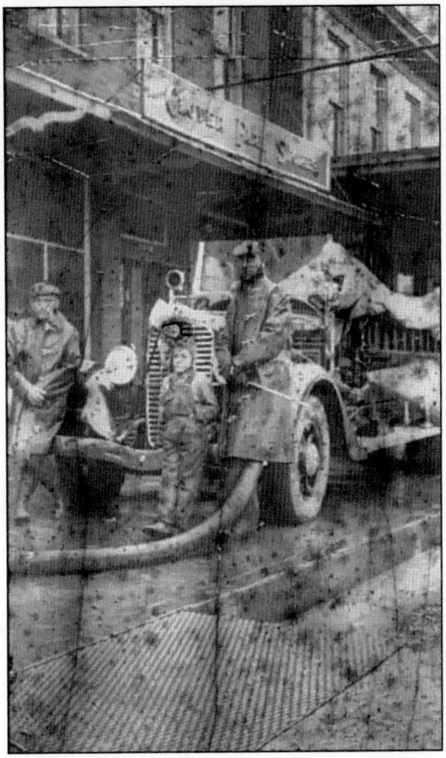

**PUMPER, 1957.** On March 30, 1957, the Rising Sun Volunteer Fire Department accepted delivery of a new pumper. The cost of the fire engine was $9,366. Fire Chief Russell Uhlmansiek stated, "Rising Sun now has the last word in fire fighting equipment." Mr. Uhlmansiek served as fire chief for 25 years. The pumper was stored in the new city building on Walnut Street.

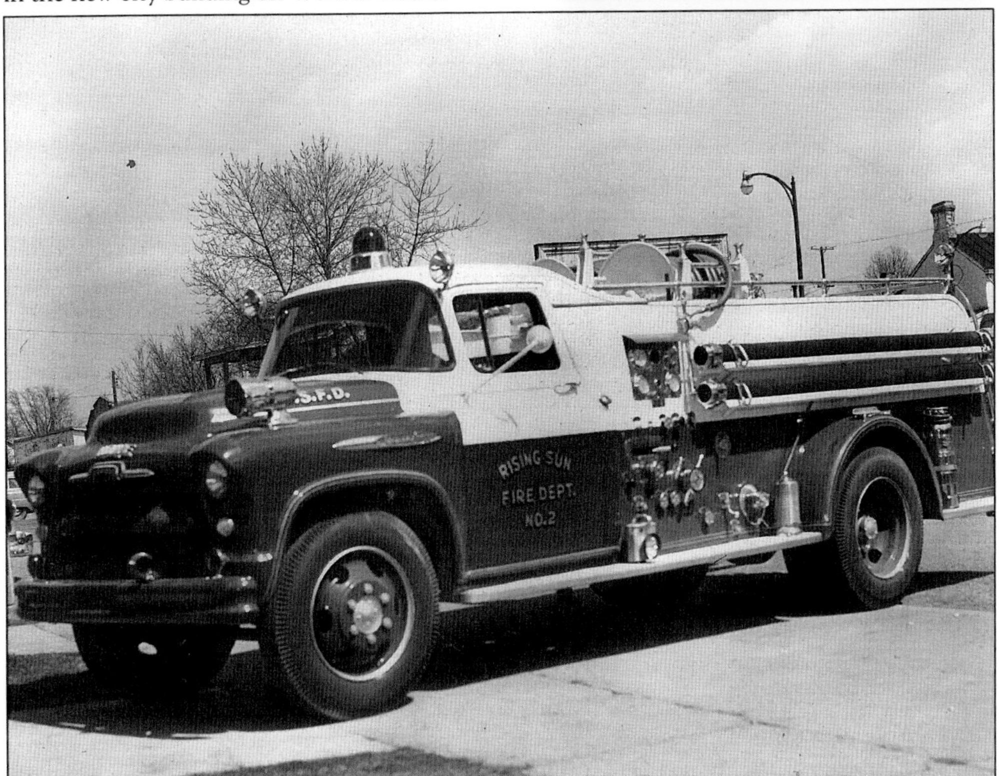

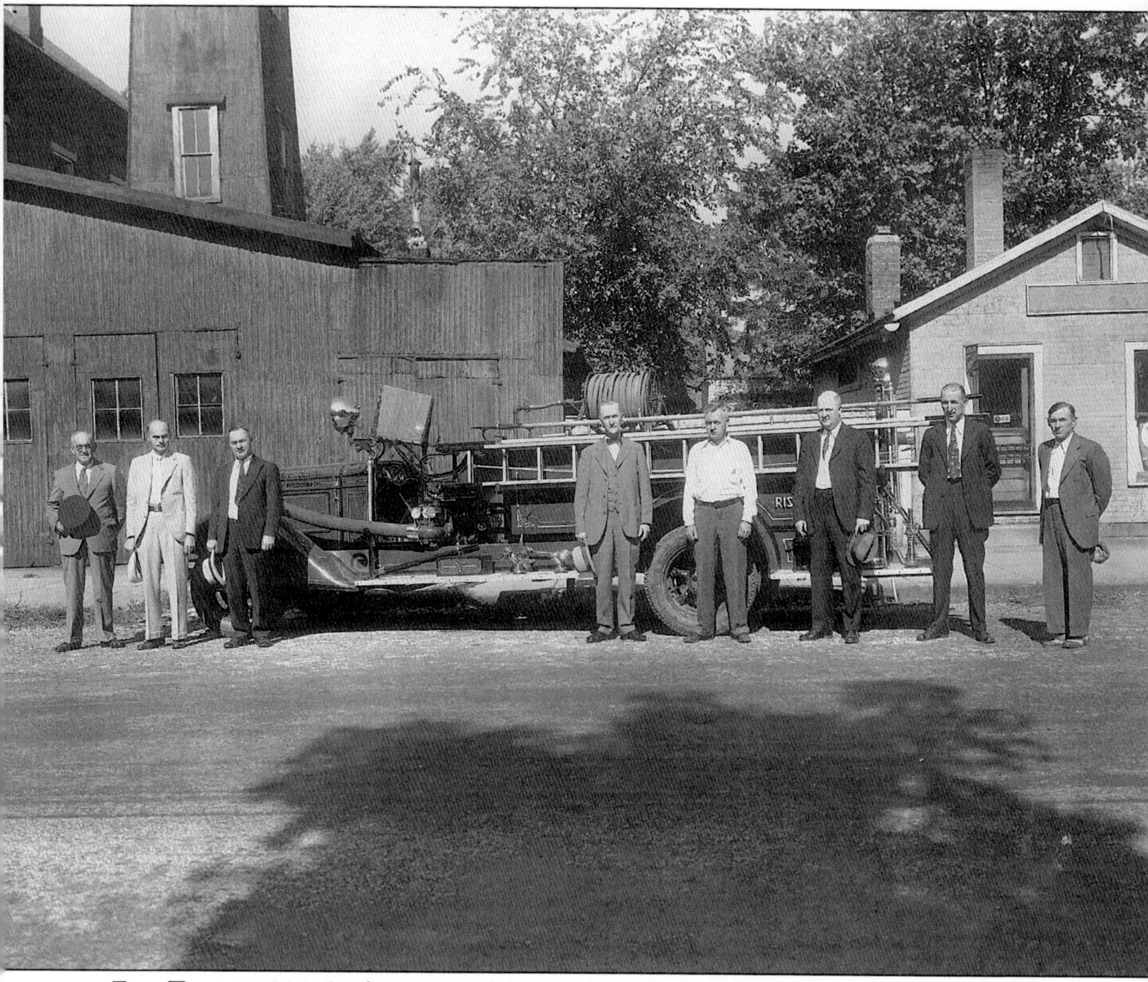

**FIRE TRUCK, 1934.** In the center of this photo is the brand new fire truck for the Rising Sun Volunteer Fire Department. The new truck poses along with city officials in front of the metal firehouse. From left to right are as follows: Harry Rump, Stanley Powell, John Durbin, Lucian Harris, Jim Green, Paris Foutty, Grant Williamson, and Sandy Baxter. The building to the right is James Fisher's Dry Cleaners. He moved the cleaners to his residence on South High Street when the new city building was erected.

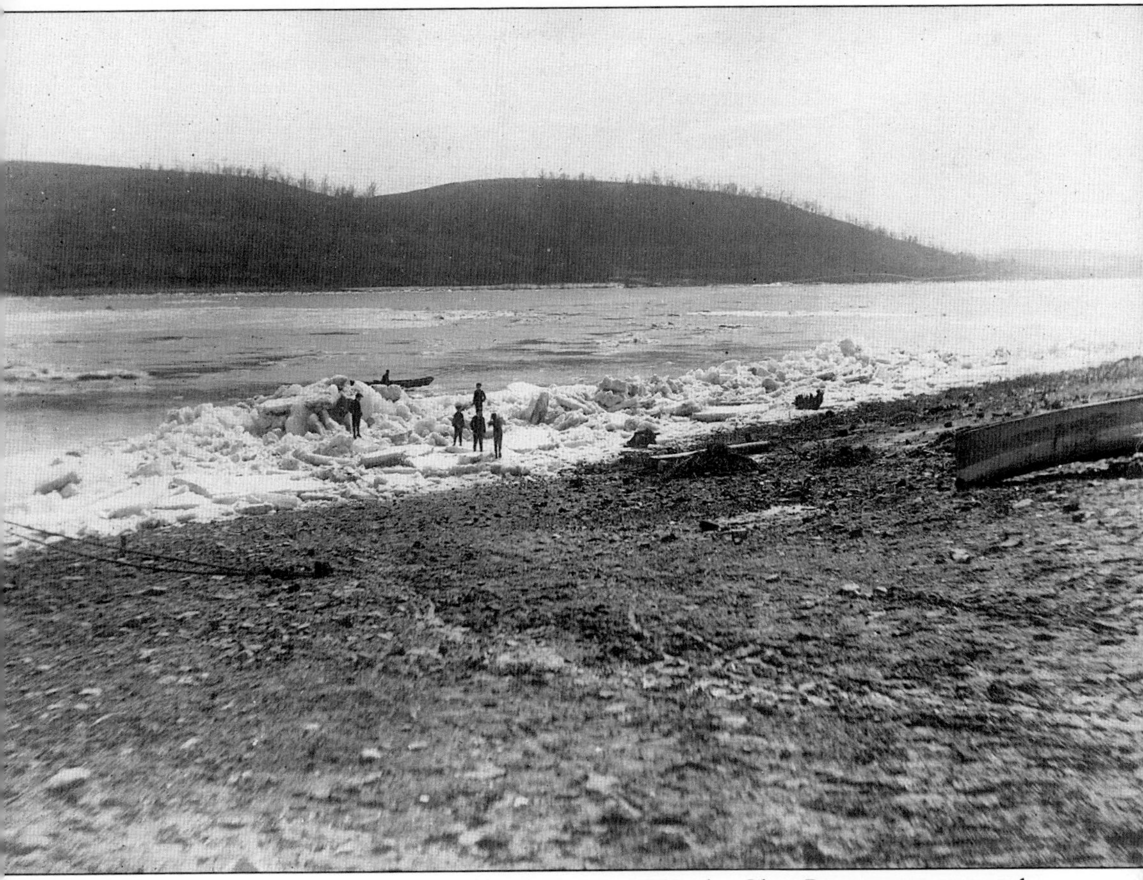

**Ice, 1918.** Prior to the building of Markland Dam in 1962, the Ohio River was not as wide or deep as it is today. The river would freeze, allowing citizens of Rabbit Hash to walk across without getting wet. However, the ice of 1918 caused serious damage to the wharfboats and smaller vessels. It was this ice that completely destroyed the steamboats *Cincinnati* and *Louisville* as they sat in dock.

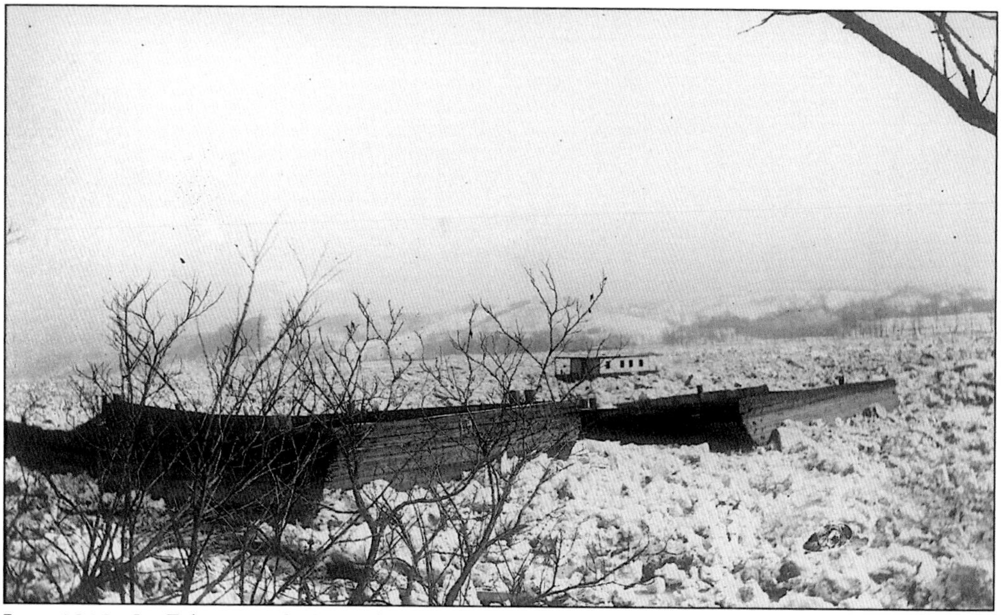

**Ice, 1918.** In February of 1918, the great ice gorge broke. Within minutes the ice began traveling along the current filled with all sort of debris. Little damage occurred along the Ohio County portion of the river. A barge was crushed when the ice drove another barge into it. The Cochran Coal and Ice Company suffered a set-back when the ice destroyed the crane during the ice's final movement. It had been weakened in earlier ice movements.

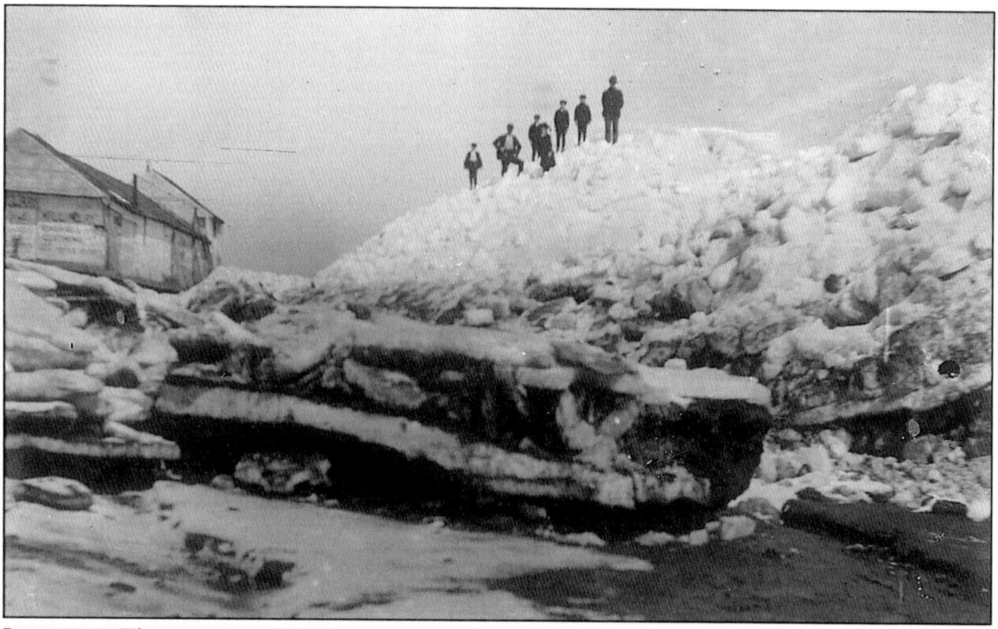

**Ice, 1918.** The great ice of 1918 was spectacular sight, especially the day it broke. Following the break through, blocks of ice made their way onto shore. In some cases the ice piled up as high as a house. This brought people to the riverbank to have their pictures taken standing on or among the ice blocks. The *Rising Sun Recorder* projected that when all the ice melted another flood of 58 feet or better would happen.

# *Six*

# Main Street

The heart of Rising Sun is Main Street. Looking at the various businesses that have occupied stores on this street and the adjoining streets gives an indication of the growth of the city. It also is a way to tell what life was like through the years and how we have developed as a society.

At first glance it may seem odd to have two or three hotels right on Front Street along the river. Today we look for lodging along the interstate or major highway. But that is due to our perspective. Nineteenth century hotels were located along a major highway—the Ohio River. In the 1800s and early 1900s, most visitors came by steamboat.

Other early businesses in town included blacksmiths, shoe and boot stores, groceries, and hardware stores. Over the years some of them were no longer necessary, while others grew and required larger accommodations outside the business district. Others eventually were put out of business by large chain stores.

Today Main Street looks much the same as it did in the early 1900s—an attractive view from the corner of High and Main streets looking down toward the Ohio River. Noticeable differences: the businesses in place today are craft shops, antique shops, and art galleries. The traditional early stores such as hardware, grocery, and shoe stores have moved away. Others like the bank, newspaper, restaurants, drug store, and insurance office are still here, creating a nice blend of commerce.

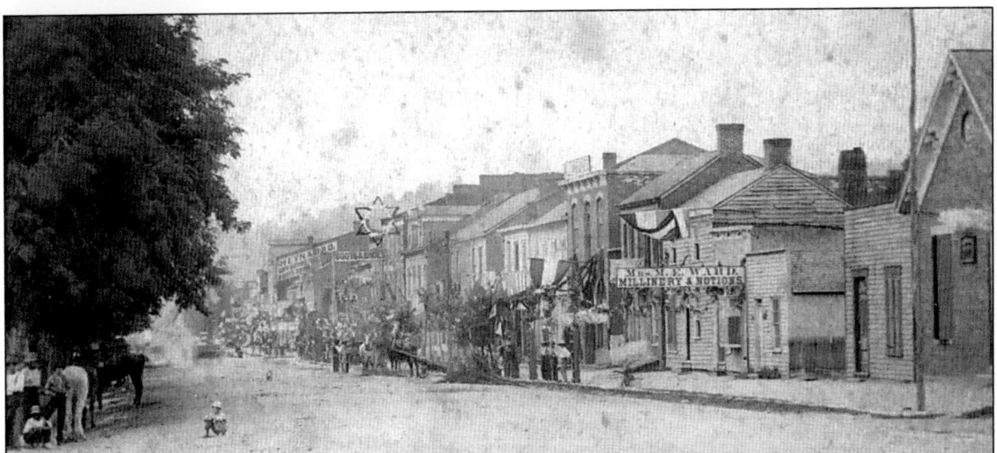


**Main Street, c. 1900.** A streetscape looking east on Main toward the river. Several businesses have signs out front. Included are Mrs. M.E. Ward's Millinery & Notions, down the block a boot and shoe store, and Heyn & Brothers dry goods and boots and shoes. The town is decorated with flags and a large star for an unknown celebration.

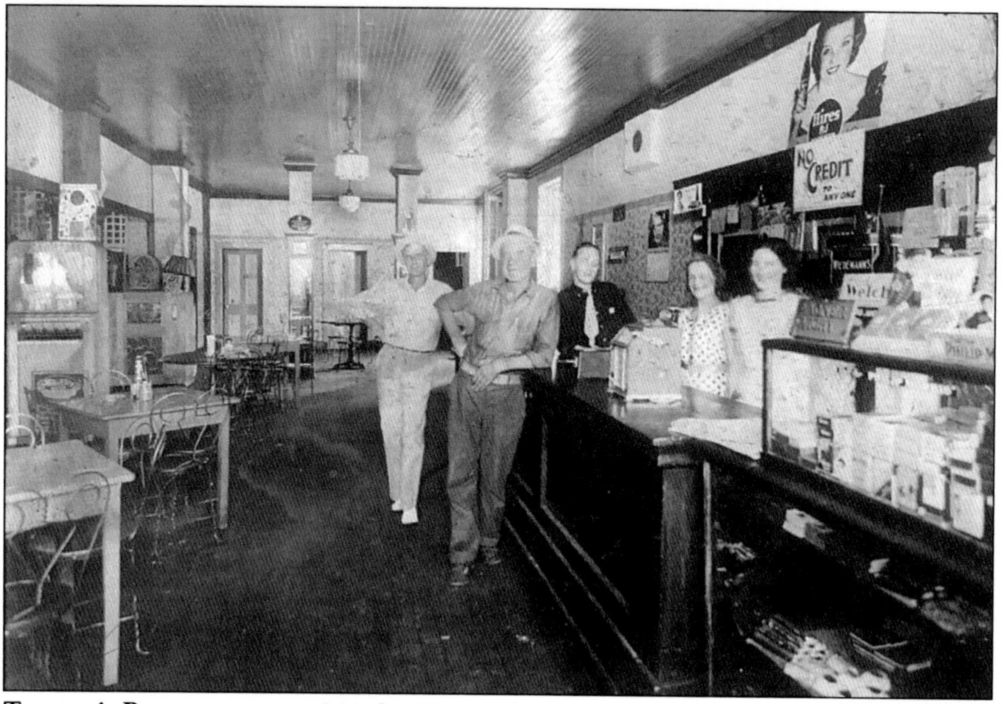


**Talbott's Restaurant, c. 1940.** Interior view of John Wesley Talbott's Restaurant located on Main Street approximately where Colonel Pepper's is today. Mr. Talbott is the gentleman behind the counter in the dark shirt. His establishment had several tables to serve his patrons. He was out of business during the 1937 flood as the water reached into his place.

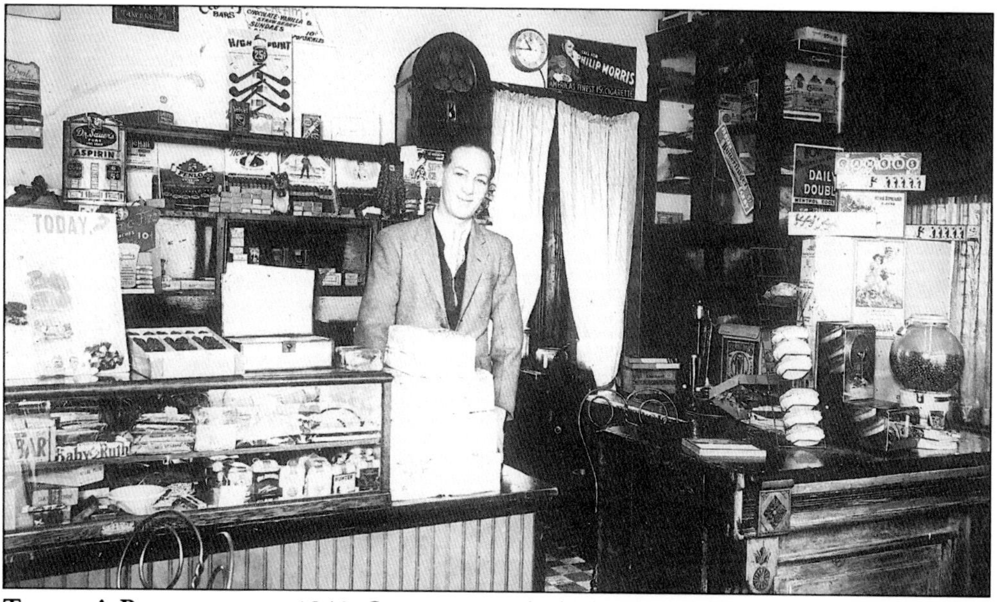


**Talbott's Restaurant, c. 1940.** Once again we find John Wesley Talbott behind the counter of his restaurant. Like many restaurants today, Mr. Talbott sold additional items such as candy, tobacco, and aspirin. Note the radio just above his head. The counter to the right is a nicely crafted piece of furniture.

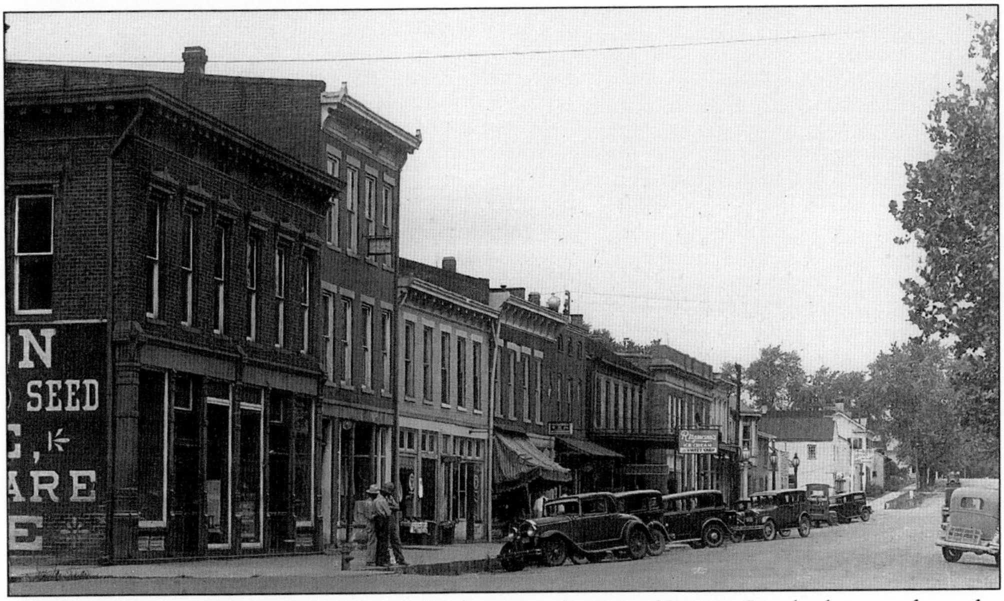


**MAIN STREET, C. 1935.** This view of the business district of Rising Sun looks west from the corner of Main and Popular streets. The business on the right is Gibson and Sons Hardware Store. The large sign hanging is Riigmann's Sweet Shop. The sign indicates that ice cream was sold here among other goodies. The seventh building from the left with the lampposts in front is the Rising Sun State Bank. Currently this is the home of the *Ohio County Recorder*. In 1988, the bank merged with the Madison Bank & Trust.

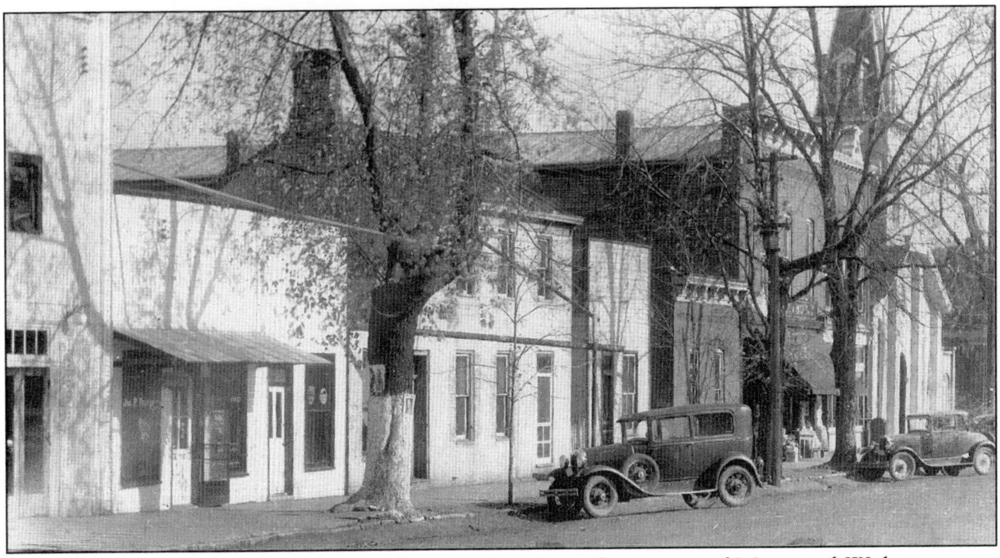

**MAIN STREET, 1935.** This photograph was taken from the corner of Main and Walnut streets looking east. The first three buildings were razed to make room for the Madison Bank & Trust. Today the remaining buildings from the left are the Snack Shack, Kraft's Rivertown Gallery, Harps On Main, Indiana Workforce Development, and the vacant Presbyterian Church. In the 1920s, the occupants included the Columbia Theater, Paris and Son Meat Market, the home and law office of Judge William Ricketts, law office of Charles French, Dr. Fessler's office, Danbury's Furniture and Appliance, the law office of Mitchell and Brown, and the Presbyterian Church.

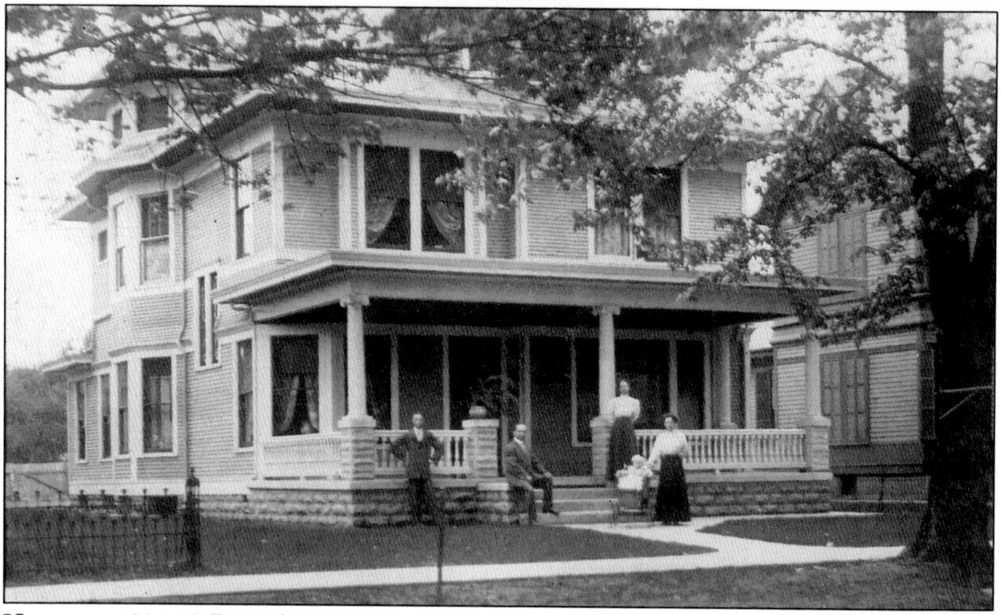

**House, c. 1920.** A Free Classic style house located on the west side of High Street. The second house from the northwest corner was built in 1910 and is known as the Rodney Davis House.

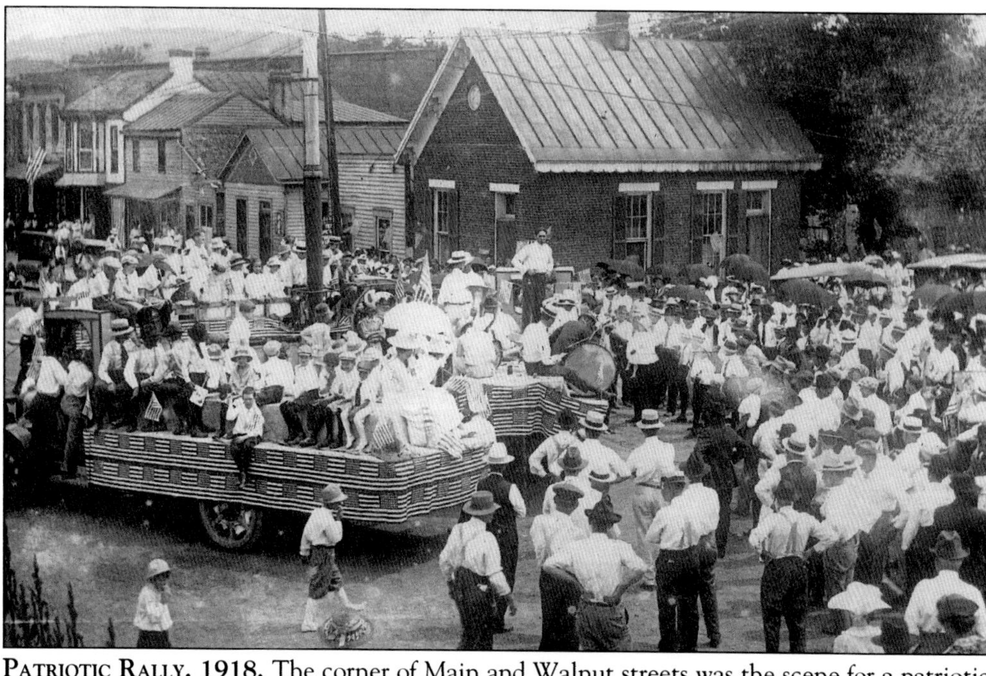

**Patriotic Rally, 1918.** The corner of Main and Walnut streets was the scene for a patriotic rally in 1918. A speaker in the center of the photograph addresses a large crowd, while standing on one of three patriotically decorated flatbed trucks. It could be part of a Fourth of July celebration or patriotic speech in support of World War I.

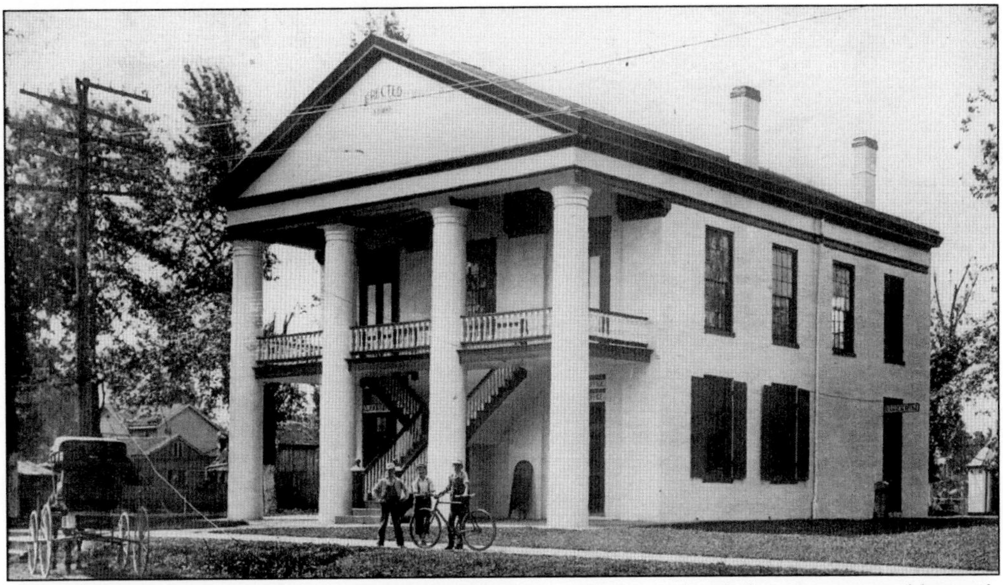

**OHIO COUNTY COURTHOUSE, c. 1920.** Rising Sun residents Col. Abel C. Pepper and his wife donated the land for the site of the courthouse. In 1844, masons laid the foundation for the Ohio County Courthouse with Colonel Pepper honored at the cornerstone laying ceremonies. He delivered the dedication address and placed the first stone. As he poured oil on the stone he declared "laid according to ancient custom."

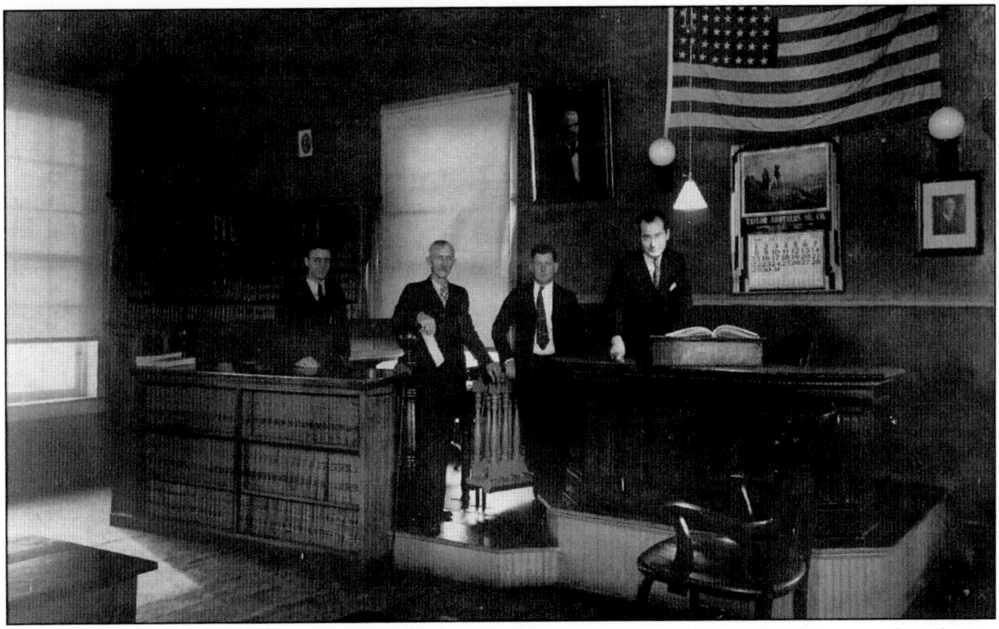

**JUDGE WILLIAM D. RICKETTS, 1935.** Judge Ricketts served as a jurist for 29 years first being elected Judge of the Seventh Judicial Court in 1926. The Seventh Court was comprised of Dearborn and Ohio counties. As a candidate for the Supreme Court of Indiana he received delegate votes in 58 of the 92 counties, and the solid delegation from 25 of the counties. The men in the photograph, from left to right, are: Austin Collins, clerk; O.B. Mitchell, sheriff; Caleb Irons, chauffeur; and Judge Ricketts. On July 5, 1940, Judge Ricketts passed away.

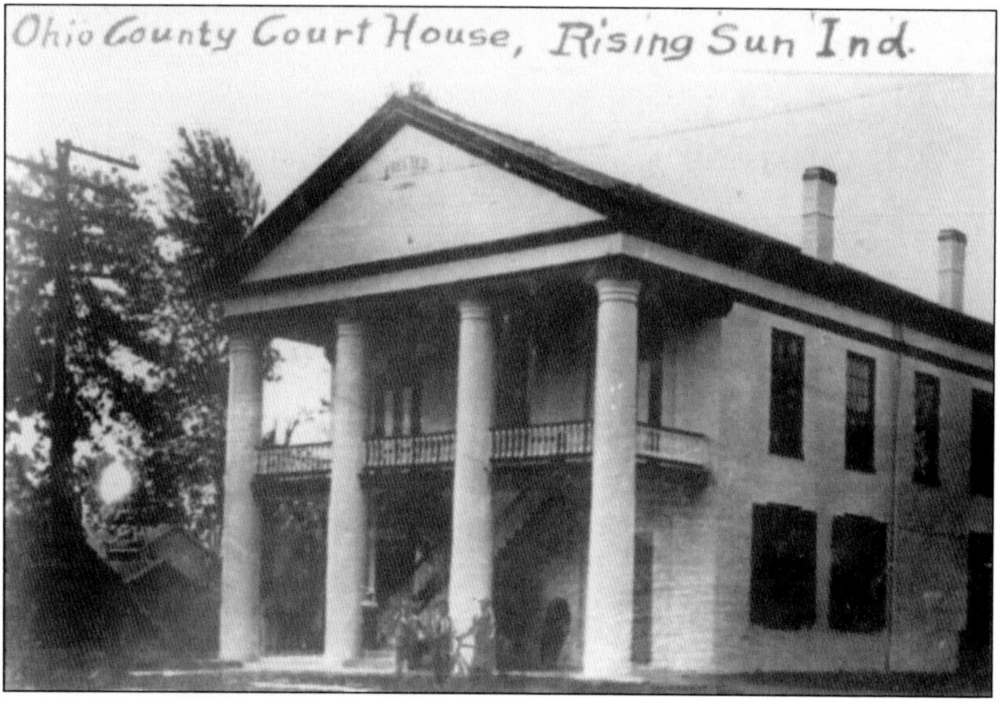


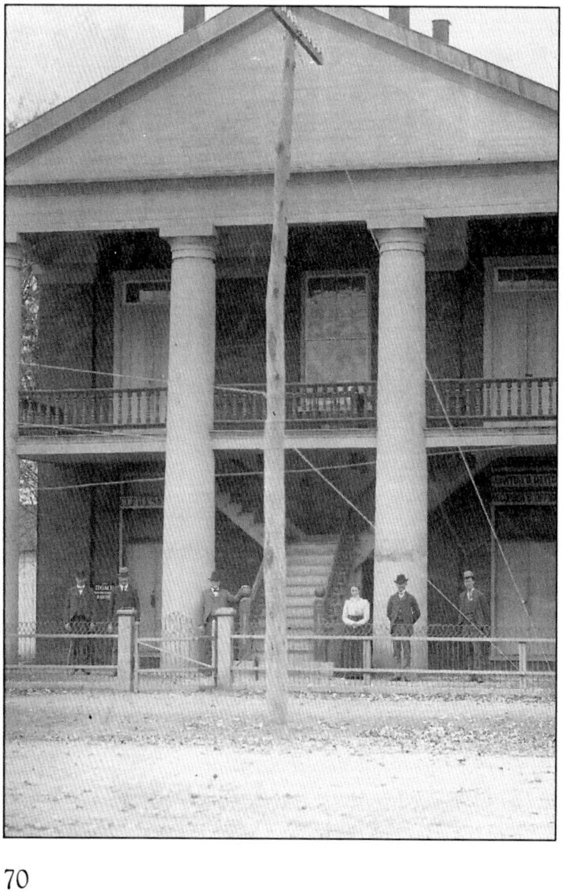

**OHIO COUNTY COURTHOUSE, C. 1910.** Sometime prior to late 1920 a coat of stucco was applied to the courthouse. The courthouse was later covered with permastone that is attached to the surface, giving the structure a stone-like appearance. In the late 1980s, plans for renovating the courthouse were formulated. Changes to the courthouse included the building of an interior hallway, which allowed access to all offices from inside the building, an addition, and the removal of the permastone.

**OHIO COUNTY COURTHOUSE, C. 1916.** The county commissioners oversaw an extensive remodeling and restoration of the county courthouse in 1987. Originally the two-story brick building stood 50 feet deep. Prior to 1987, the courthouse had no interior halls. Each of the county offices had to be accessed via an outside entrance. To the left of the staircase is the clerk's office, and the door to the right is the auditor and recorder's office. Sometime around 1909 the porch was added to the front.

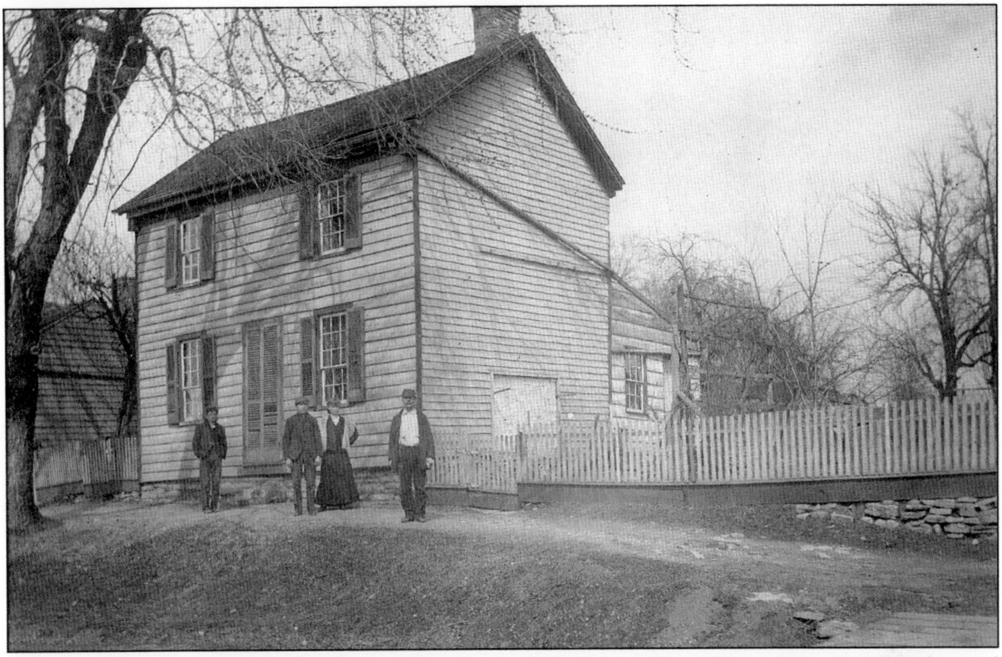

**Beatty House, c. 1910.** The Beatty House was located on First Street between Popular and Front streets. It is Beatty's first name that is unknown. In 1888 according to the *History of Dearborn, Ohio, and Switzerland Counties, Indiana*, George Beatty was superintendent of the Rising Sun Cotton Mill at the corner of Front and Fifth streets. The mill employed 45 people.

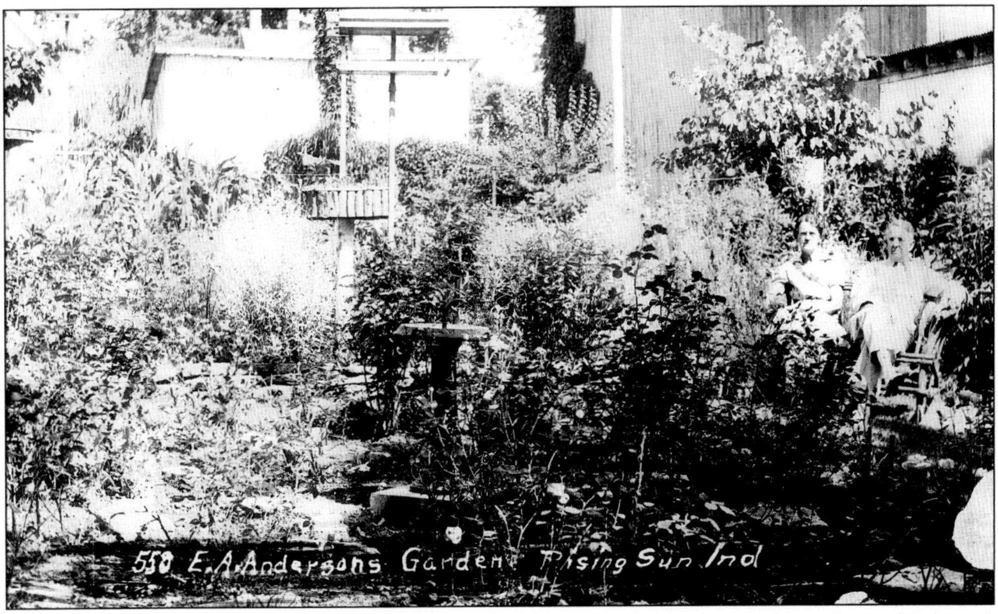


**Gardens, c. 1930.** Mr. and Mrs. E.A. Anderson sit in chairs in the garden of their backyard. The well-landscaped garden is complete with bird feeders and a sundial in the center of the yard. Even with a beautiful garden, industry still can occupy the view. To the right is the large lumber shed of the Whitlock Furniture Factory. Mr. Anderson owned E.A. Anderson Clothing Store on Main Street and lived in the home that the Whitlocks built.

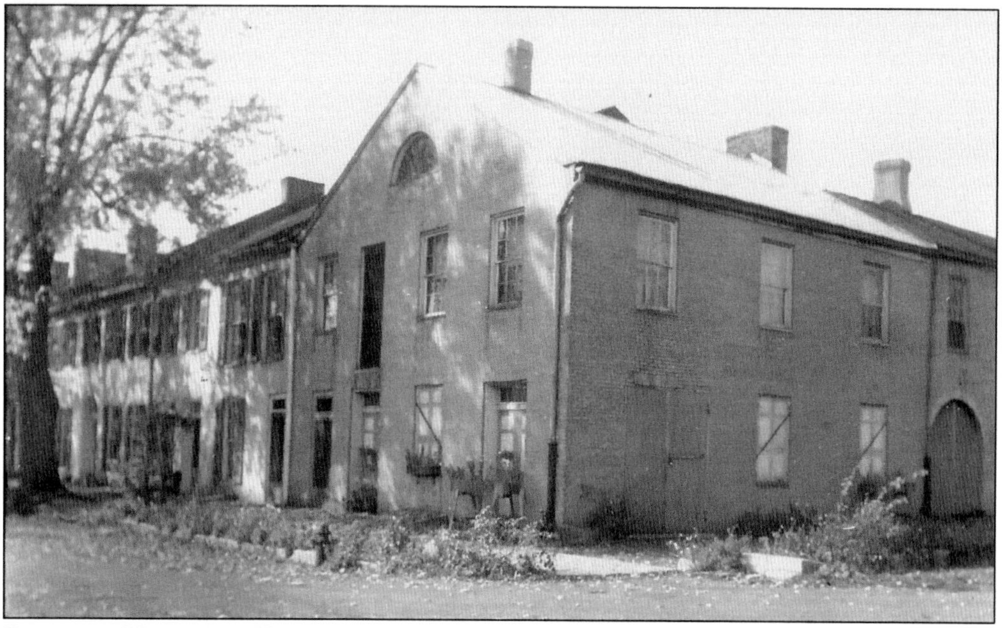

**SHADRACH HATHAWAY HOUSE, c. 1930.** While on a visit to Cincinnati in 1814 he met the proprietor of the new town of Rising Sun, John James. Mr. Hathaway purchased a lot at the corner of Front and Fourth streets for $100. It was here that he opened up his shoe business and later a general merchandising store. In 1840, he replaced the log house he was working out of with a Greek Revival building that served both as his residence and business. It is said that this was a stop on the Underground Railroad. Today the Courtyard Restaurant occupies the building.

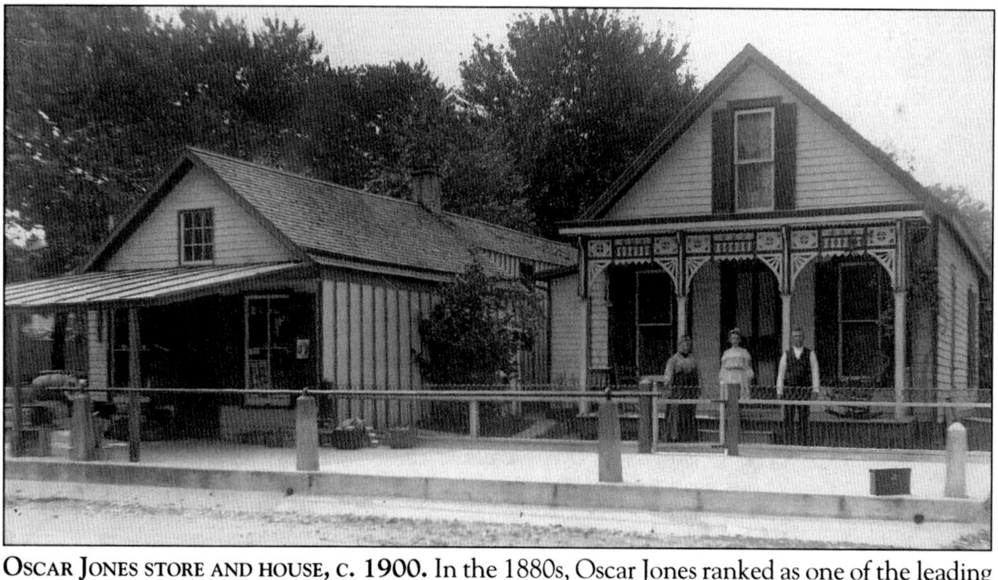

**OSCAR JONES STORE AND HOUSE, c. 1900.** In the 1880s, Oscar Jones ranked as one of the leading dealers in staple and fancy groceries. His store and home were located at the corner of Walnut and Second streets. In 1921, Oscar Jones' nephew, Oscar Baxter, had the store razed and a brick building constructed. The building currently is a laundromat, but over the years had seen service as a store, restaurant, and bus station. The following year Mr. Baxter replaced the frame home with a brick house.

**PRESBYTERIAN CHURCH, c. 1910.** According to the records of the church, the building was built in 1833, although the cornerstone indicates 1832. The trustees closed a contract with Joshua Wills to do the masonry work, which included the brick and stone work at a cost of $500. They also hired Furman Vinup to do the carpenter work for a fee of $480. Though the church was still under construction the congregation was already using it for worship.

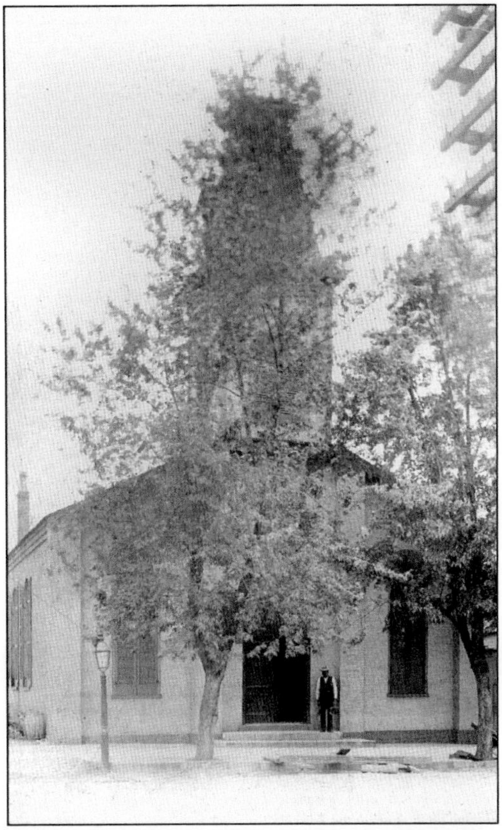

**FIRST PRESBYTERIAN CHURCH, c. 1900.** Interior of the First Presbyterian Church located on Main Street. The church is currently unoccupied. The church was organized in 1816 with James Steward, William McCord, and Hugh Espey, Jr. as elected elders. They began in a schoolhouse located across from the courthouse. Until the church was built in 1833, the congregation met in the schoolhouse, stores, private homes, and even in the woods. After 174 years as a church, the First Presbyterian Church closed its doors in 1990 after membership dwindled to 14 persons.

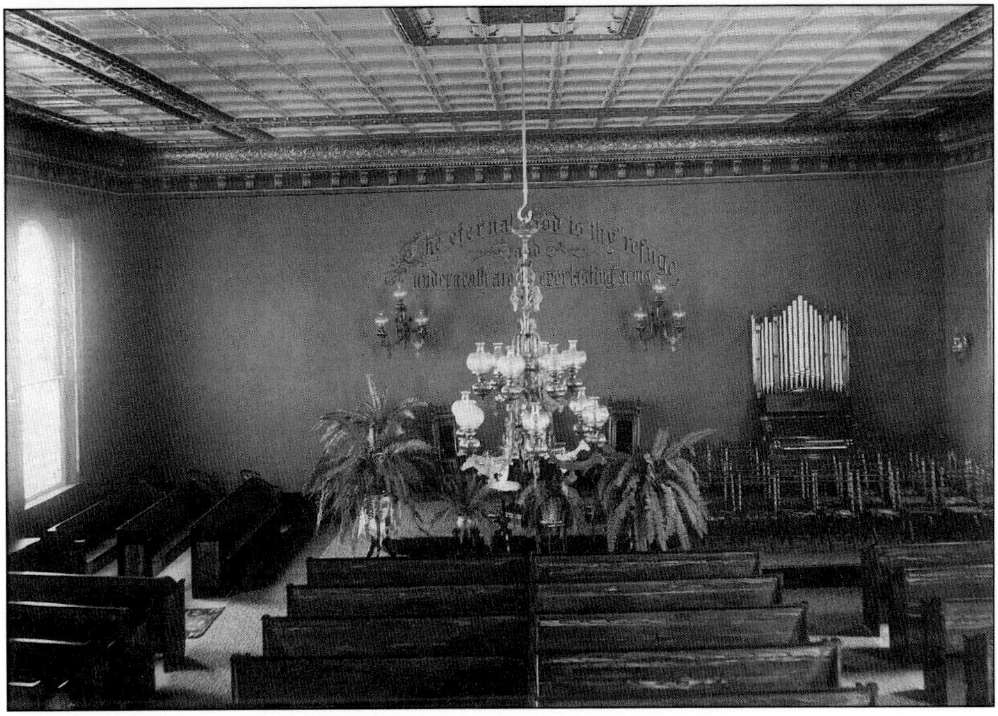

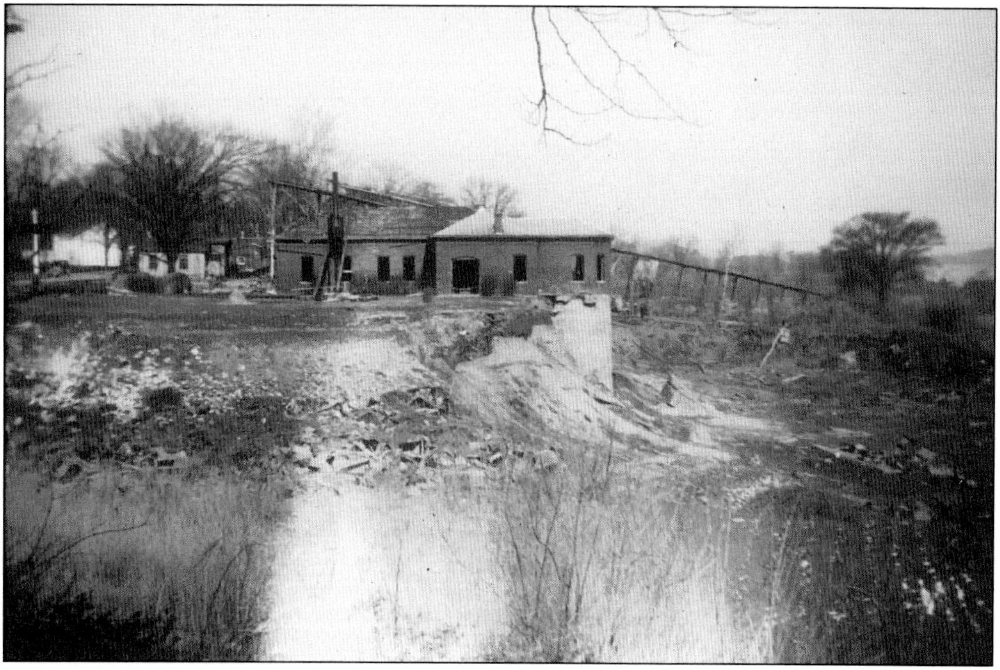

**Bottom of Main Street, c. 1937.** At one time both sides of Front Street had buildings. This included the Talbott Mill, which stood a little north of the brick building in the center of the picture. In 1937, the flood washed away much of the riverbank that supported buildings. As is the case with rivers, the landscape for towns located along them will change.

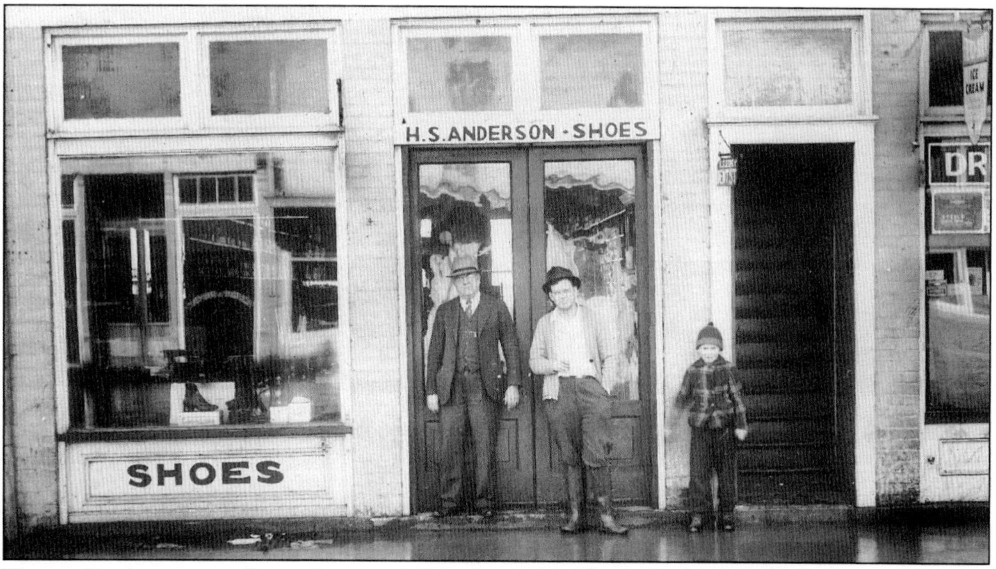


**Harry S. Anderson Shoe Store, 1937.** In 1915, Harry S. Anderson (man on the left) purchased the shoe store where he once worked as a salesman for W.H. Rogers. Mr. Anderson kept the store at the same location, which was the third store from the southwest corner of Main and Popular streets. In the 1920s, Samuel Truitt worked for Mr. Anderson for $2.50 a week. Mr. Truitt said one half the store carried shoes for everyone in the family, while the other side had items for men only such as hats, ties, and overshoes.

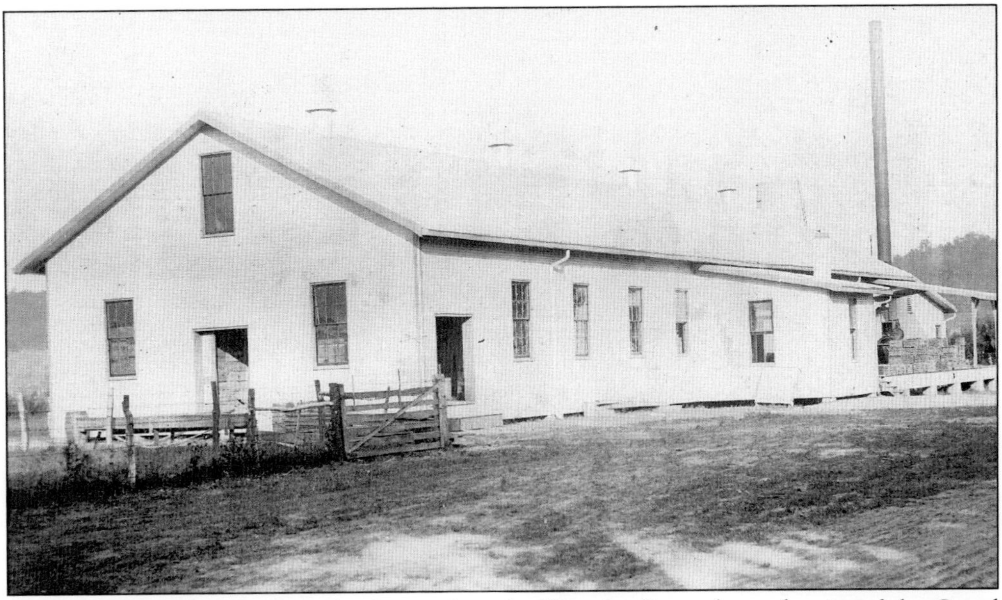

**CANNING FACTORY, C. 1937.** At the north end of Popular Street (now the site of the Grand Victoria Casino parking lot) Ralph J. Mattingly and his sons, John, Paul, and Richard, started a canning business. They began canning tomatoes, green beans, and corn in the old Gibson Hardware Company warehouse in 1937. The Gibsons used the warehouse to store wagons, buggies, and farm machinery. In 1940, they relocated the canning process to the old American Tobacco Company and later the Shepherd Lathe building on Front Street. This building still stands today.

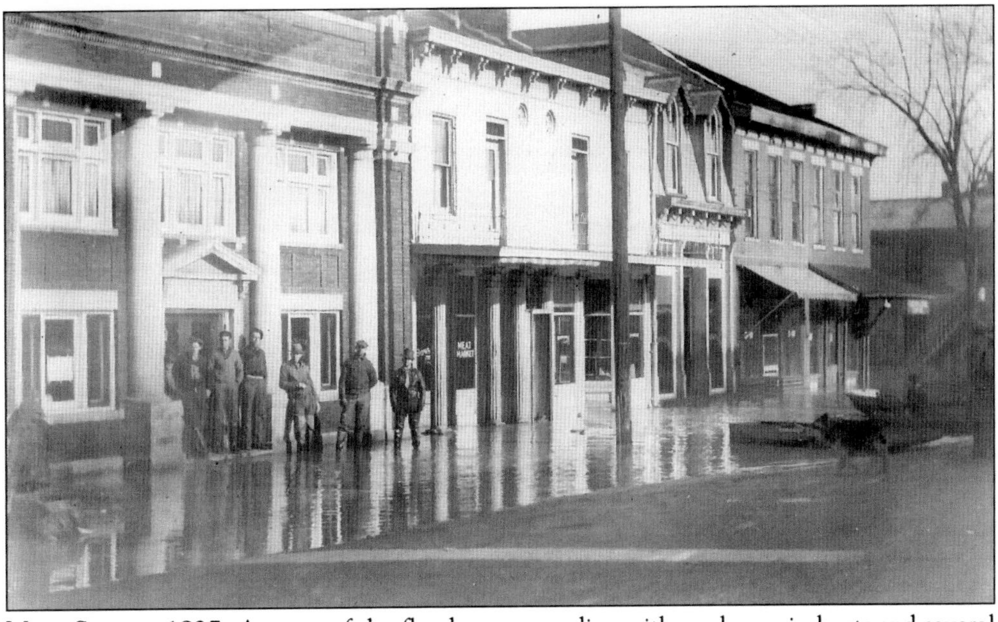

**MAIN STREET, 1937.** A scene of the floodwaters receding with workmen in boats and several boats used to transport workers to the affected areas. The building on the left is the national Bank of Rising Sun built in 1923–1924. The bank was chartered in 1872 with A.C. Downey as president and a capital stock of $100,000. The business of the bank had been constant and strong suffering no problems during the late 1800s panics or the Depression.

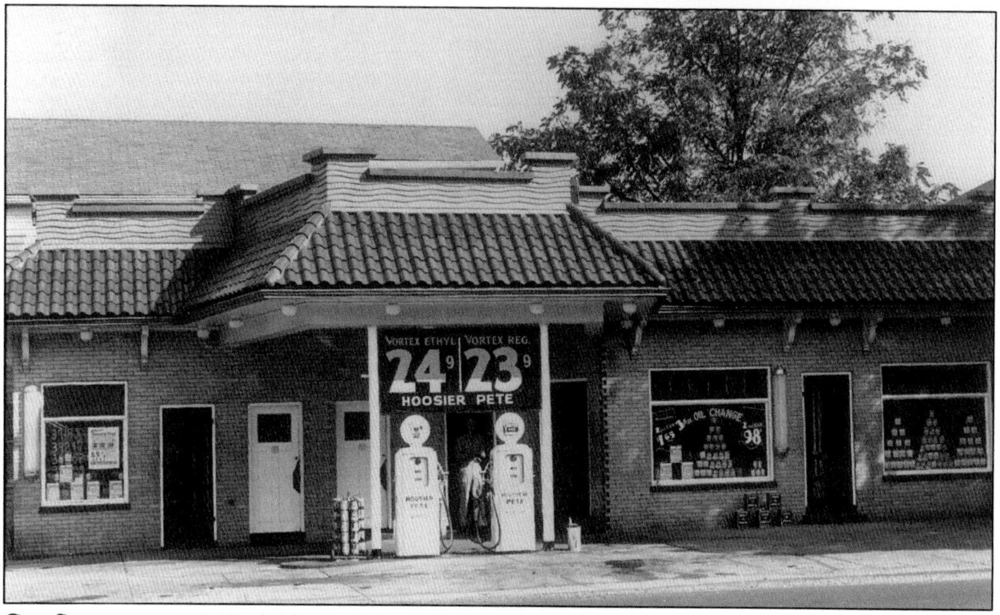


**Gas Station, c. 1949.** A Hoosier Pete gas station stood at the southeast corner of Walnut and Main streets. In current times with the gas price on the rise we often long for the days for these gas prices. In 1951, kerosene was sold for 18¢ a gallon and the other gas prices remained the same as they were in 1949. Ray Smoot is the attendant on duty standing in the doorway. Today the former gas station serves as headquarters for Historic Downtown.

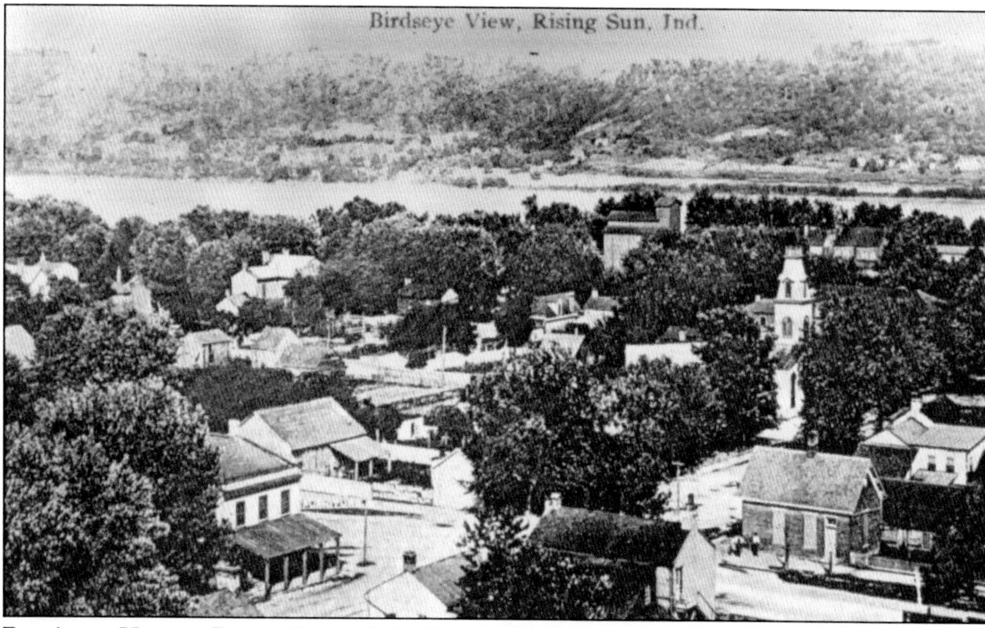


**Bird's-eye View of Rising Sun, 1912.** This is a bird's-eye view taken from the high school on High Street looking east toward the Ohio River. The lower center of the picture is the corner of Main and Walnut streets. In the lower right is a building with two men in front. This was a doctor's office, then later a gas station, and today Historic Downtown offices. Above this building is the Presbyterian Church. Across the street to the west is the city building.

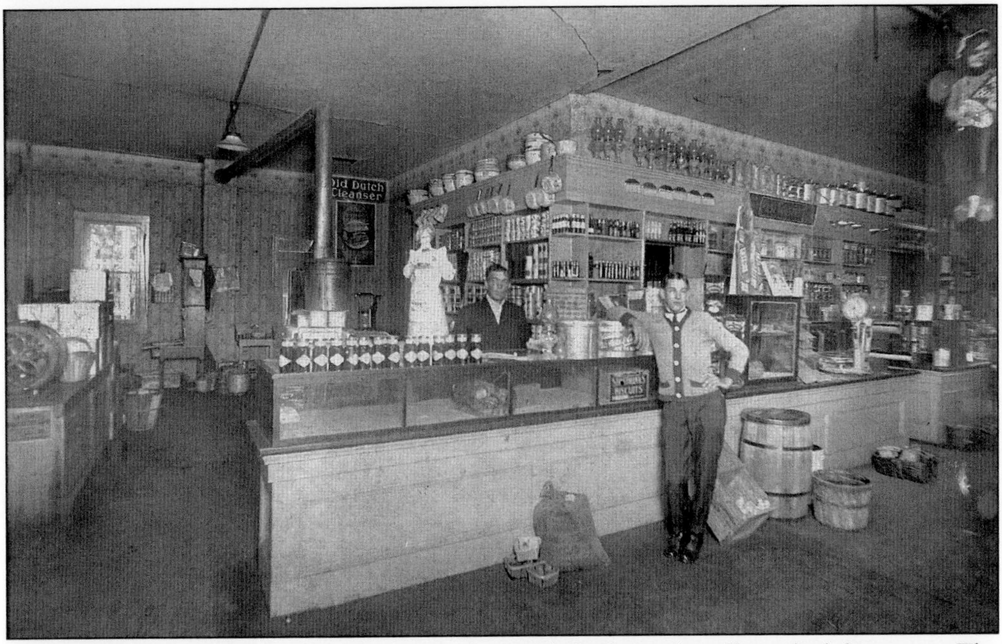


**DRUG STORE, C. 1910.** An interior view of a Frank Buchanan's well-stocked drug store. The northeast corner of Main and Popular streets was the site for the drug store. By the 1920s Buchanan was no longer in business, but several others had drug stores in Rising Sun. They include Hemphill Drug Store and one owned by Lew Thorn. A gazebo occupies the site today.

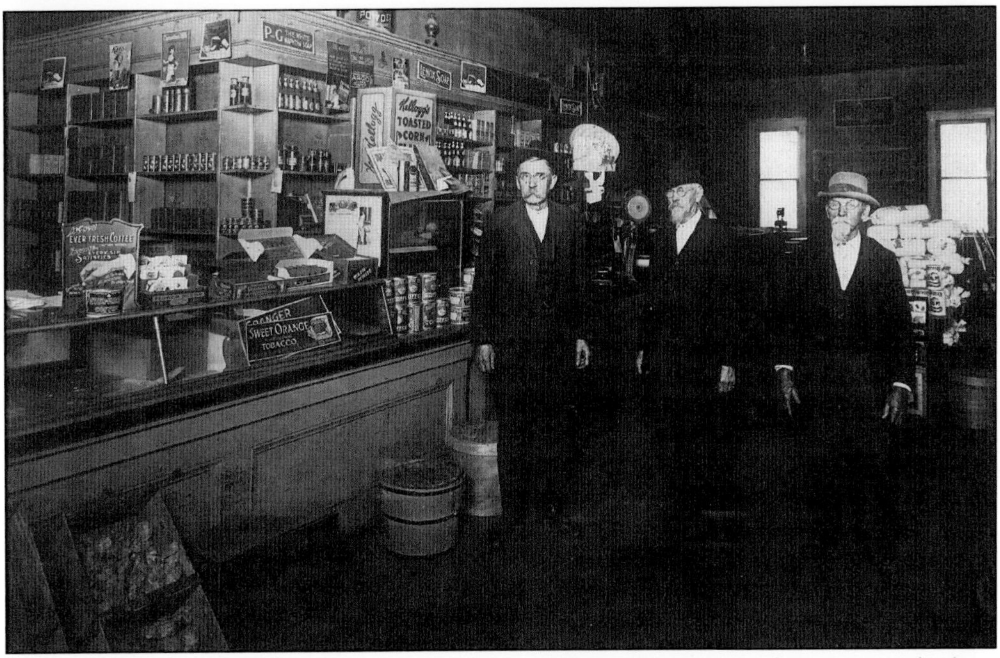


**DRUG STORE, C. 1910.** Another interior view of Frank Buchanan's drug store with three unidentified men. On the shelves are some well-known products and company names. The large box is Kellogg's Toasted Corn Flakes and on the wall in back of the counter is Proctor and Gamble's "the white naphtha soap." Sitting on the display case are coffee, flower seeds, and soap.

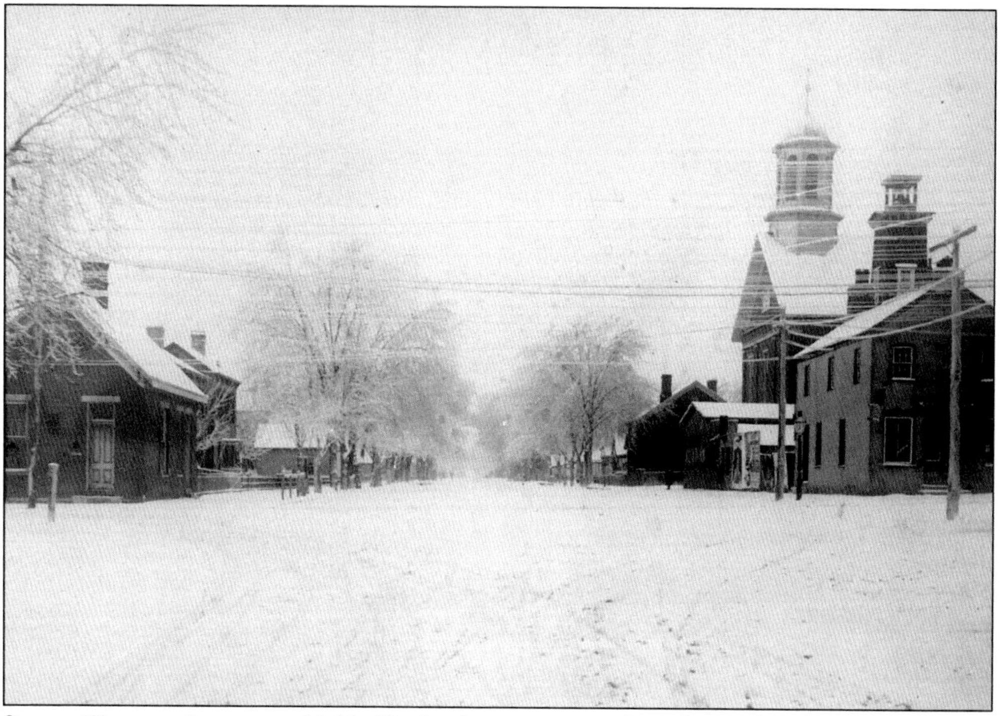

**SOUTH WALNUT STREET, C. 1900.** The brick structure on the left was the office of Dr. Cowen and later Dr. Hall. Even later it became the barbershop of Everett Downey. Still later the building was replaced with a filling station. On the right is the city building. The small structure next to the city building is Fisher's Cobbler Shop, followed by the familiar towers of the fire station and the Methodist Church.

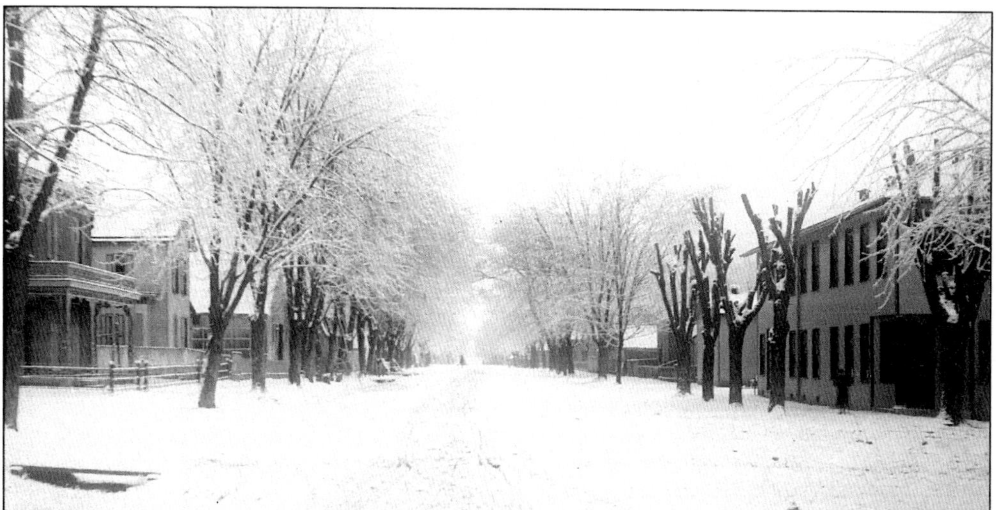

**WALNUT STREET LOOKING NORTH, C. 1910.** A winter scene looking north up Walnut Street from Third Street. The two houses on the left were residences for the Whitlock family. The one on the immediate left is currently the Jelly House Bed & Breakfast. The Whitlock Furniture Factory is the two-story building on the right. Currently this is the Hoosier Boy Senior Housing. It is interesting to note that the trees in front of the building have all been trimmed.

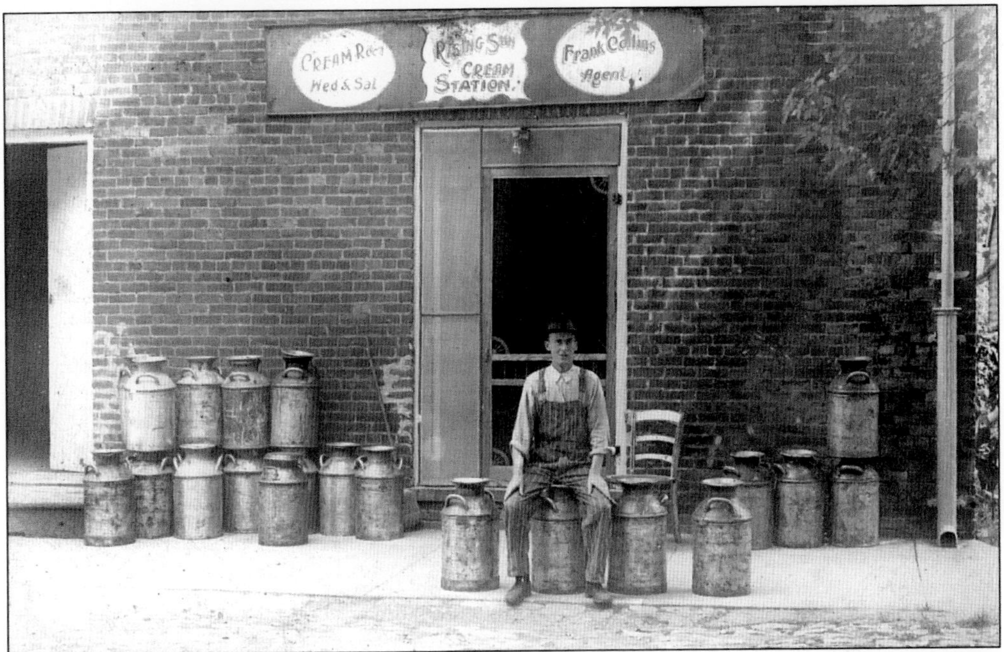


**MERCHANT'S CREAMERY, C. 1920.** William Smith owned the Merchant's Creamery with Frank Collins as the agent. The cream station received cream on Wednesdays and Saturdays from local farmers. Most farms owned a dairy cow or two for their personal use. Some farmers possessed an evaporating cream separator that allowed the milk to sit until the cream separated from the milk naturally.

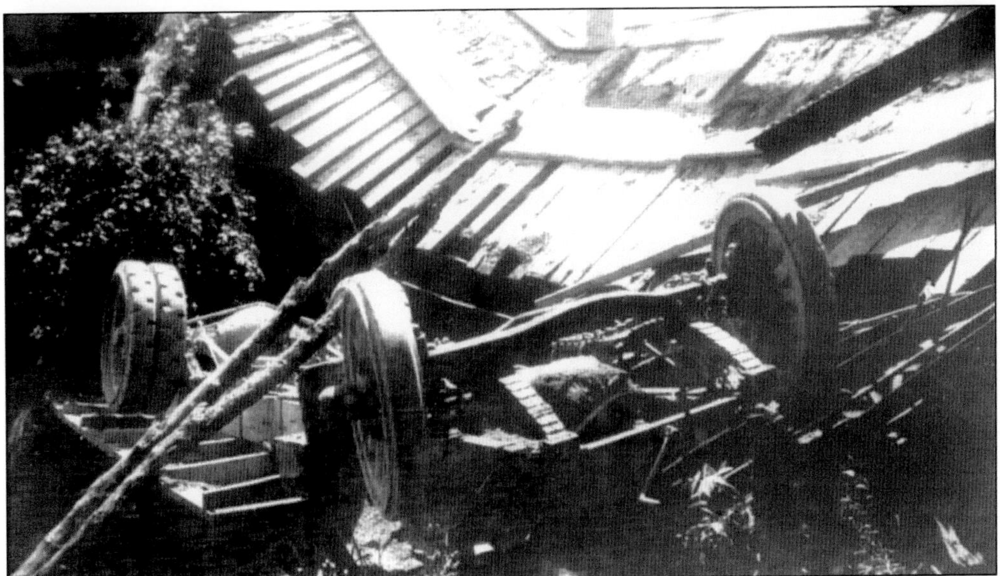

**MERCHANT'S CREAMERY TRUCK, 1922.** There were many hazards of driving in the early 1900s. This Merchant's Creamery truck went over the side of an old plank bridge. Possibly the driver approached the edge a little too closely or the structure was no longer sound. The accident occurred between Florence and Barkworks, also known as Quercus Grove (located in Switzerland County).

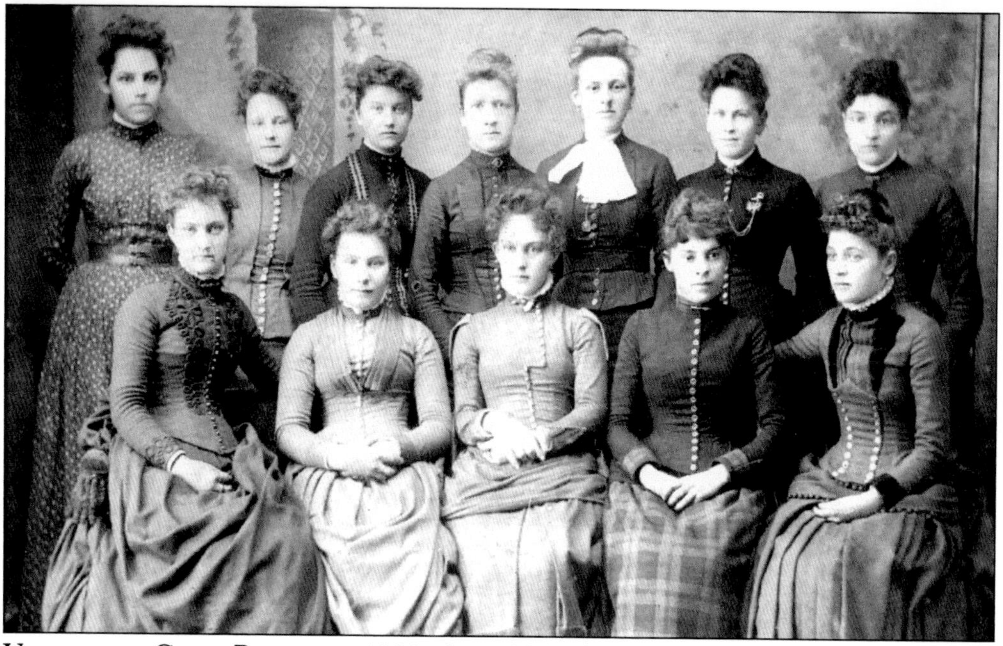

**Unidentified Group Picture, c. 1890s.** James N. Walton, born and raised on a farm in Ohio County, took lessons in the art of photography at the age of 18. The following year, in 1861, he opened a small gallery in Rising Sun. Shortly afterward, he gave up the gallery and traveled with William Davis in a portable photograph car.

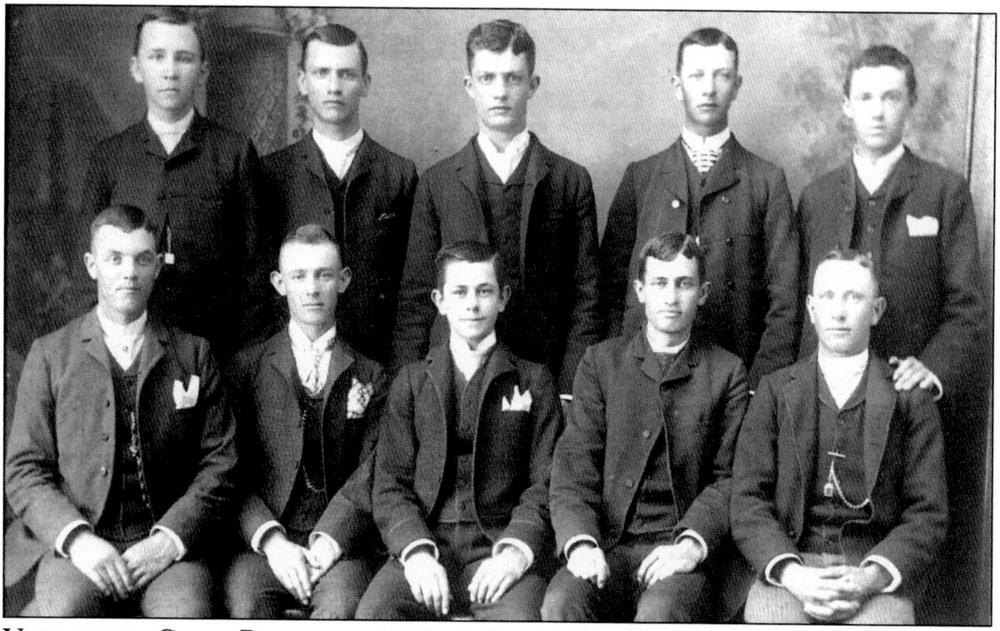

**Unidentified Group Picture, c. 1890s.** Following the invention of photography by Louis Jacques Mandes Dauerre in 1839, the United States saw a proliferation of photographers come and go. Ohio County saw at least 11 photographers between 1852 and 1916. The first to arrive in Rising Sun was Anthony Jaquay who came in May 1852 from Pittsburgh. Some of the photographers established studios while others traveled the country.

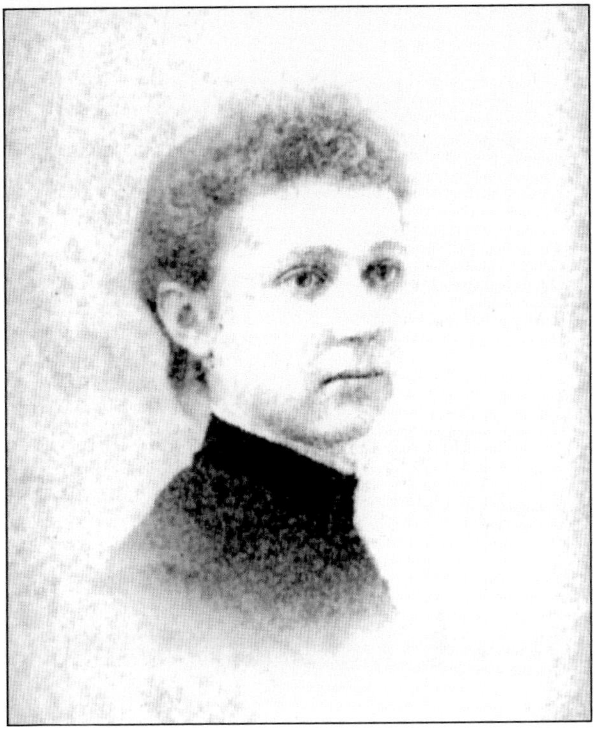

**Unidentified Woman, c. 1890s.** James N. Walton did his work in a small wood building that was located on the lot where the gazebo stands. A brick building was next to it at the northeast corner of Main and Popular streets.

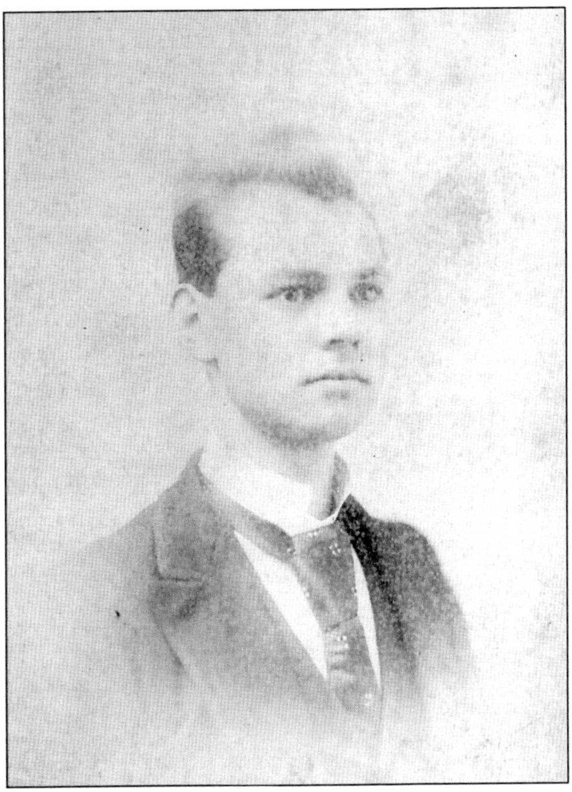

**Unidentified Man, c. 1890s.** Dan K. Walton produced these four cabinet cards of unidentified people. Earliest records indicate that Walton established his art studio in 1880. The art studio was located on lower Main Street until his death in 1922. Busch McQuithy used the former studio as a Kodak Finishing Room for a time until Rising Sun's fourth barbershop began operation there.

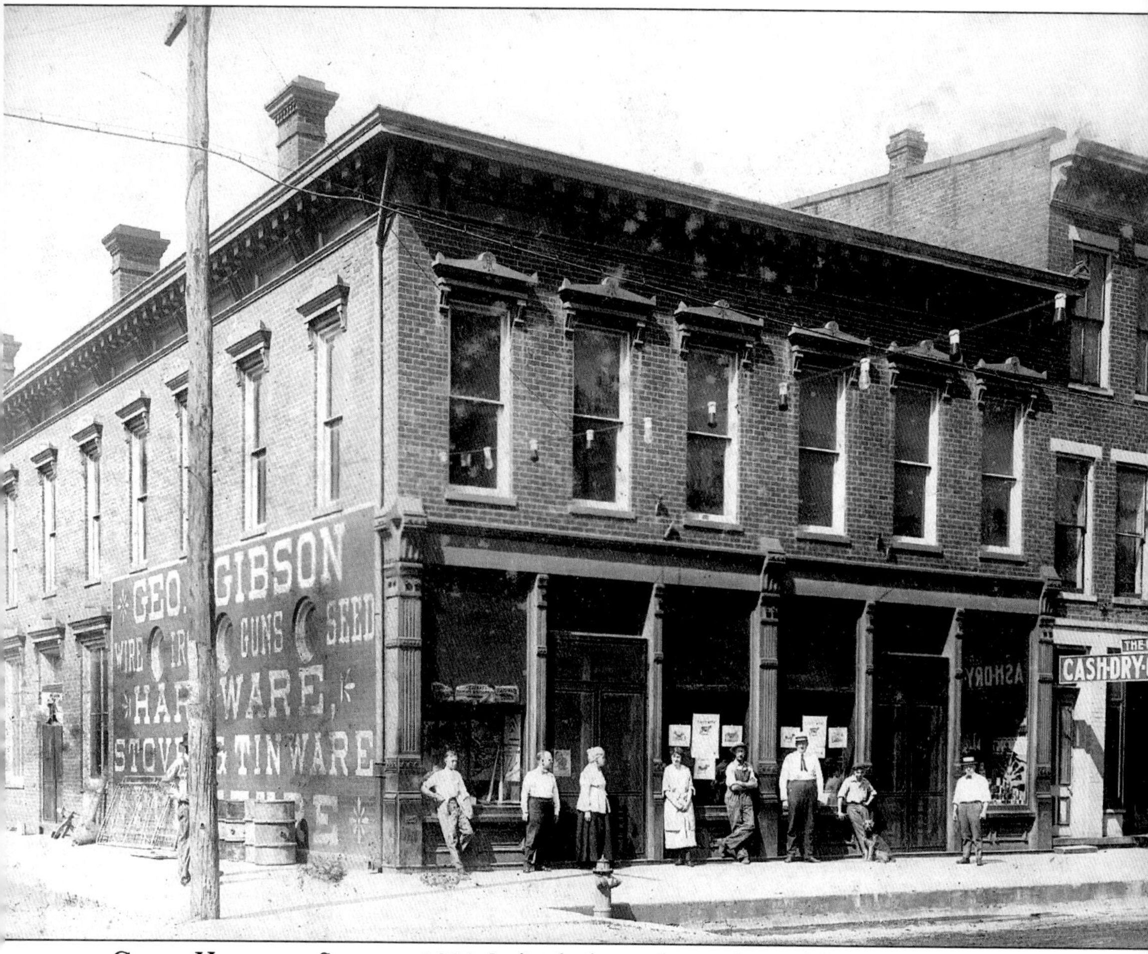


**Gibson Hardware Store, c. 1920.** Individuals standing in front of the Gibson Hardware Store, from left to right, are Roy Gibson, Leonard Gibson, unidentified, unidentified, Grant Williamson, Andy Henschen, Wilbur Gibson, and Oscar Baxter. The store, located at the southwest corner of Popular and Main streets, had an attractive advertising sign on the building that is still evident today. According to the sign they sold wire, iron, guns, seed, stoves, and tinware. The Griswold sisters who operated a dry goods store owned the business to the right.

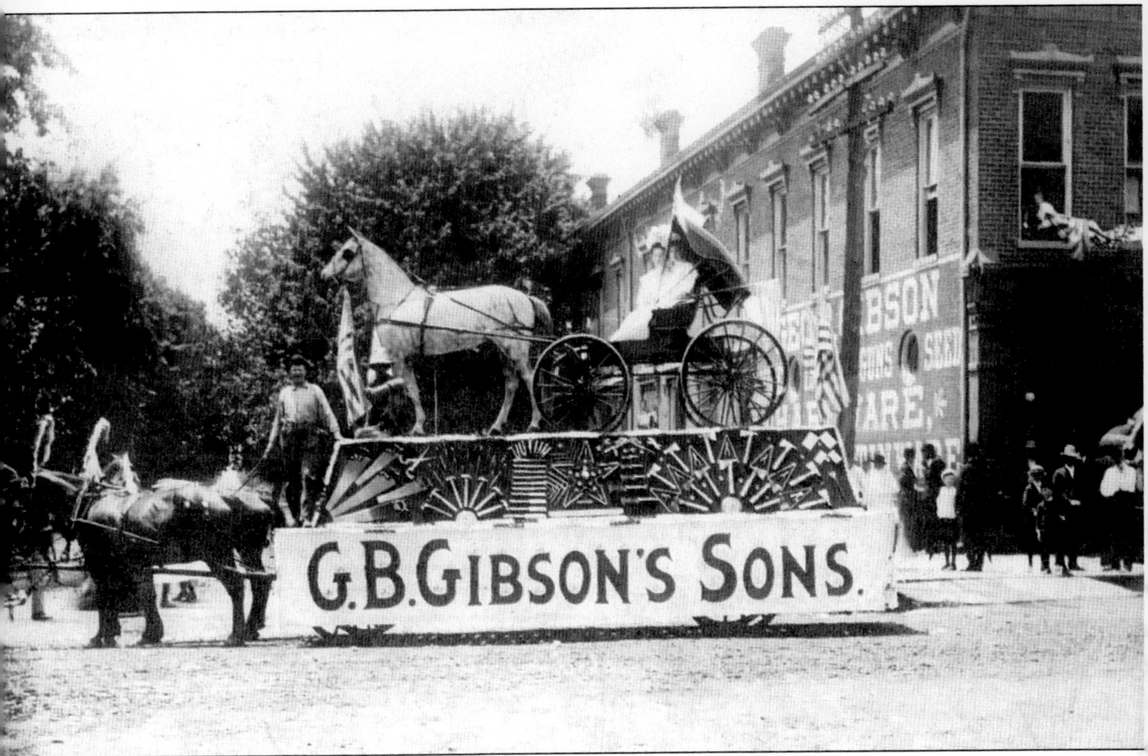


**Parade, 1907.** G.B. Gibson's Sons participated in what appears to be a Fourth of July parade celebration. The float with a horse and buggy with two women riding is being pulled by at least four horses with plumes. The Gibson Building is to the right as you look down Popular Street.

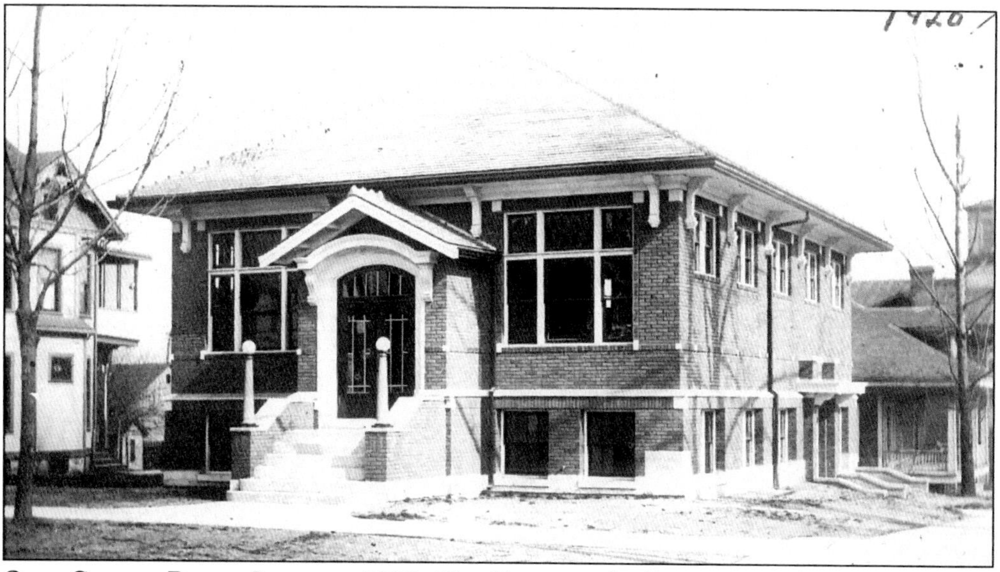


**Ohio County Public Library, 1920.** The library in the Rising Sun school was officially established when the mayor of Rising Sun, Joshua M. Spencer, signed and approved an ordinance on December 14, 1898. It was to be known as the Mahlon Brown Library after a local citizen who had created a trust fund to educate the poor and indigent of the city. The Public Library building was erected in 1916 after the Carnegie Foundation gave a grant for $10,000.

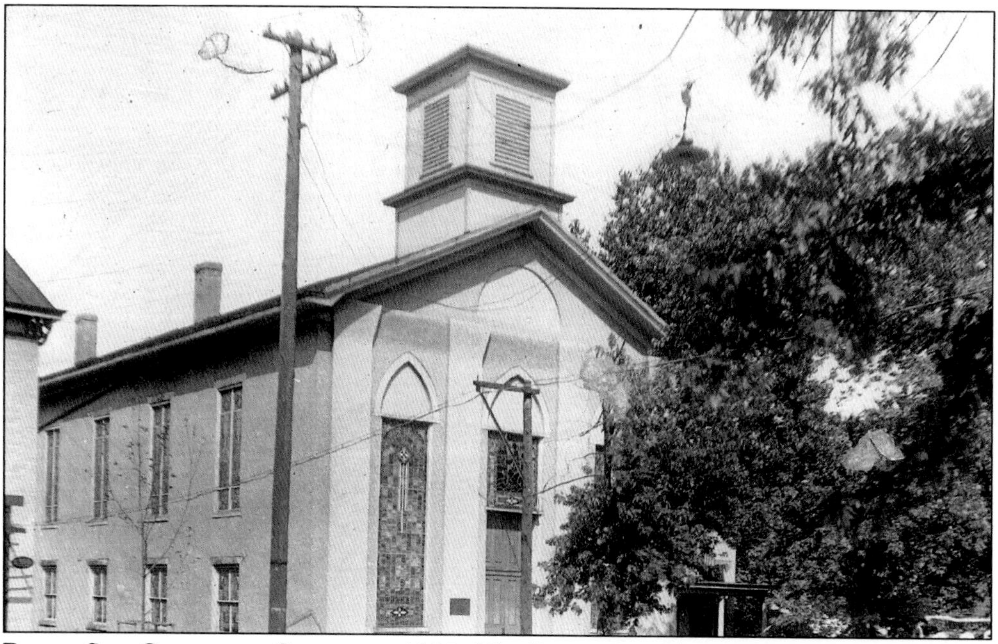

**Rising Sun Church of Christ, c. 1920.** The Rising Sun Church of Christ congregation organized on December 16, 1832. The first meetings were held in the Masonic Hall over Craft's store located on the riverbank north of Main Street. The first Church of Christ building was built on Walnut Street between Fourth and Fifth streets. In 1860, the congregation moved to the newly built church on Main Street, now home to the Bethel Unity Baptist Church. The Rising Sun Church of Christ worships today on Fifth Street.

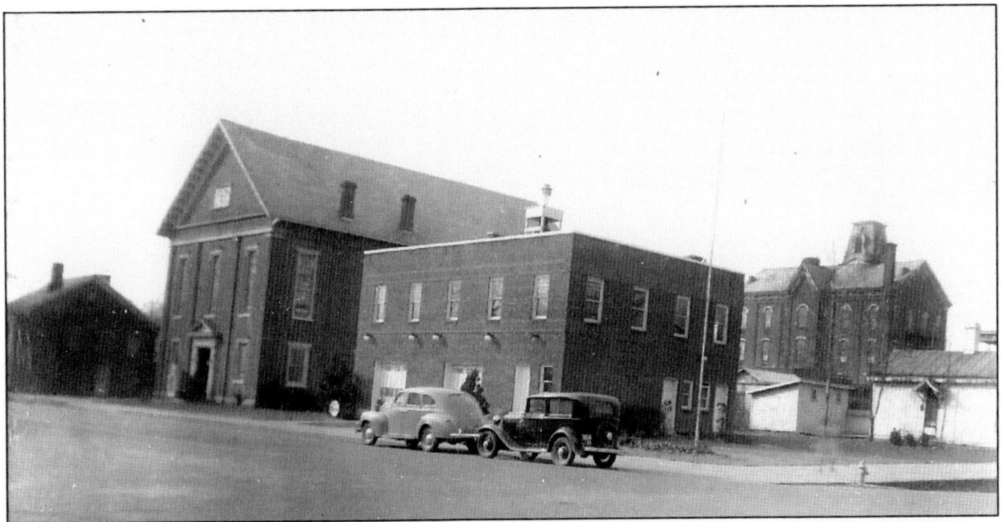

**City Building, c. 1935.** This photograph shows the recently built city building at the southwest corner of Main and Walnut streets. The old high school can be seen in the distance to the right. To the left of the city building is the Methodist Church built in 1865. This is the third Methodist church to occupy this site dating back to 1821.

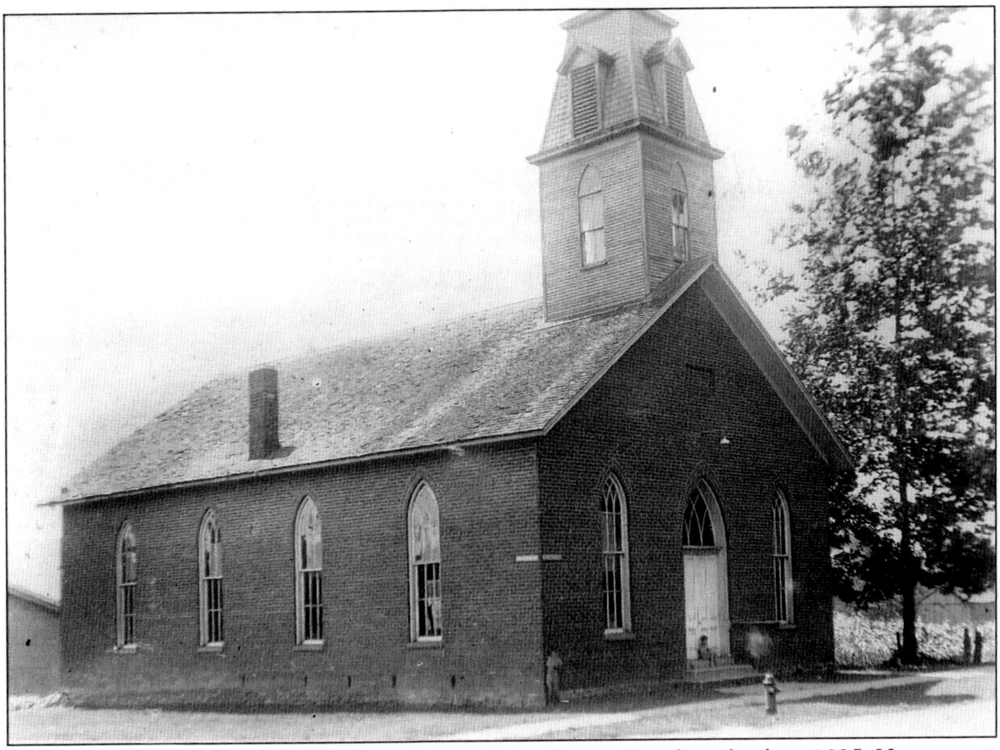

**Baptist Church, c. 1935.** The Baptist Church in Rising Sun dates back to 1825. However, it was not until 1863 that a church was constructed for worship. The church was erected at Fifth and High streets and was sold in 1881 to the Reformed Church. A second church was dedicated in 1892 at the corner of Walnut and William streets. During excavation of a basement in 1949, the church collapsed. The present church's cornerstone was laid in October, 1949.

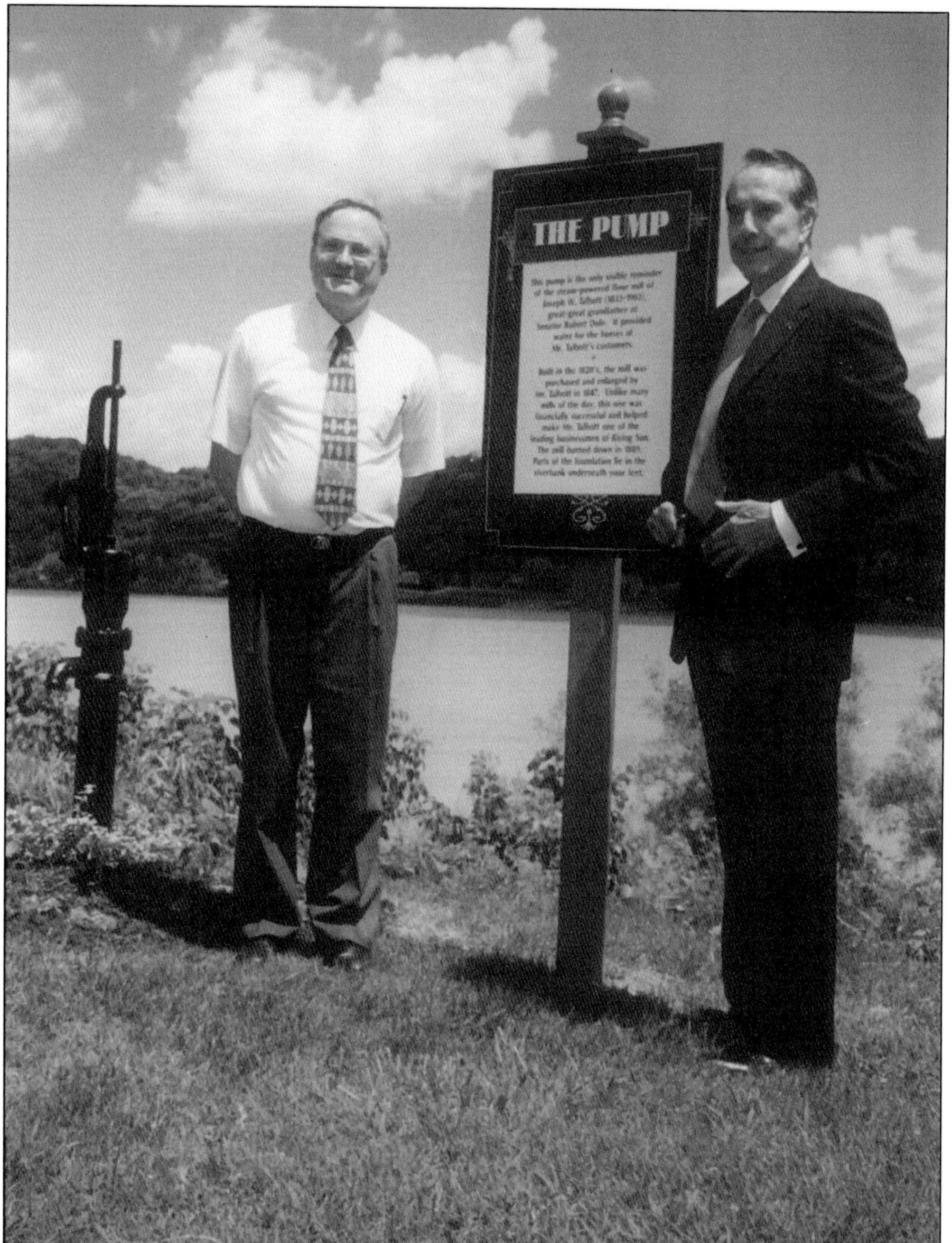


**Robert Dole at site of Talbott's Mill, 1998.** The flour mill originally built in 1827 by Moses Turner was sold to J.W. Talbott in 1847. Senator Dole, a descendant of J.W. Talbott, was invited to Rising Sun in 1998. His grandparents lived in the Ohio County community in the early part of the 20th century. The pump is all that remains of the Talbott Mill. Also in the picture is John Dorrell of Indianapolis whose ancestor was also J.W. Talbott.

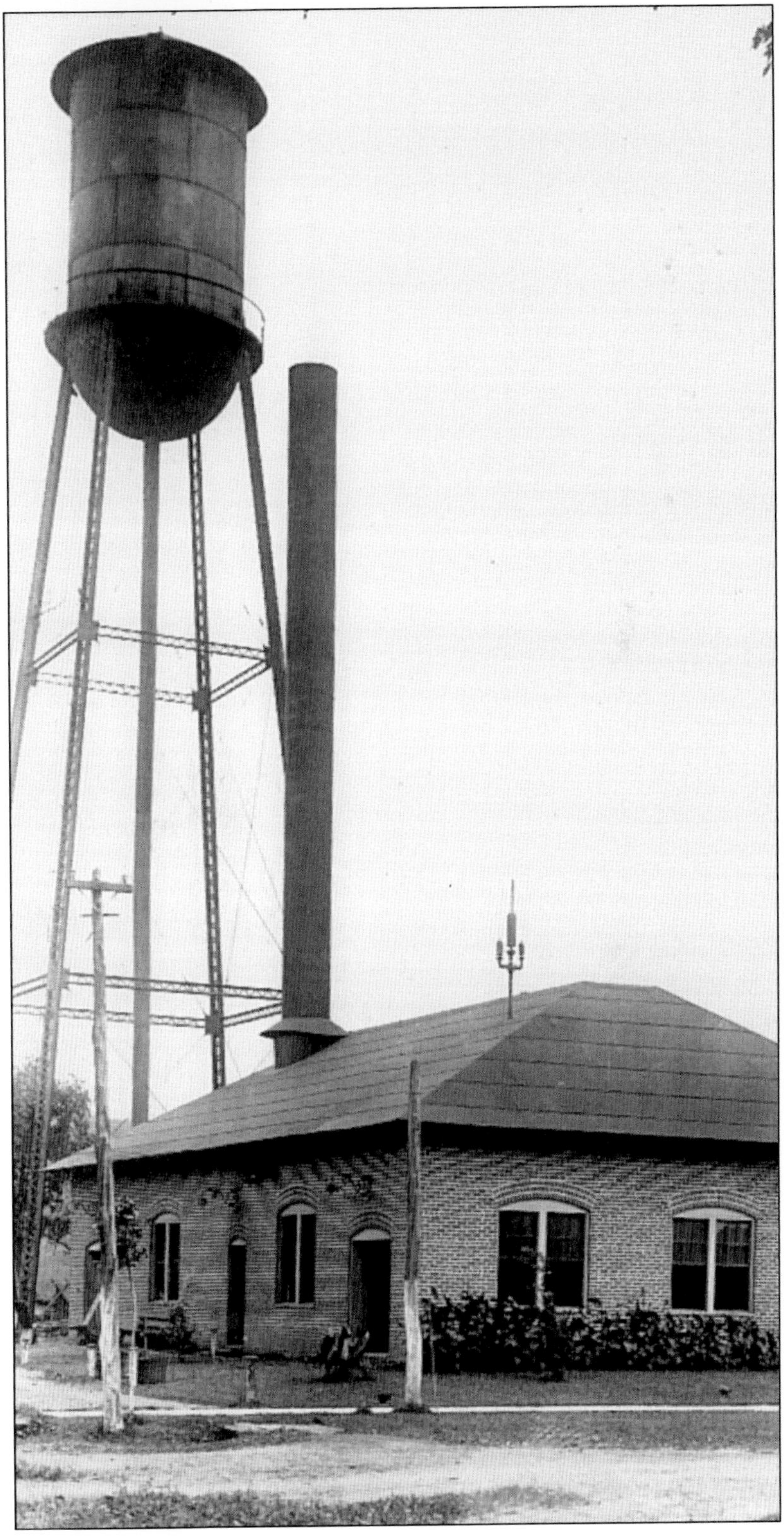

**LIGHT AND WATER PLANT, C. 1915.** Prior to electricity coming to Rising Sun, the streetlights were lit each night by the city lamplighter. He would travel up and down the streets of town in his wagon filled with gasoline and his apparatus for lighting the wicks in the streetlights. In 1912, E.V. Menefee became city utilities manager overseeing the Rising Sun Water & Light Company. The company was privately owned until it was sold in 1929 to Associated Gas & Electric Company of New York.

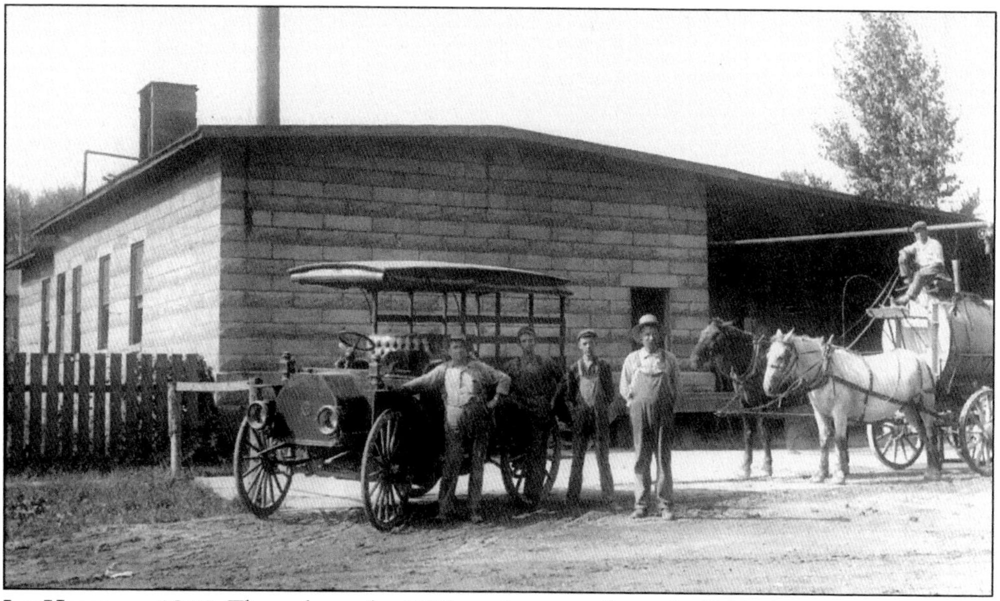

**Ice House, c. 1910.** Throughout the 1800s and on into the early 1900s, harvesting ice from a frozen lake or river was a major operation. But by 1900, production of artificial ice began to be popular in some areas. Rising Sun had John Cochran's artificial ice plant. Mr. Cochran's brother, Harry, is driving the water wagon. After loading up with water he would drive up and down sprinkling the streets to keep the dust down.

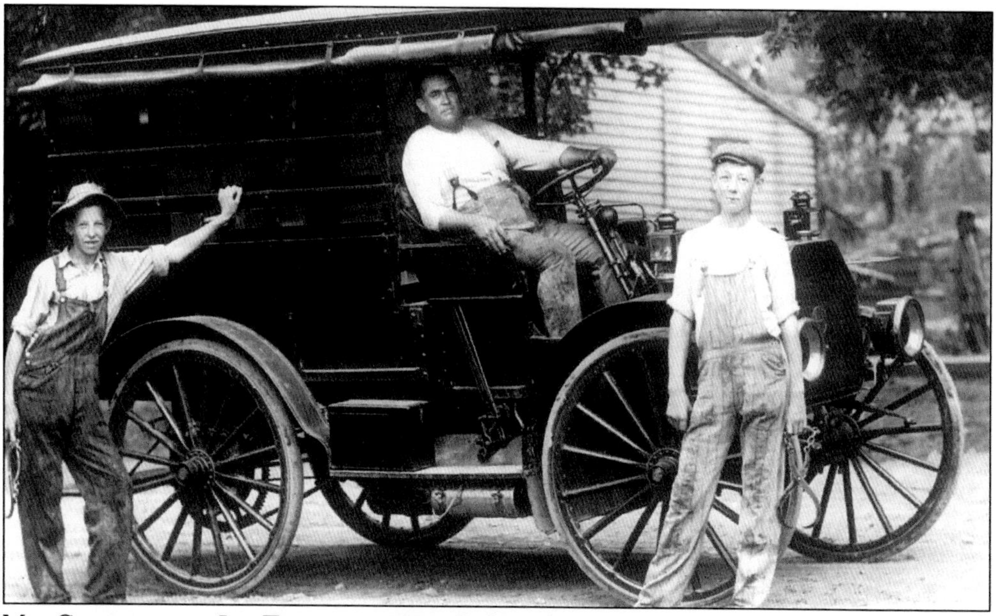

**Mr. Cochran and Ice Truck, c. 1910.** Before electric refrigerators the place most people kept food cold was in an icebox. To fill up the icebox, ice would need to be purchased from the iceman. Every morning the driver would load up with ice from Cochran's Icehouse and drive around town. The driver used tongs to carry the block of ice and place it in the icebox. Mr. Cochran's truck had curtains that could be rolled down in inclement weather. Note the toolbox by the rear fender used in case of a breakdown.

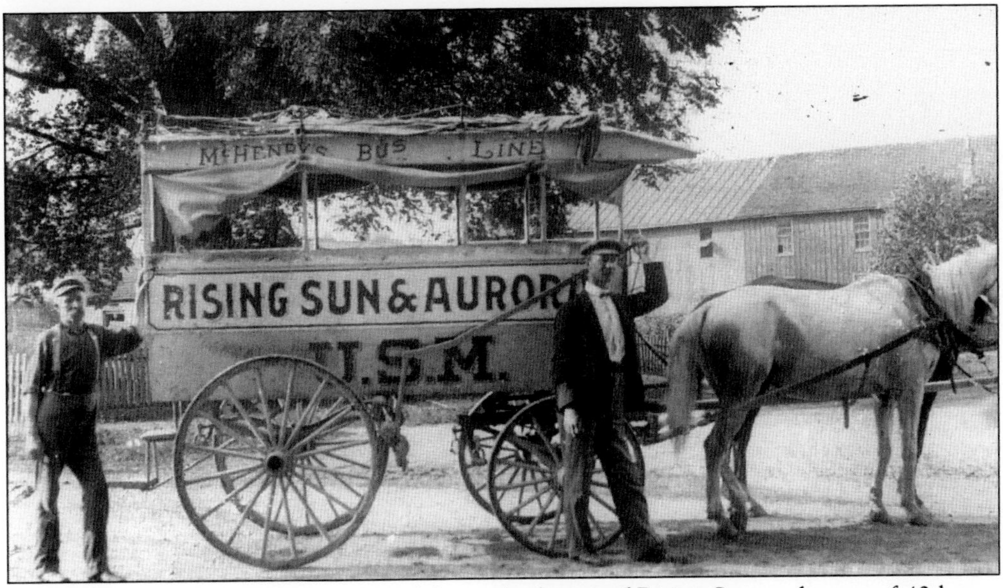


**TIM MCHENRY'S BUS LINE, C. 1905.** Mason Anderson of Rising Sun at the age of 40 began operating on a limited schedule the Aurora & Rising Sun Omnibus Line. In 1879, Tim McHenry purchased a half-interest in the bus line, forming a partnership. The bus line was a means for local people to travel to Aurora for various activities and to catch a train to Cincinnati. Note the man on the right has his hand on the brake that when pulled up would apply pressure to the wheel and slow it to a stop.

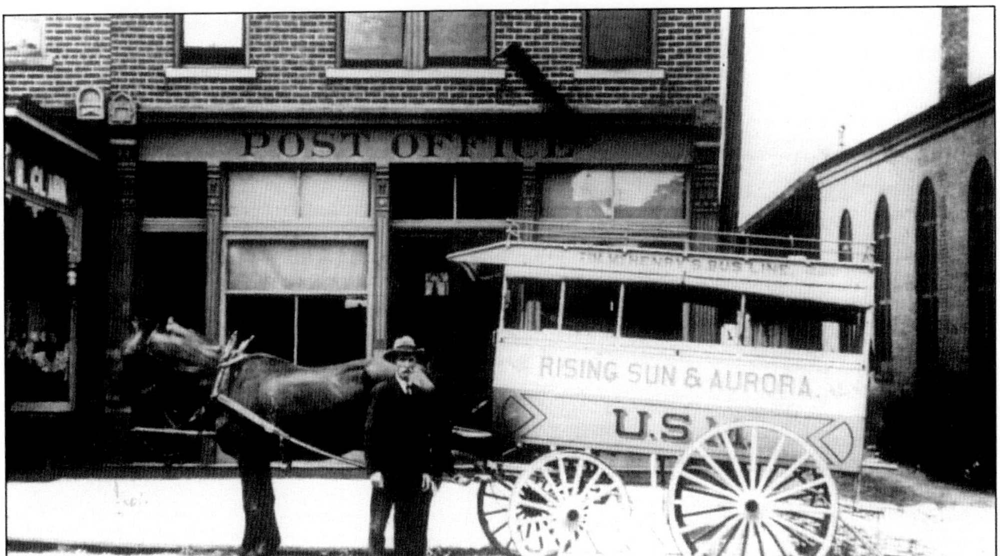


**TIM MCHENRY'S BUS LINE, C. 1905.** At some unknown time Tim McHenry purchased the bus line from Mason Anderson. McHenry operated the service until 1905. This picture is in front of the post office on Main Street (Indiana Workforce Development occupies the building today). To the right is the Presbyterian Church. Note the bus has the large letters U.S.M. This stands for United States Mail. The bus line would take anywhere from two to three hours to carry passengers or the mail to Aurora.

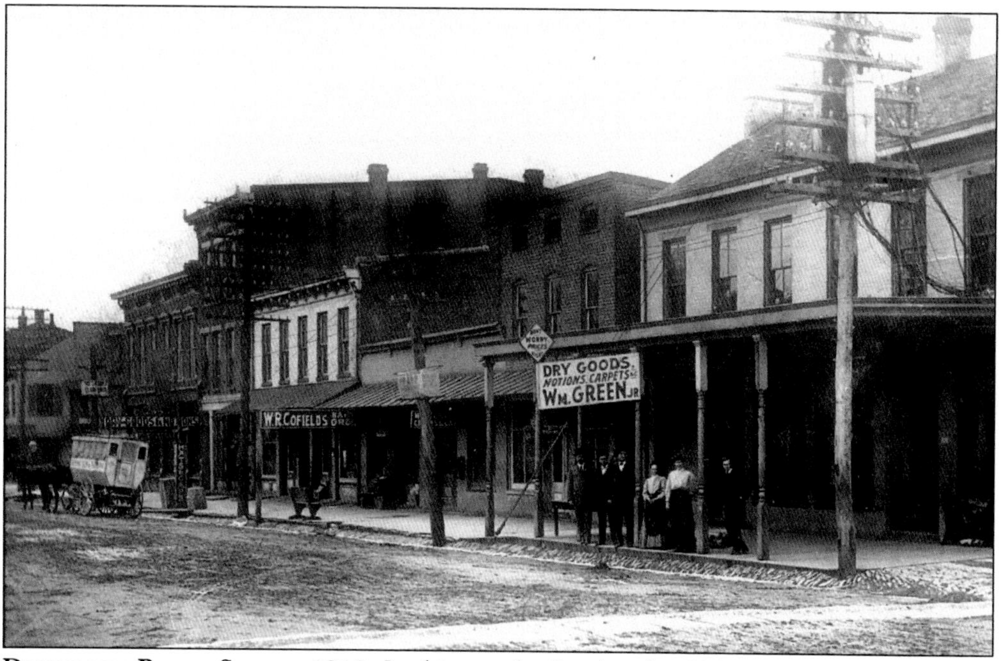


**DOWNTOWN RISING SUN, C. 1910.** Looking at the South side of Main Street of 1910 and of today we see for the most part the buildings have remained the same. Exceptions include the middle building, which is now two-stories, and the structure on the right no longer has the covered walk. The electric poles no longer grace the streets. This one block has two dry goods and notions stores, a grocery, a shop selling hats, and another selling candy. Today you will find art galleries, a coffee shop, an herb store, and a printer.

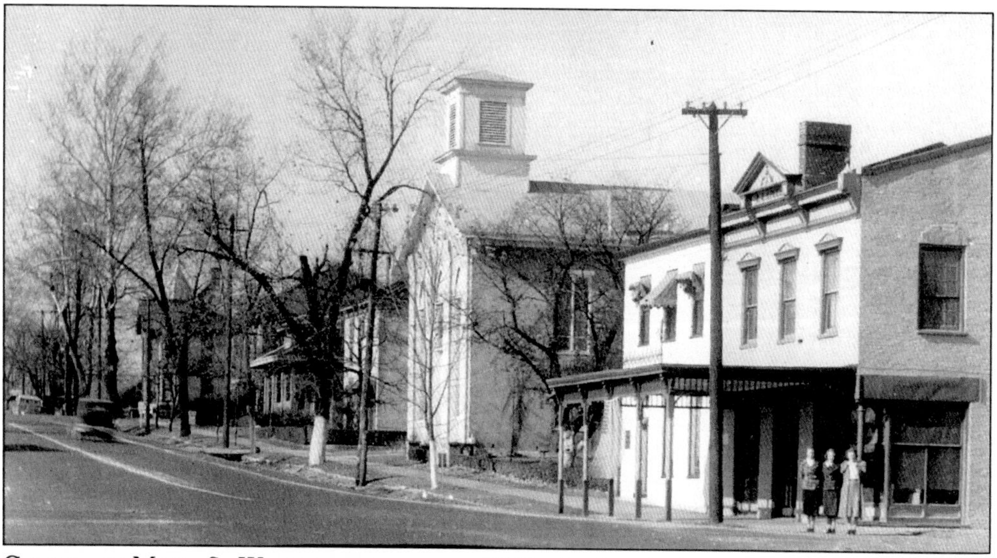

**CORNER OF MAIN & WALNUT STREETS, C. 1930.** A view looking west along Main Street toward the courthouse. At the top of the hill on the left barely visible is a Texaco gas station sign near where Jeff's Carpet is currently located. The corner building has seen service as a restaurant and appliance store. The sidewalk covering is longer there. The church is the Bethel Unity Baptist Church.

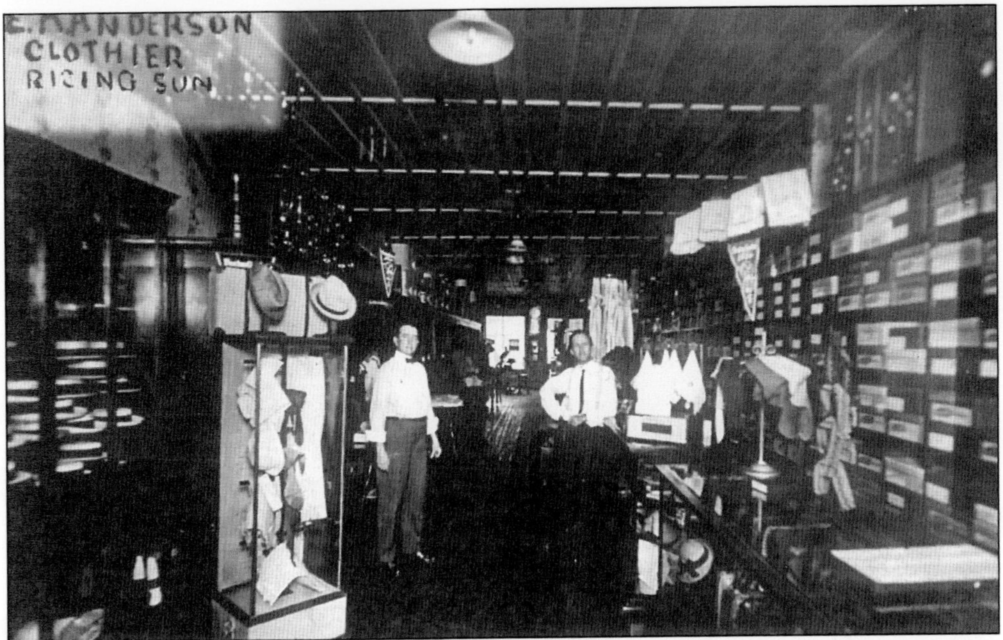


**E.A. ANDERSON'S CLOTHIER, C. 1913.** As with many towns, many of the everyday businesses have left for a variety of reasons. Sometimes it is hard to imagine a town the size of Rising Sun supporting two shoe stores, a couple of groceries, a dry goods store and a clothier. But we also tend to forget that traveling to the next larger town was not a convenient trip. So it was feasible to have a few businesses that duplicated services because there was competition. E.A. Anderson located his store on the south side of Main Street between the alley and Popular Street during the time period of 1910–1930.

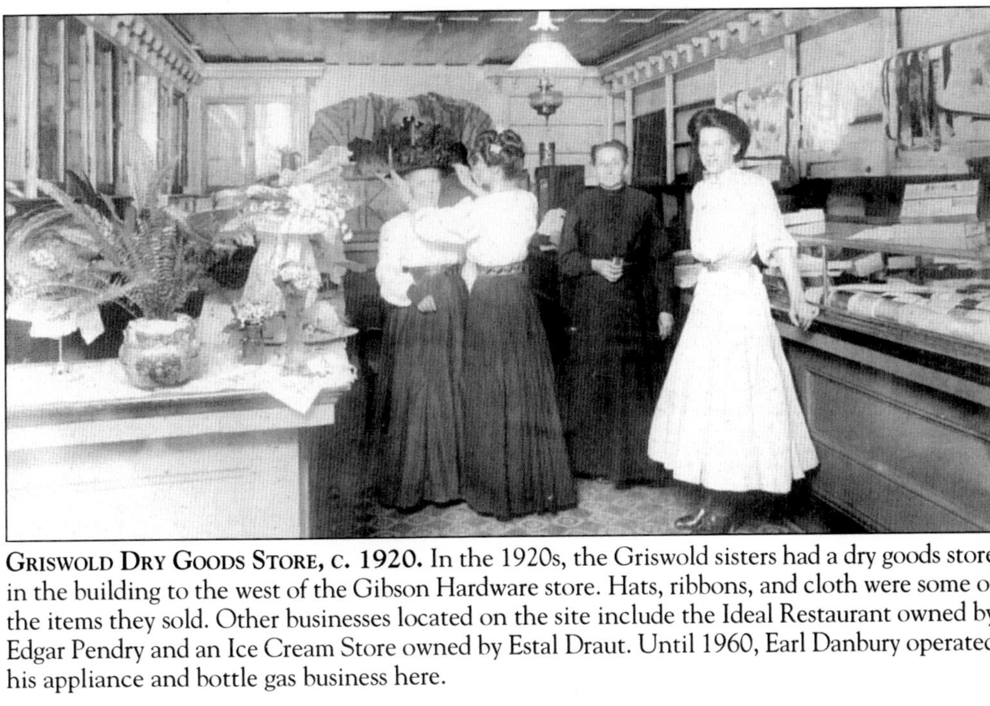

**GRISWOLD DRY GOODS STORE, C. 1920.** In the 1920s, the Griswold sisters had a dry goods store in the building to the west of the Gibson Hardware store. Hats, ribbons, and cloth were some of the items they sold. Other businesses located on the site include the Ideal Restaurant owned by Edgar Pendry and an Ice Cream Store owned by Estal Draut. Until 1960, Earl Danbury operated his appliance and bottle gas business here.

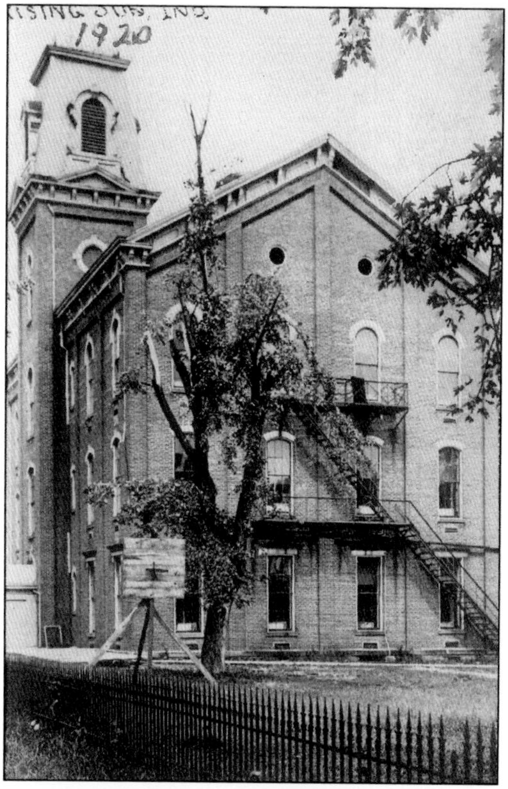


**RISING SUN PUBLIC SCHOOL—1920.** Rising Sun's first public school opened in 1851, 37 years after the founding of the city. The building located on High Street between Main and South streets (today the site of the Emergency Services Building) was destroyed by fire in 1872. The new school building opened in 1872, as both the elementary and high school. The high school continued in the three-story brick building until 1925 when it became too crowded and a new high school was built.

**RISING SUN HIGH SCHOOL, C. 1900.** When the high school was built in 1875, it operated initially like an overgrown country school, with the pupils choosing the teacher they would like to have. Students graduated in three years. This eventually changed to a four-year program. The first to graduate included Fannie Rabb, Lillie Smith, Jones J. Seward, Lou Espey, and Maggie Matson. In 1929, the first school buses brought the pupils to the school from throughout the county.

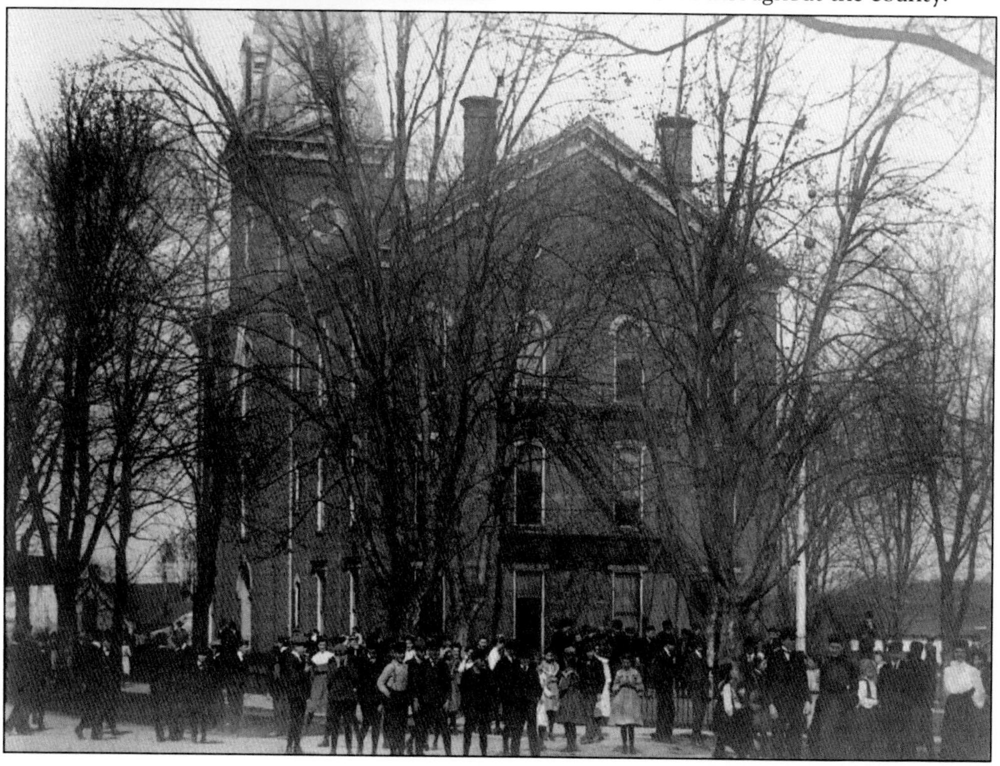

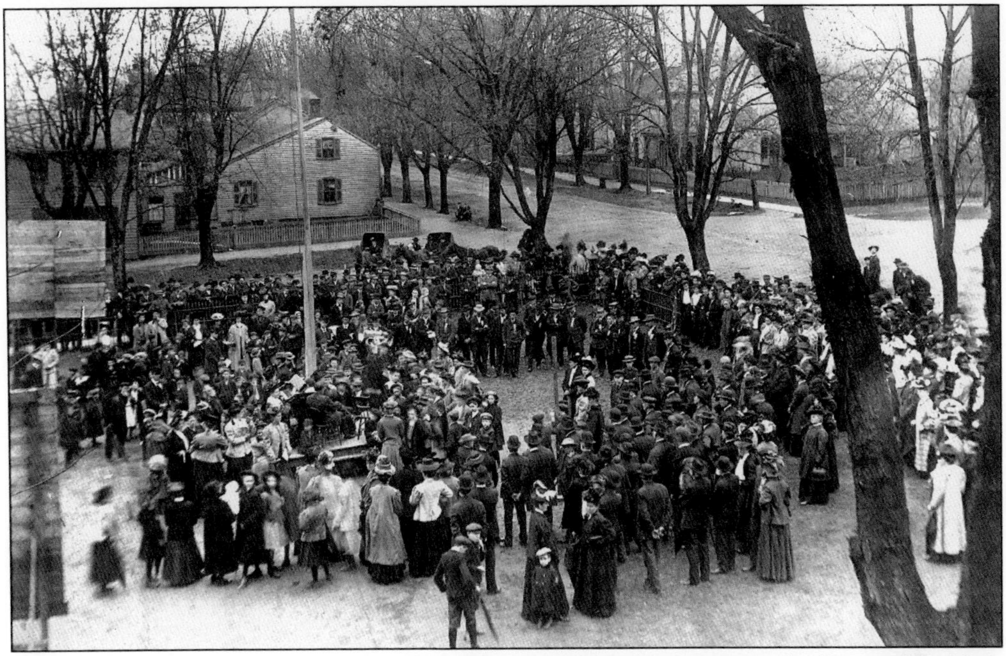

**RISING SUN HIGH SCHOOL, 1923.** The gathering of local citizens on the Rising Sun High School playground was for an unknown purpose. The high school itself (unseen in the picture) was built in 1875. In 1924, the building was razed to be replaced by a new larger high school and gym on the same site. The picture shows the basketball goals. The basketball team played outdoors because the previous school had no gym. The current Life Squad building is situated on the former high school land.

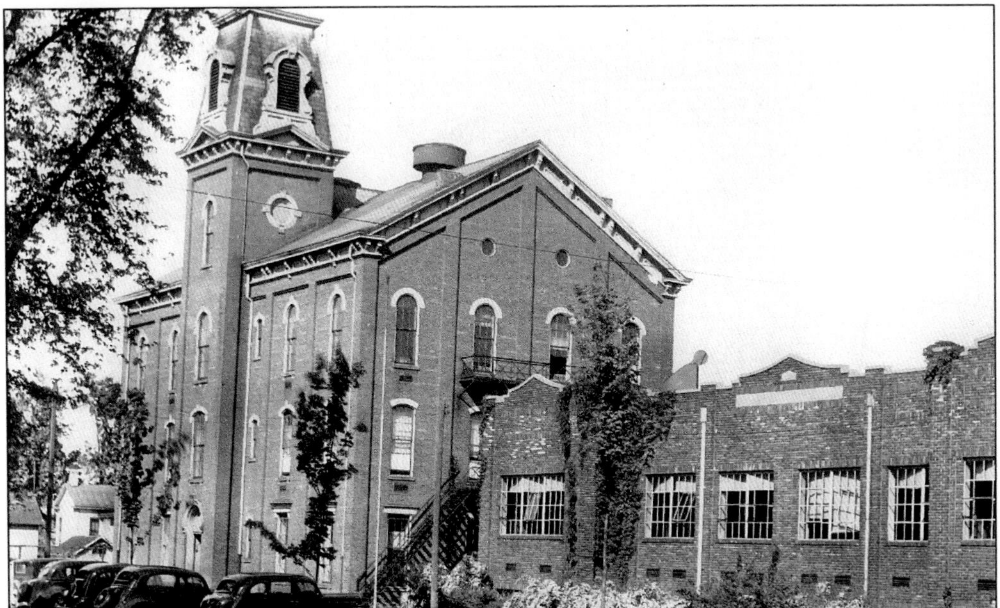

**HIGH SCHOOL, 1935.** The building to the right of the old high school, built in 1875, is the new high school. The school and gym were built in 1924 and razed in 1960.

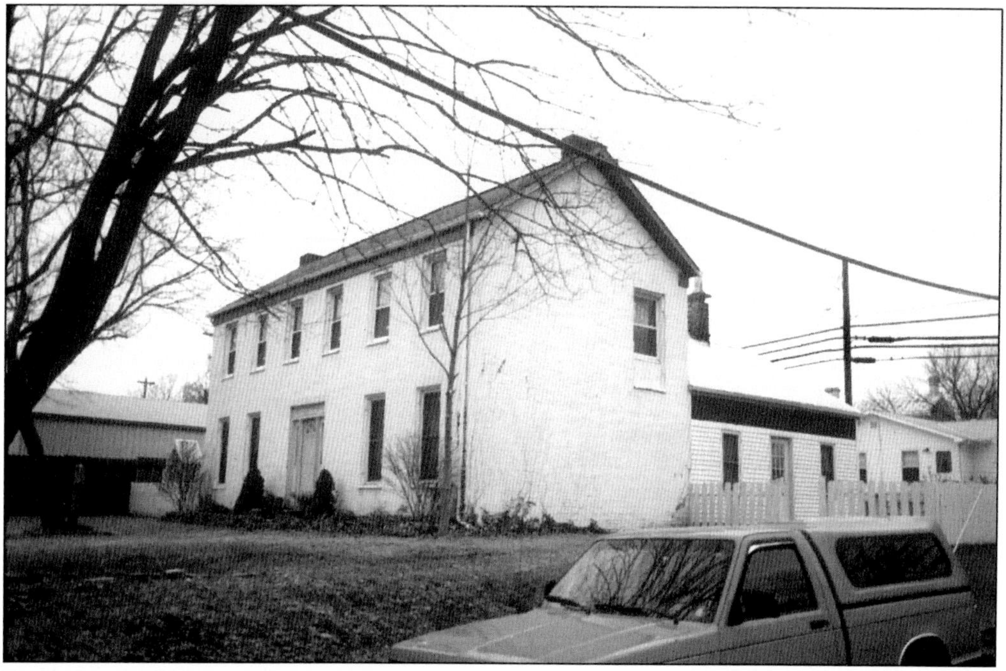

**PRESBYTERIAN SEMINARY, MARCH 2001.** Prior to the first public school being built in 1851, private schools provided education for children. In 1827, a Seminary was organized to fill the void. A building was constructed on Fourth Street between High and Walnut streets. The institution prepared youngsters to enter any of the country's colleges. The school underwent several changes until it came under the authority of the Presbyterian Church in 1854. The "window" on the side of the building's second floor originally was a door that led to the outside stairs.

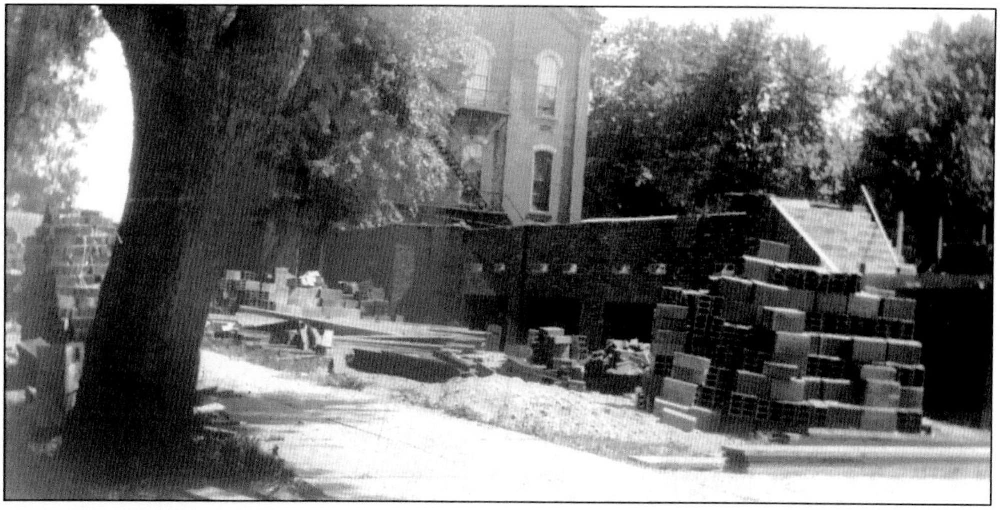

**NEW HIGH SCHOOL, 1923.** In the background is the old high school, soon to be replaced with a new building. The new school superintendent J.G. Turner oversaw the construction and restructuring of the high school. The new high school sat on land that held the outdoor basketball court. Only four classrooms, a study hall, a shop, and home economics rooms were in the new school, therefore forcing the high school to continue using the third floor of the old school for classes.

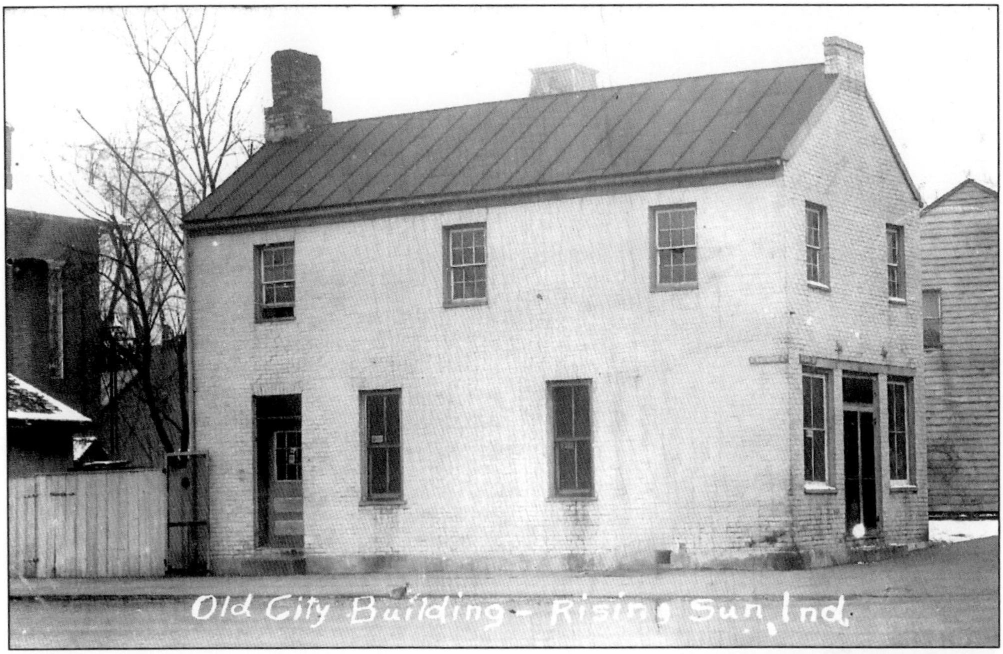


**OLD CITY BUILDING, C. 1915.** The first of two city buildings to occupy the southwest corner of Main and Walnut streets was this two-story brick structure. As Rising Sun grew and the staff needed to run the city increased, this building became obsolete. A new city building was built on the same site. The fire department was combined into one building. Previously, the fire department was a separate building standing next to the Methodist Church.

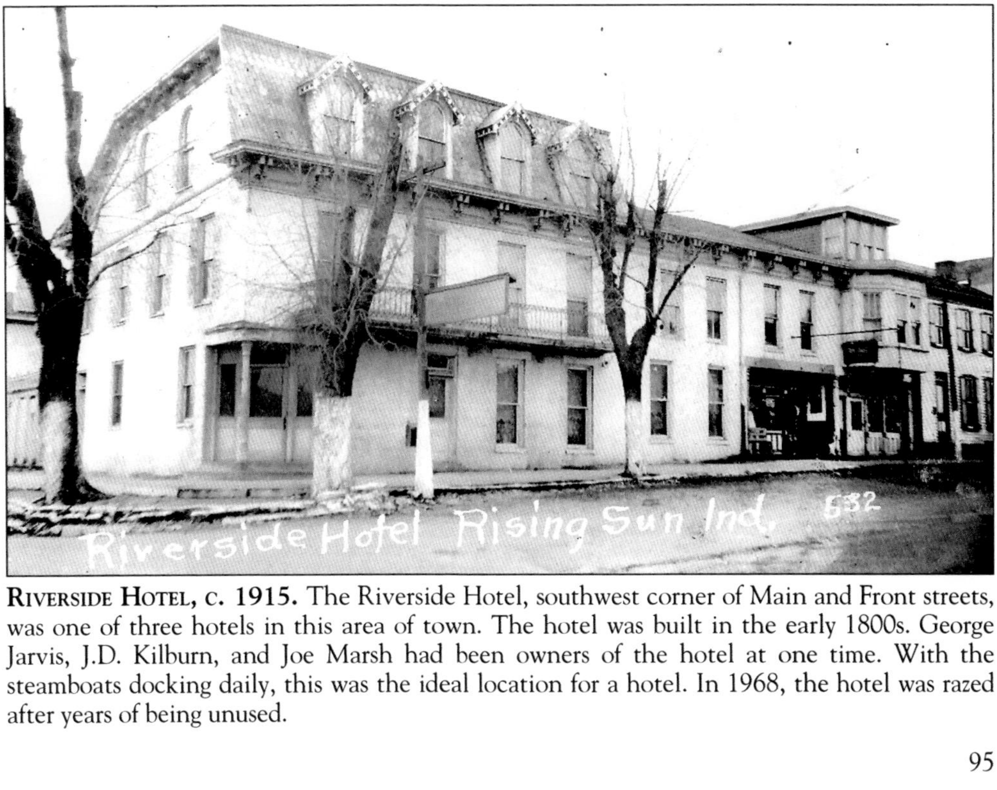


**RIVERSIDE HOTEL, C. 1915.** The Riverside Hotel, southwest corner of Main and Front streets, was one of three hotels in this area of town. The hotel was built in the early 1800s. George Jarvis, J.D. Kilburn, and Joe Marsh had been owners of the hotel at one time. With the steamboats docking daily, this was the ideal location for a hotel. In 1968, the hotel was razed after years of being unused.

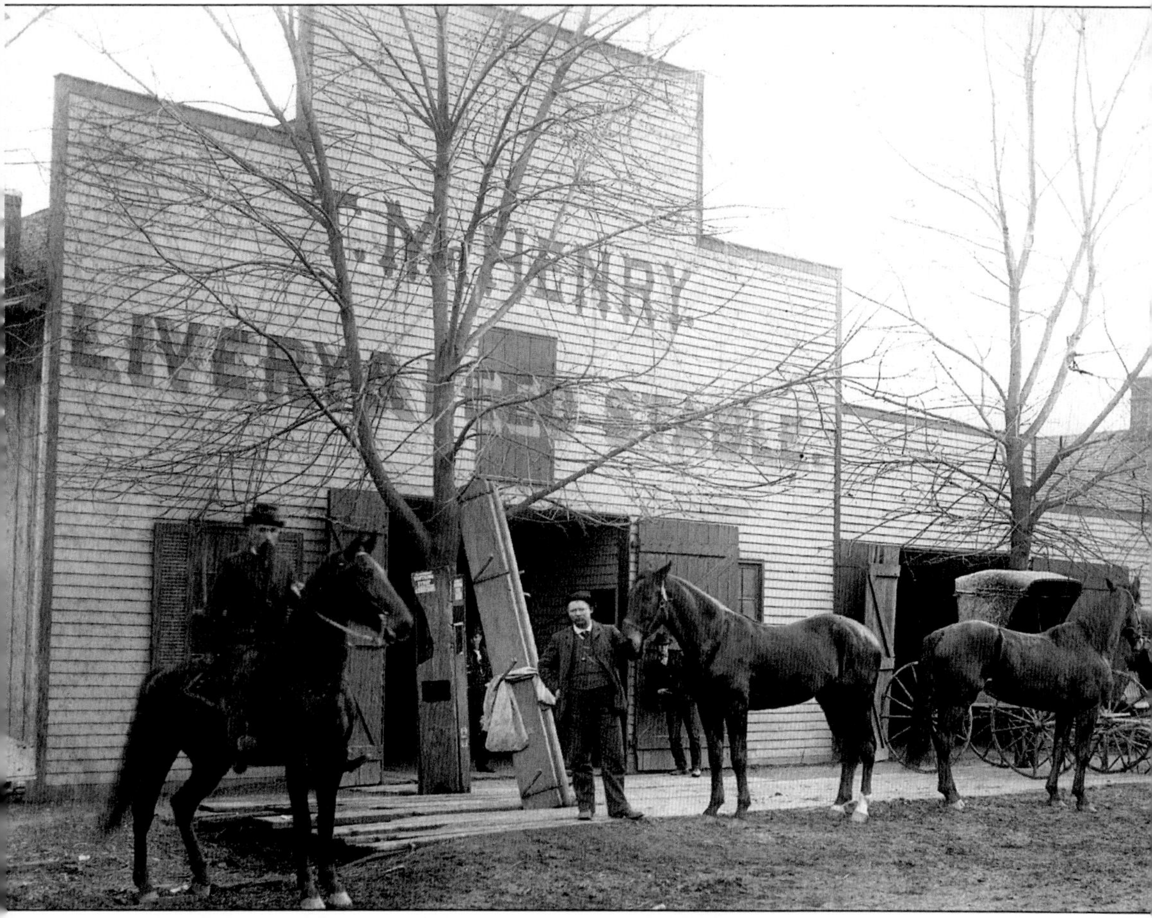


**LIVERY STABLE, C. 1900.** Tim McHenry started the T. McHenry Livery and Feed Stable operation in 1882. The livery and feed stable was located where Rising Sun/Ohio County Convention & Tourism Bureau is currently on Walnut Street. McHenry started this business after purchasing a half interest in the Aurora & Rising Sun Omnibus Line in 1879. The man second from the left is Tim McHenry. Horses, buggies, and surreys could also be rented from McHenry.

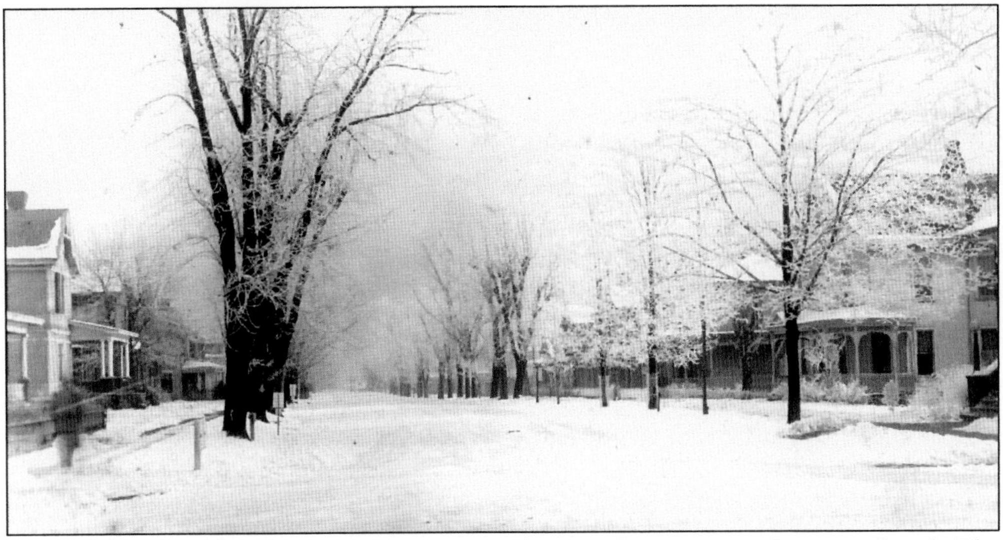

**High Street, c. 1920.** A pleasant winter scene shown with snow covered street and yards. The view is looking north on High Street (State Road 56). The Ohio County Public Library is barely visible on the right. Traffic at the time the photograph was taken was slow, but by the looks of the streets there has been considerable traffic. The lone person in the picture is blurred, as is the case with photographs of the time. If the person did not hold still a blurred image would be captured.

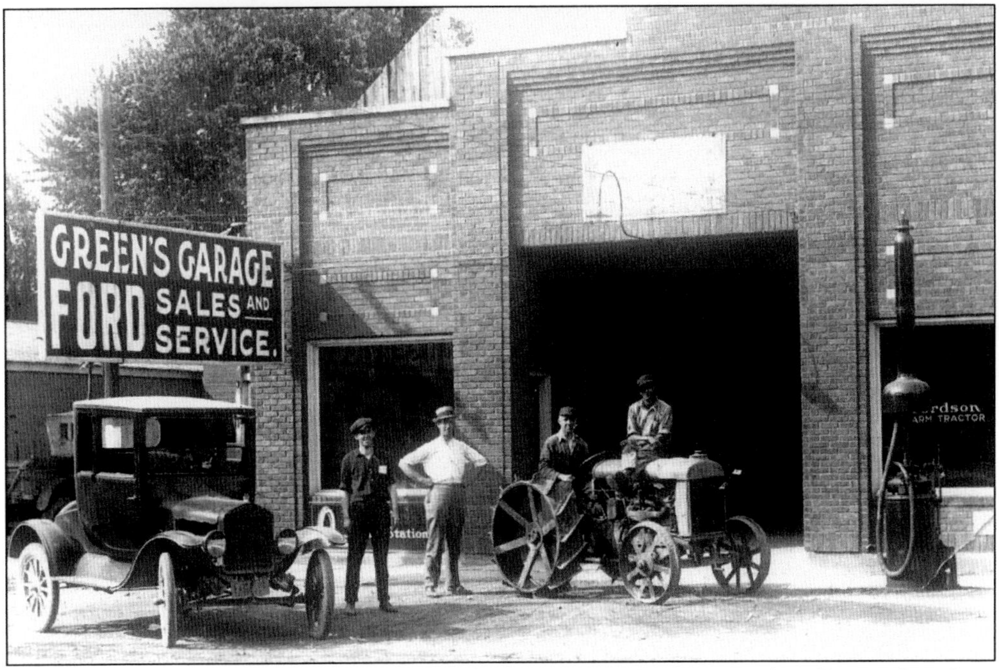


**Ford Garage, c. 1924.** Sometime around 1915, Harry Green moved to Rising Sun from Patriot, Indiana. At this time this building was built on Main Street across from the courthouse. Mr. Green is the gentleman in the white shirt and straw hat. Green's Ford Garage was a place to purchase Fords such as the up-to-date 1924 Ford or the Fordson tractor with the metal wheels. The gas pump was the type you pumped the amount of gas you wanted prior to filling your car. The garage is now home to Jeff's Carpet.

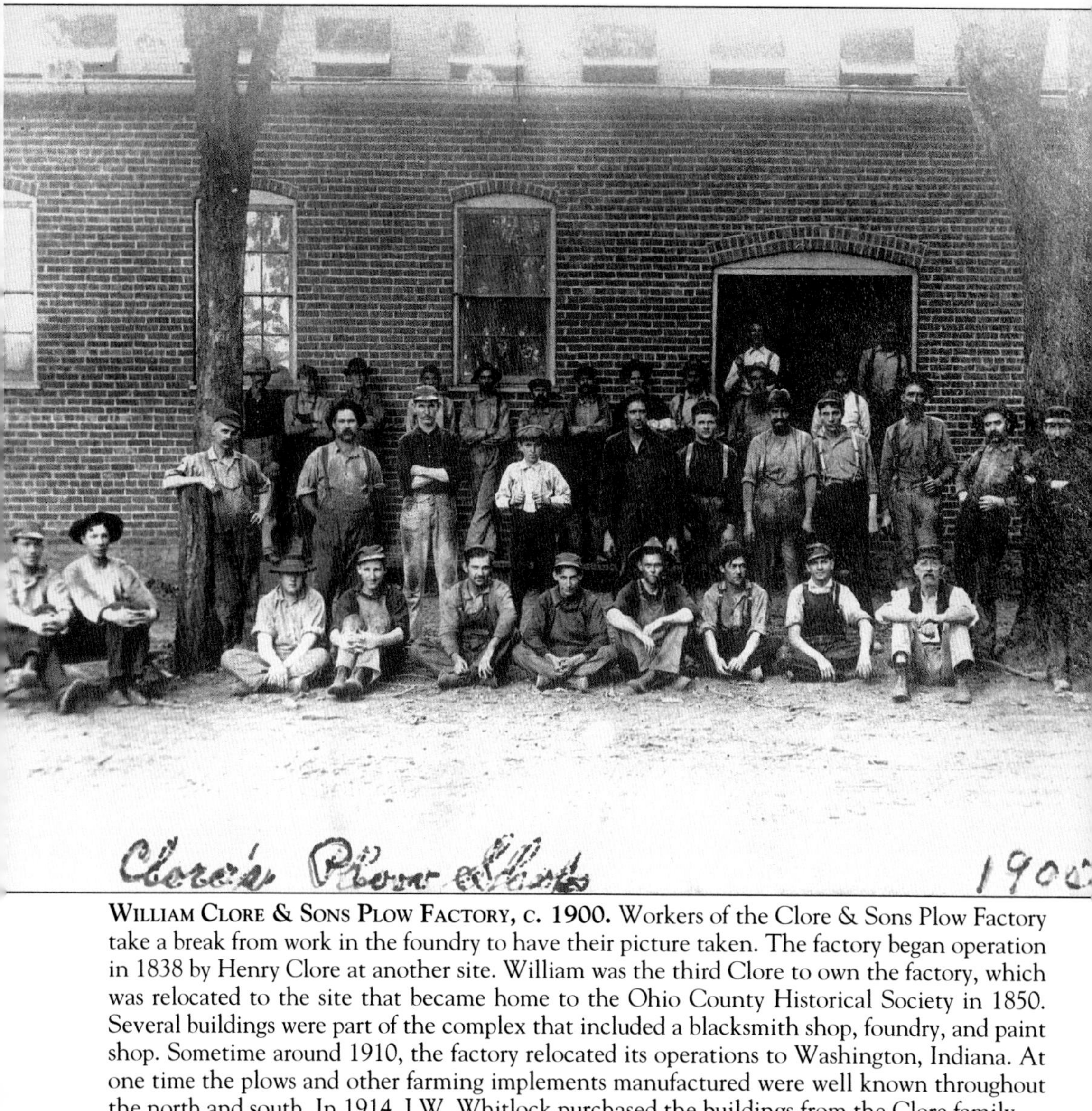

**William Clore & Sons Plow Factory, c. 1900.** Workers of the Clore & Sons Plow Factory take a break from work in the foundry to have their picture taken. The factory began operation in 1838 by Henry Clore at another site. William was the third Clore to own the factory, which was relocated to the site that became home to the Ohio County Historical Society in 1850. Several buildings were part of the complex that included a blacksmith shop, foundry, and paint shop. Sometime around 1910, the factory relocated its operations to Washington, Indiana. At one time the plows and other farming implements manufactured were well known throughout the north and south. In 1914, J.W. Whitlock purchased the buildings from the Clore family.

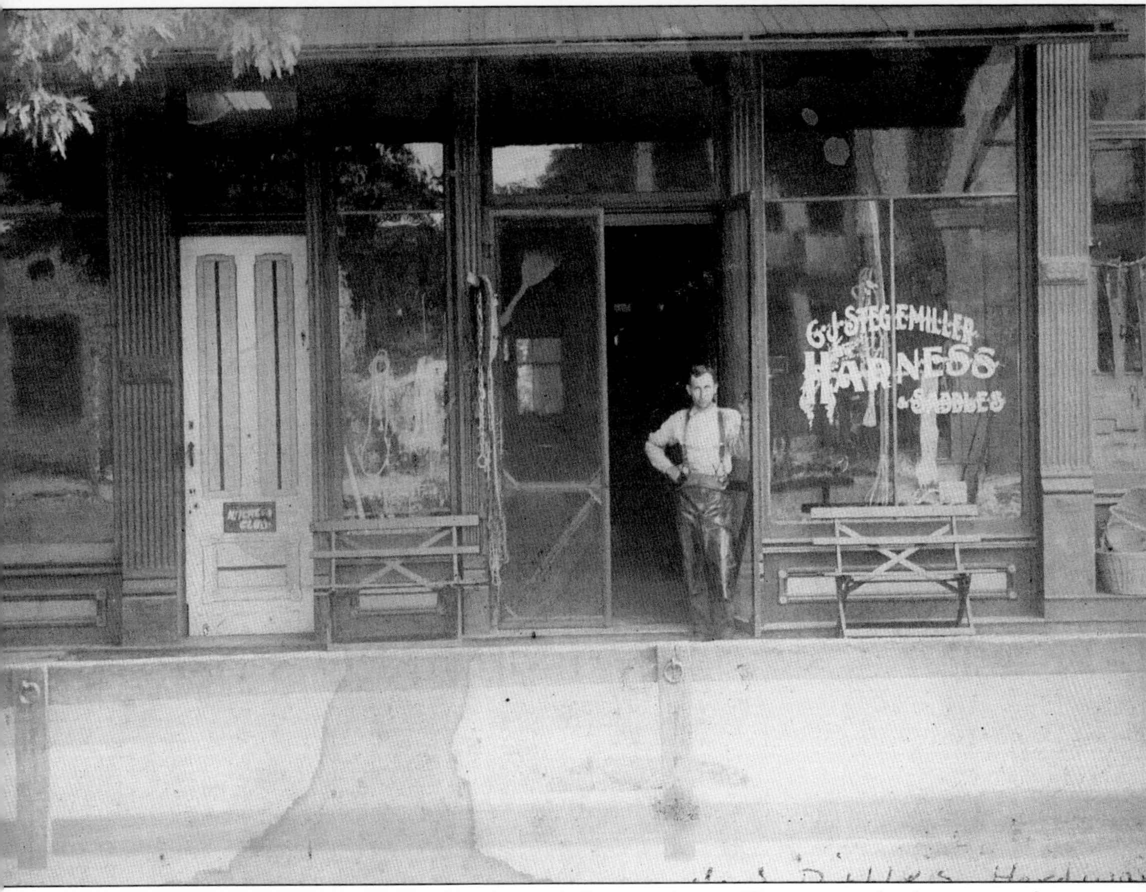


**STEGEMILLER HARDWARE, C. 1910.** Charles and George Stegemiller operated a harness and saddle repair shop on Main Street where Daniel's Total Physique is currently located. The man standing in the doorway is Charles Stegemiller. He is wearing leather pants to protect himself and his clothing while he completes the repair work. Out in front of the shop, which also was a hardware store, is a fence with rings to tie a horse to. Later it became Dibble Hardware Store. On the door to the left is a sign—"Nitche Club."

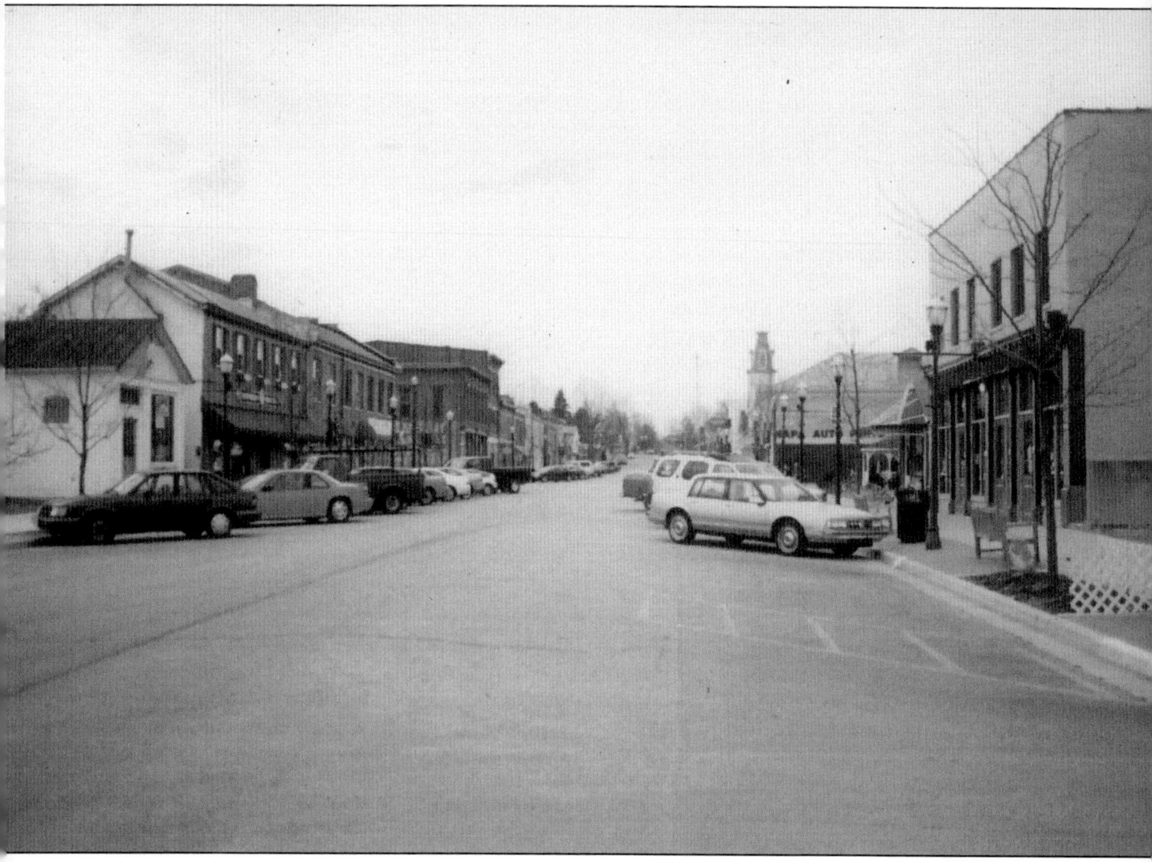

**DOWNTOWN RISING SUN, MARCH, 2001.** This view of downtown is taken from the eastern edge in front of the American Legion Post (to the right). The Historic Downtown Program is blending existing service businesses with art galleries, craft shops, and music-related businesses. The idea is to bring tourists to town to mingle with local people to shop and enjoy events in town and along the riverfront.

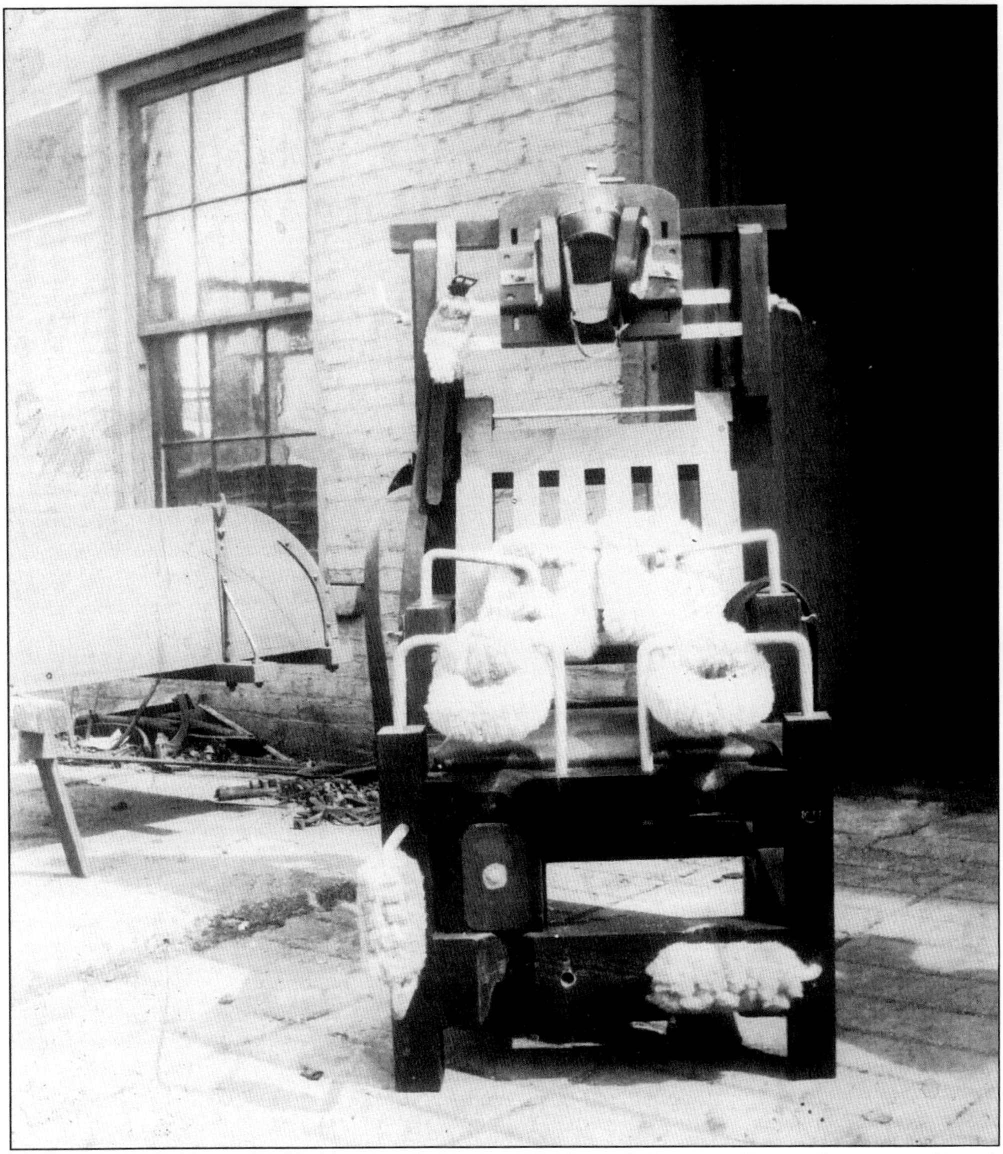

**Electric Chair, 1928.** In 1928, Smith Riggs, a blacksmith living in Rising Sun, was selected to construct two electric chairs. A hospital consultant in Indianapolis overseeing the project, J.F. Gregries, contacted Riggs. He was chosen because the particular lumber to be used could be found in Rising Sun. It was one of the few places where the heavy three-inch, air-dried white oak could be obtained. The new chairs were to be more humane. The electric chairs in use at the time took between 5 and 10 minutes to fasten the man into the chair. The new chairs would take less than a minute. When completed, one of the chairs went to the Joliet, Illinois penitentiary and the other to the Menard, Illinois penitentiary.

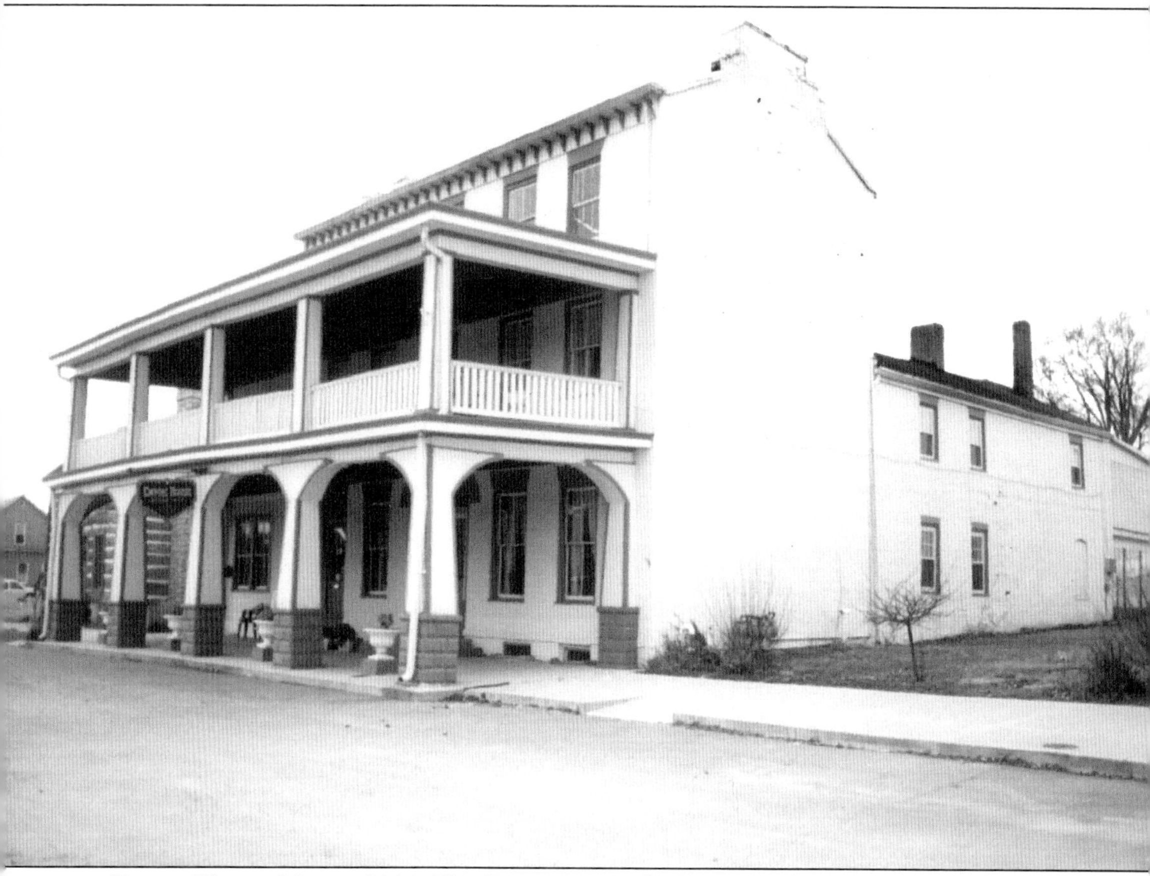

**Empire House, March 2001.** The Empire House, built in 1816, has had a unique long history. The original owner, Daniel Brown, had it built as his home. For 50 years Mr. Brown operated a general store out of a portion of the building. For a time during Mr. Brown's ownership, the upper floor served as the Masonic Lodge. Other uses for the building included a church and tavern. Several different owners used it as a hotel, for which it is most noted. From 1885–1920, the Schroeder family owned the Empire House. Every member of the family assisted in the operation of the hotel and restaurant.

# *Seven*

# Ohio County People and Places

The majority of the photographs included in this book pertain to Rising Sun, but the rest of Ohio County is just as important to the growth of the area. The towns of Aberdeen, Pate, Bear Branch, Milton, French, and Hartford all had an influence on the everyday life of people in the county. As you drive through any of these towns today, you need to use your imagination to see them as thriving communities of the 1800s and early 1900s. They were filled with activity. The trip to Rising Sun took a half day or more from most of the smaller towns. So they had their own post offices, groceries, mills, blacksmiths, and eating establishments. At one time steamboats were built in Milton. In Hartford there was a hotel for travelers, and in Aberdeen there were two gunsmiths. There were churches in each local community and some of them are still active. One-room schools dotted the county until school consolidation became necessary in the mid-1900s. All of the county's schools were then relocated to Rising Sun.

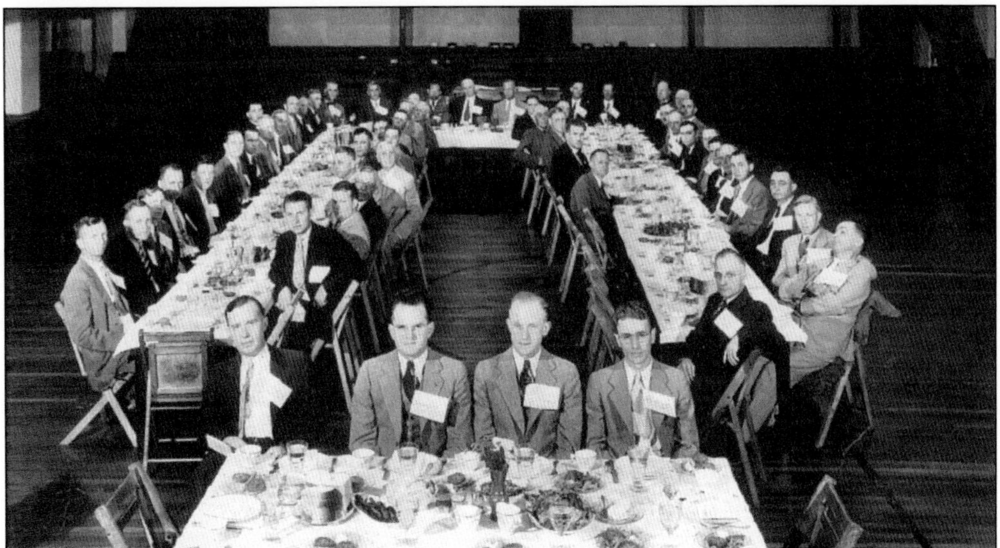

**Rotary Banquet, 1935.** The annual Rotary Banquet was held in the old high school gym. On July 18, 1933, the Rotary was formed by local businessmen lead by Lucian Harris along with Roy Gibson and Earl Danbury. Mr. Harris was president in August 1933, when the Rising Sun Rotary was presented its charter and became the smallest city in the world to receive a charter. Mr. Gibson and his father, Leonard, both would become Rotary presidents. Leonard Gibson is the first man in the third row from the left.

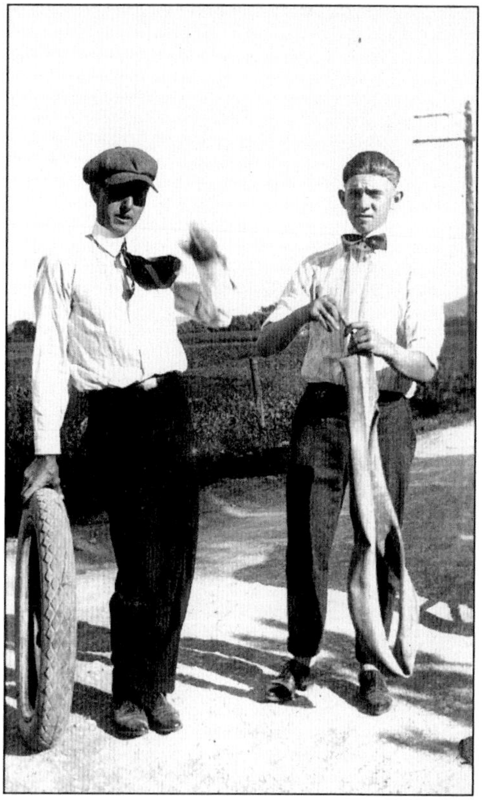

**Fixing tire, 1920.** Traveling by automobile in the early part of the 20th century was new and done by very few. There were some that used it for leisure such as going for a picnic or simply going for a drive. The early roads in Ohio County like those in most areas of the country were in poor condition. When it rained they would become muddy, sometimes trapping the motorist and car in the middle of the road. The automobiles themselves would often breakdown, many times with tire problems. Unfortunately, on this particular day, Glenn Dorrell (left) and Russell Dorrell had recurring tire troubles.

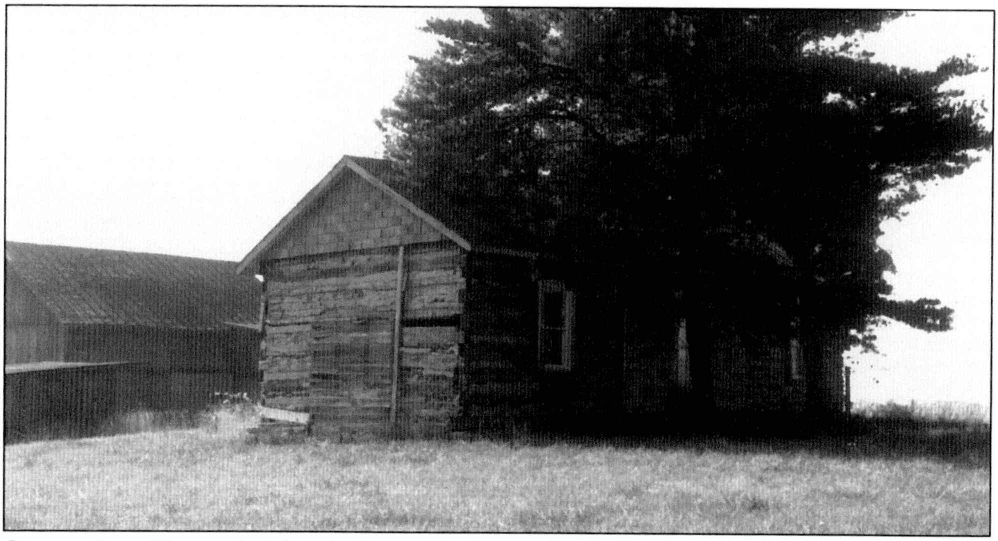

**Corson Log House, 1988.** The James K. Corson family lived in this log house from 1857–1870. James, born June 9, 1838, married Mary Jane Spore on March 10, 1857. They had seven children before moving to Illinois sometime around 1870. The house built *c.* 1830 is located on Homes Hill Road in Randolph Township. Often structures like this are called log cabins, however, that is not accurate. A log cabin is a crudely constructed for temporary housing. A log house would have the logs squared, smoothed, and clapboard placed over it covering the construction. Sometimes a log cabin would be incorporated into a house.

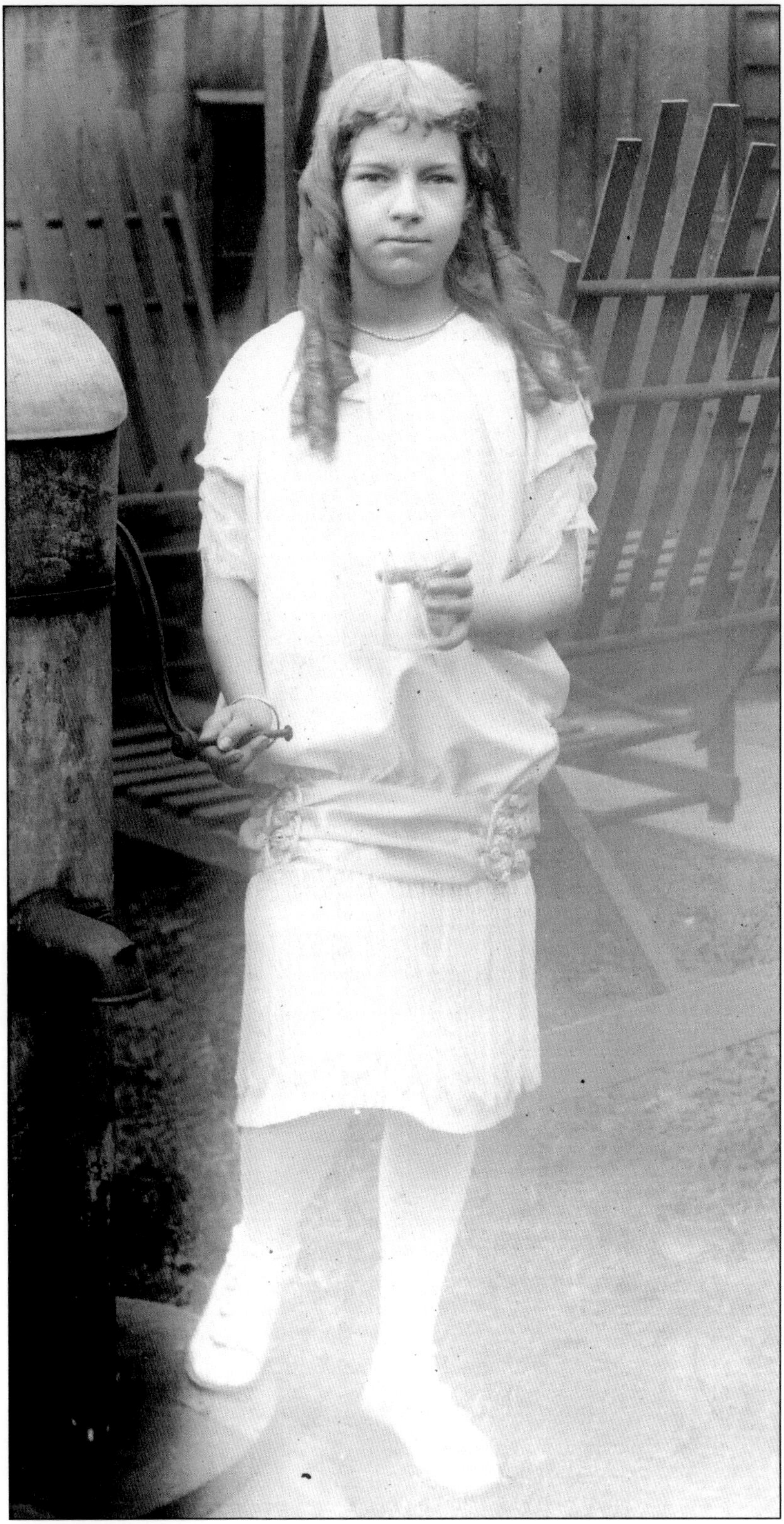

**FREDA DEVERS DUCKWORTH, C. 1920.** Freda Duckworth stands in her backyard with a glass. She is preparing to get a drink of water from the cistern pump. These pumps were one of the styles popular in the late 1800s to early 1900s. Of note is the glider directly behind Ms. Duckworth.

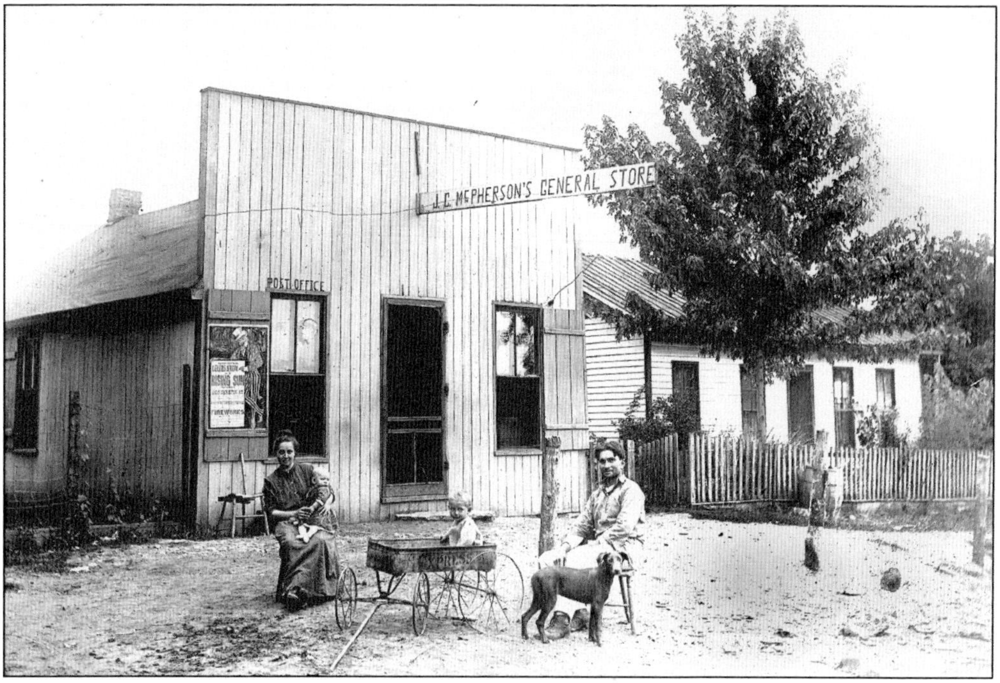


**J.C. McPherson's General Store, 1911.** Aberdeen became the name of the crossroads in Cass Township where the Gillespie family lived in the mid-1800s. The Gillespies and their neighbors all came from Aberdeen, Scotland. The area had been settled since 1819. Joe C. McPherson operated a general store there, which also served as the town's post office. Note the broadside announcing a celebration in Rising Sun that included fireworks.

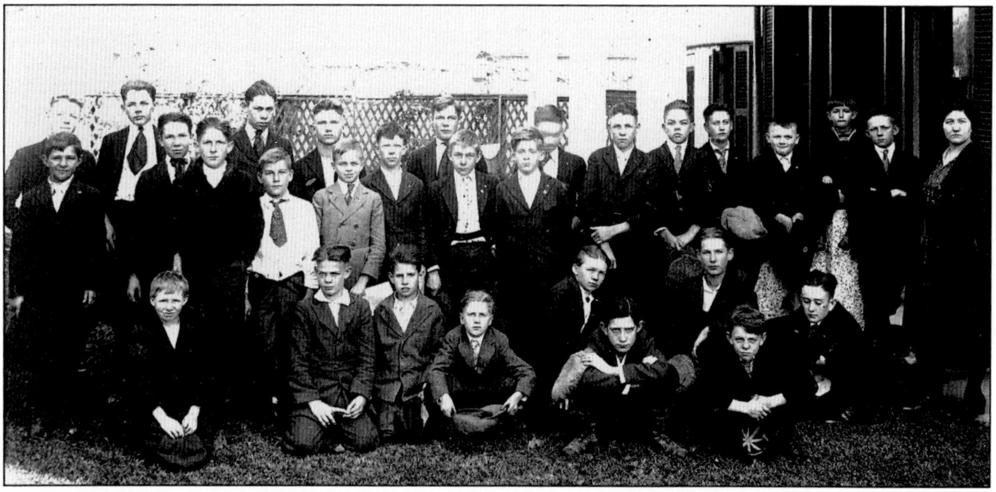

**Sunday School, c. 1920.** Freda Gibson and her Christian Church Sunday School class pose at the home of Frank Steeles. From left to right are as follows: (front row) (?) Ryan, Murray Talbott, Louis Ricketts, Stewart Whitlock, (?) McClellan, Frank Bodle, Powell Byran, William Buchanan, and John T. Whitlock; (second row) Carlisle Hall, Leslie Campbell, Lyston Bright, (?) Baxter, Roy Gibson, James Irons, Harry Baxter, and Lawrence Scott; (third row) Willard Becht, Roy Dugle, Elmo Heath, (?) Marble, Ralph Rollins, Pete Feegitt, Lora Pavy, Raymond Dugle, Bud Whitlock, Lucian Lineback, Wilford Hall, Rudolph Hall, and Freda Gibson.

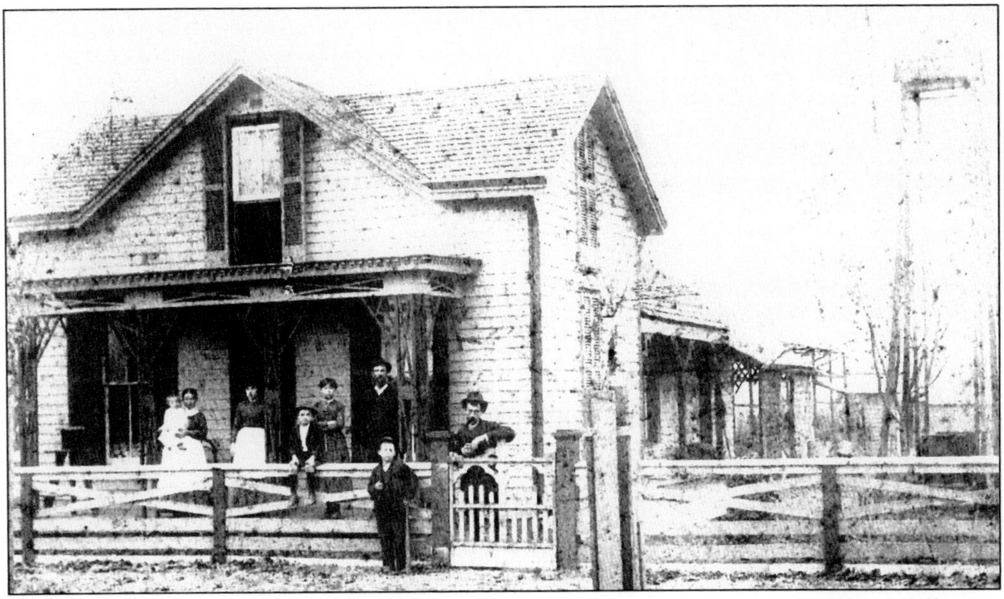

**HOFFNER HOMESTEAD, LATE 1800s.** This photograph depicts the home of Walter Hoffner in the late 1800s. The house is typical of the time period. The eight people in front of the house are unidentified. Interesting items within the picture include the well structure to the right, the fancy gate, and the two trees in front of the house. Boards fastened around the trees protect the bark from being eaten by horses.

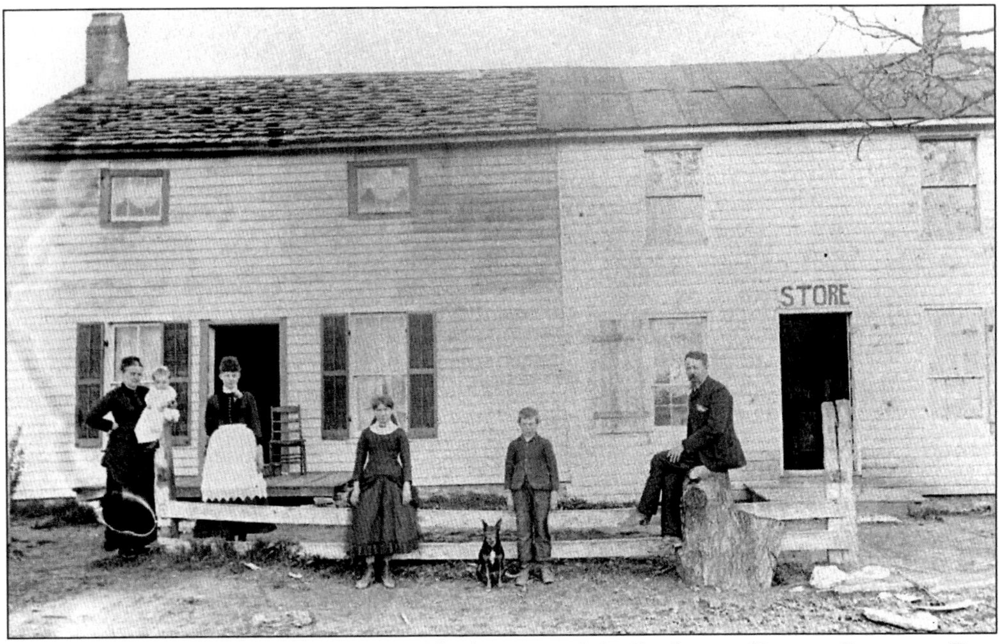


**BUCHANAN GROCERY STORE, C. 1900.** The location of the Buchanan Grocery Store is in Pate along Cass-Union Road. However, the photograph is still interesting because the building served two purposes. The portion on the left was the house and the one on the right with the sign above the doorway serves as the store. The paint color of the clapboards and type of shingles on the roof are different.

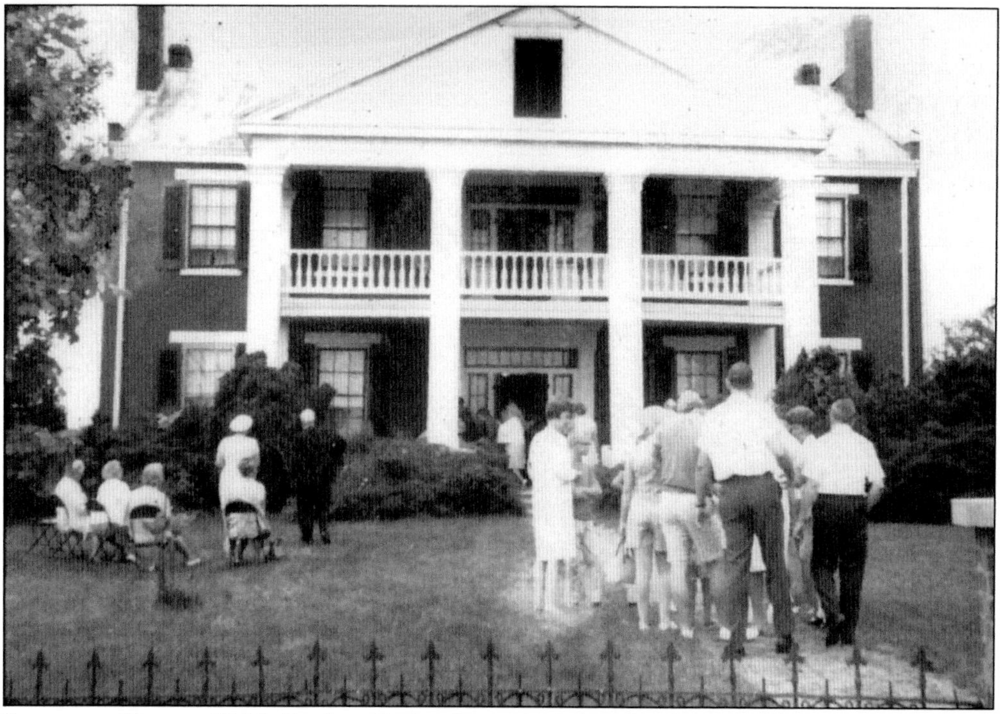

**SPEAKMAN HOUSE, 1966.** Stephen S. Speakman had this Greek Revival house built in 1846. He built it for a young Kentucky belle who agreed to marry him if he built her a showplace. Mr. Speakman owned 500 acres located near Laughery Creek, and a Native American mound was discovered in the front yard. Later Henry Miller owned the house. He was a strong abolitionist, and it was said that President Lincoln paid him a visit at the house. Legend states that it was a stop on the Underground Railroad. A tunnel leading from the house to the icehouse lends support to this claim.

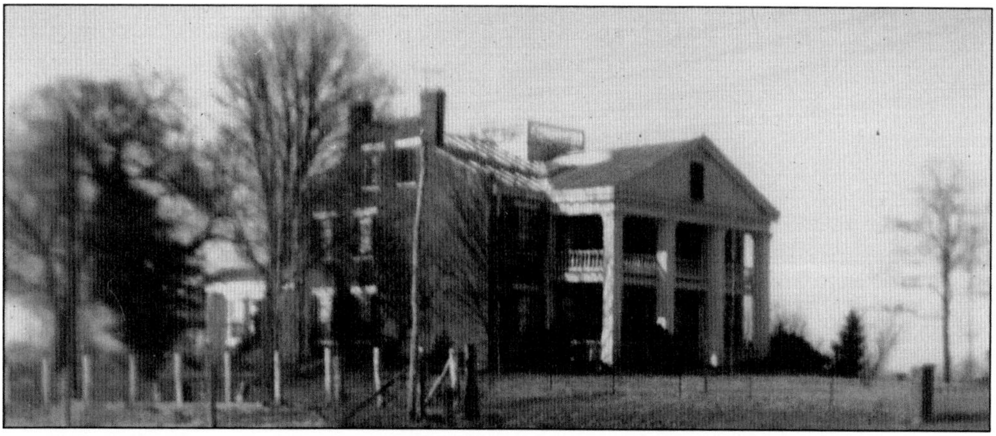

**THE FISHER-BARRICKLOW HOME, C. 1960.** This is known as the Fisher-Barricklow Home. John and Agnes Fisher had purchased the land, and then in 1844 had the Greek Revivial house built. Materials such as the bricks were made on site and the timber was cut on the farm. The three-story home had a dance hall on the top floor, which was common in many houses of the time. A legend states that the house was part of the Underground Railroad. William Taylor Barricklow married one of the Fisher girls and purchased the house later.

**Freda Gibson, 1889.** Her father was William Taylor Barricklow who, along with his wife Agnes, lived on and operated the Fisher Farm. This was Agnes' father's farm. When Agnes died, in 1912, William sold the farm to Freda and her husband and moved to Rising Sun. For a few years he operated a small hardware store in town.

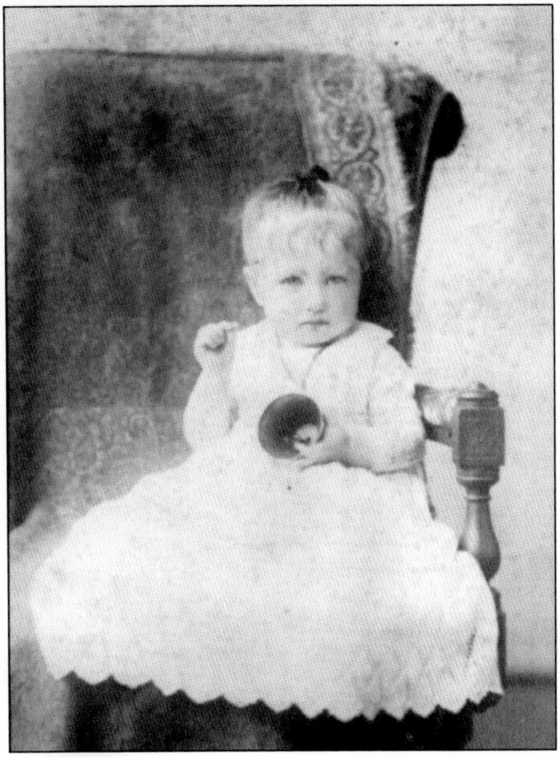

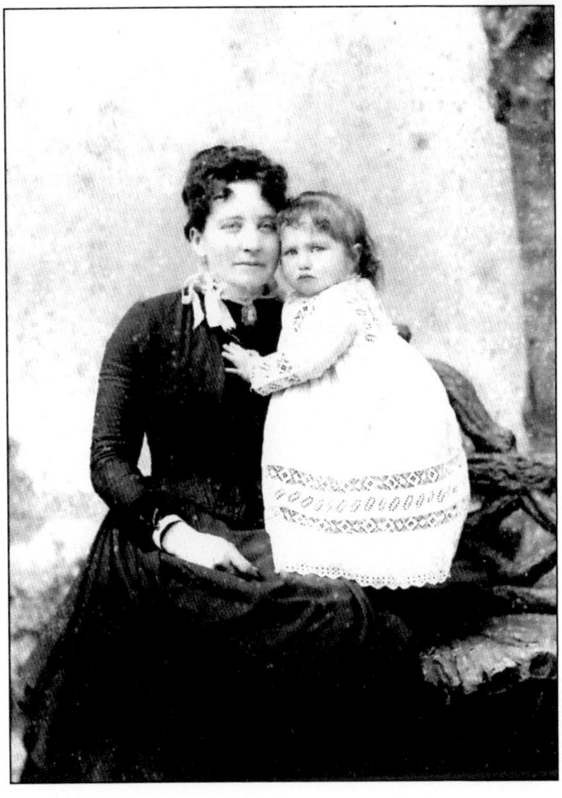

**Freda Barricklow Gibson, 1889.** This photo shows Freda Barricklow Gibson with her mother, Agnes Barricklow. Freda was two years old at the time photographer J.N. Walton took her picture. Freda married Leonard Gibson. Leonard Gibson's ill health forced him to the sell the hardware store in 1945. Both Leonard and Freda moved to Florida where Leonard died in 1966, and Freda Gibson in 1978.

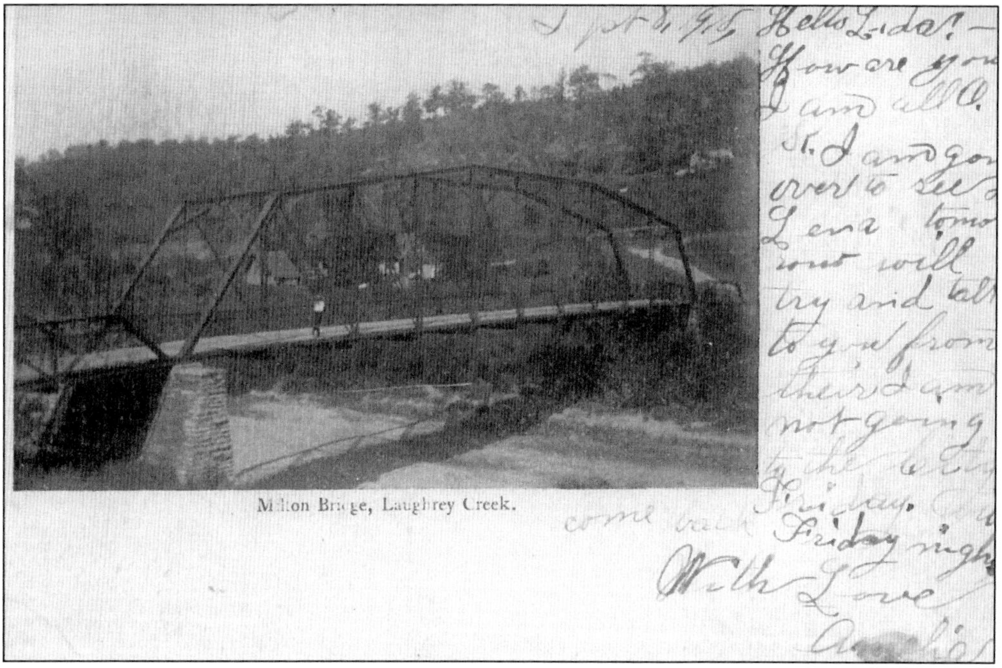


**MILTON BRIDGE, C. 1910.** Originally, Milton had been known as James' Mill or Jamestown, so called because John James founded it. Pinkey James, son of John James, and Prince Athearn built two steamboats (the *Renown* and *Dolphin*) in Milton. Several business establishments were located in Milton. Among them were a grocery, blacksmith shop, and a gristmill. The iron bridge over Laughery Creek was built in 1898, and replaced in the 1980s.

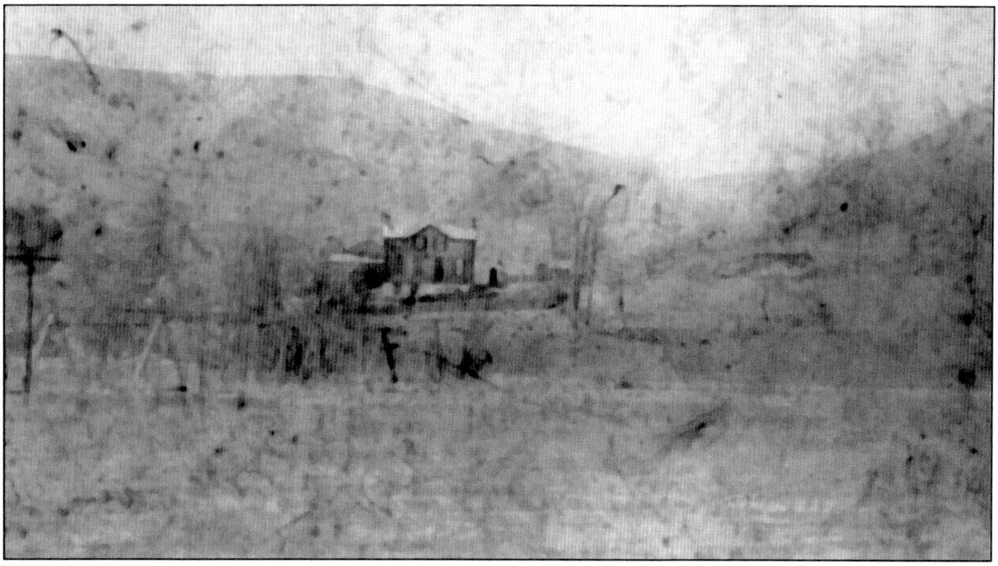

**STEGEMILLER HOME, C. 1900.** The old Stegemiller Home was located on Miller Brick Hill. State Road 56 runs near the home. Jack Gallager later owned the house. In the middle left of the photograph faintly visible is a bridge that crosses Arnold's Creek. It's interesting to note that the water is over the bed of the bridge and it appears there are two people in a rowboat to the left of the bridge.

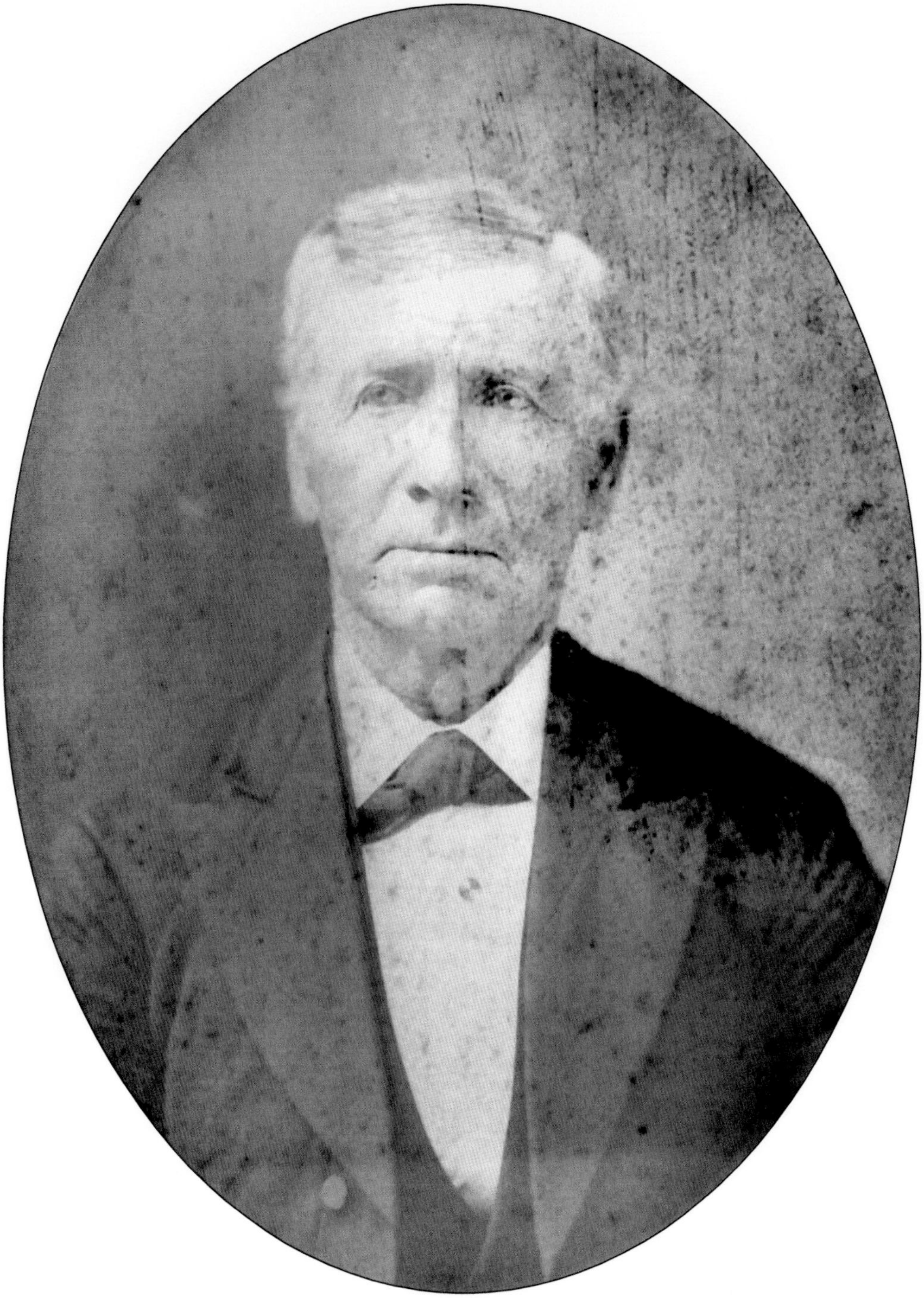

**James North, c. 1880.** James North, born March 23, 1811, lived at North's Landing until his death August 4, 1890. He spent his life as a farmer with time given for civic duties in 1867 in the House of the General Assembly and in 1879 as a County Commissioner.

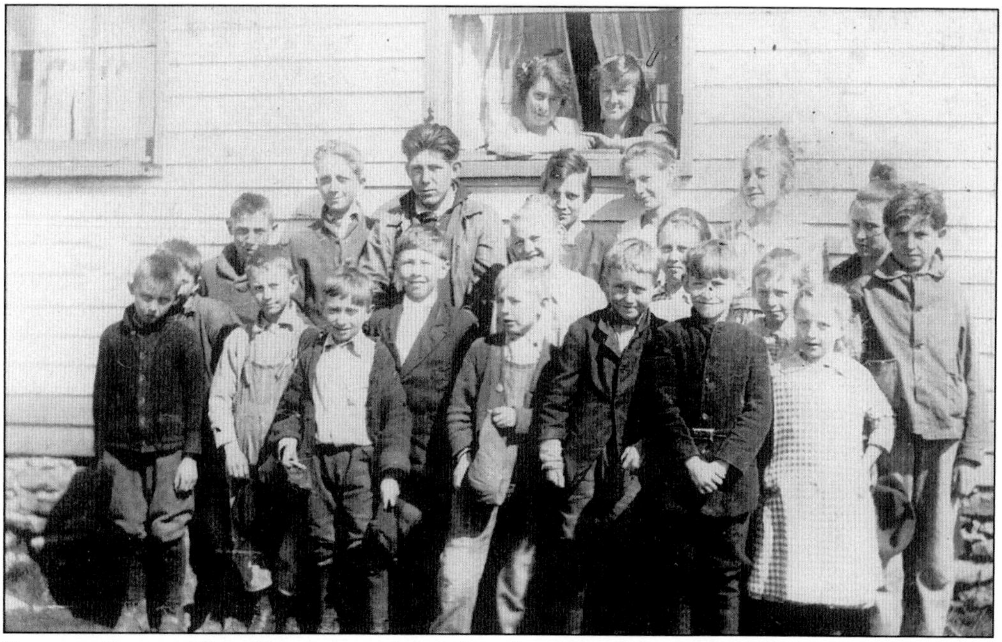

**Freedom School, Bear Branch, c. 1910.** Freedom School located in Pike Township was one of four one-room schools in the township. In 1950 a new school replaced the school pictured. That school closed in 1964, when all pupils were sent to Cass Union. This was part of the county school consolidation process.

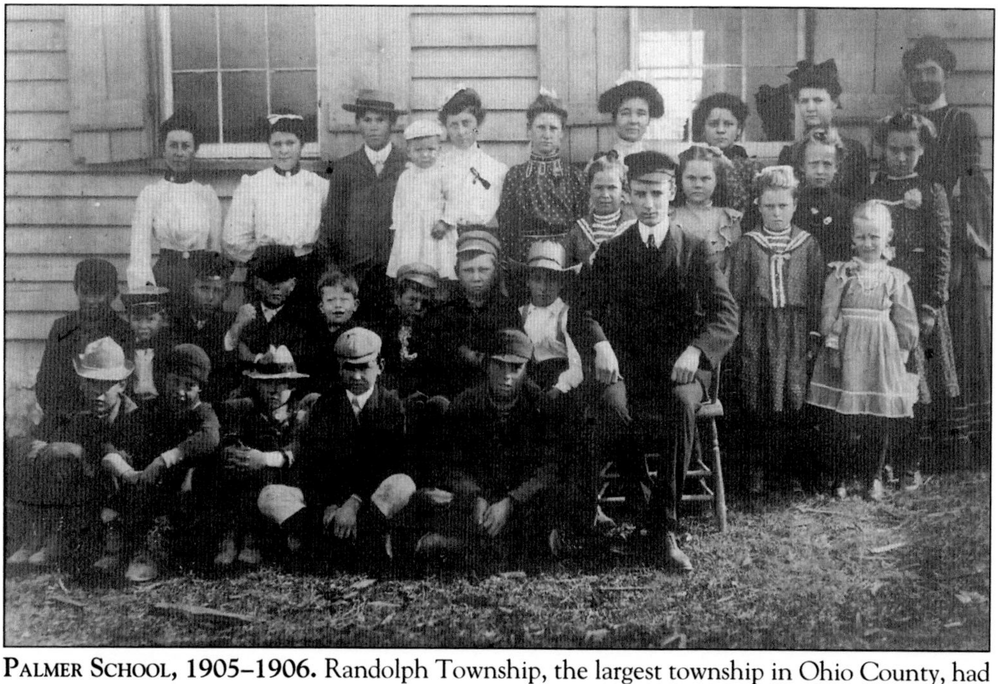

**Palmer School, 1905–1906.** Randolph Township, the largest township in Ohio County, had its first school built prior to 1830. This log school was located near Salem Church. Another school added along the way was Palmer School. Robert Tumy was the teacher who taught in the Palmer one-room school, covering grades one though eight in the early 1900s.

**Cream Station in Aberdeen, 1920.** Farmers living in the vicinity of Aberdeen brought their cream to this cream station. At one time Glenn Dorrell operated the cream station. Earl Green operated the station depicted in this photograph. Note the cream cans on the porch. It is hard to believe, but Aberdeen was home to two gun makers at the same time in the 1800s. Other businesses in town included blacksmith shops, broom makers, a cooper, and a grocer, to name a few.

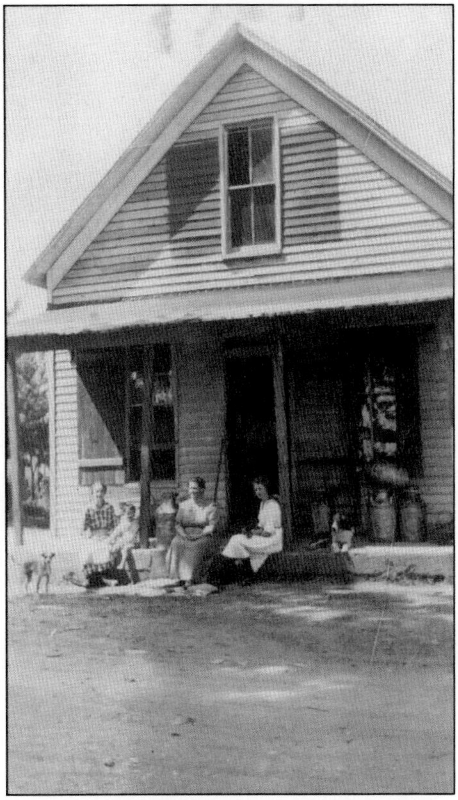

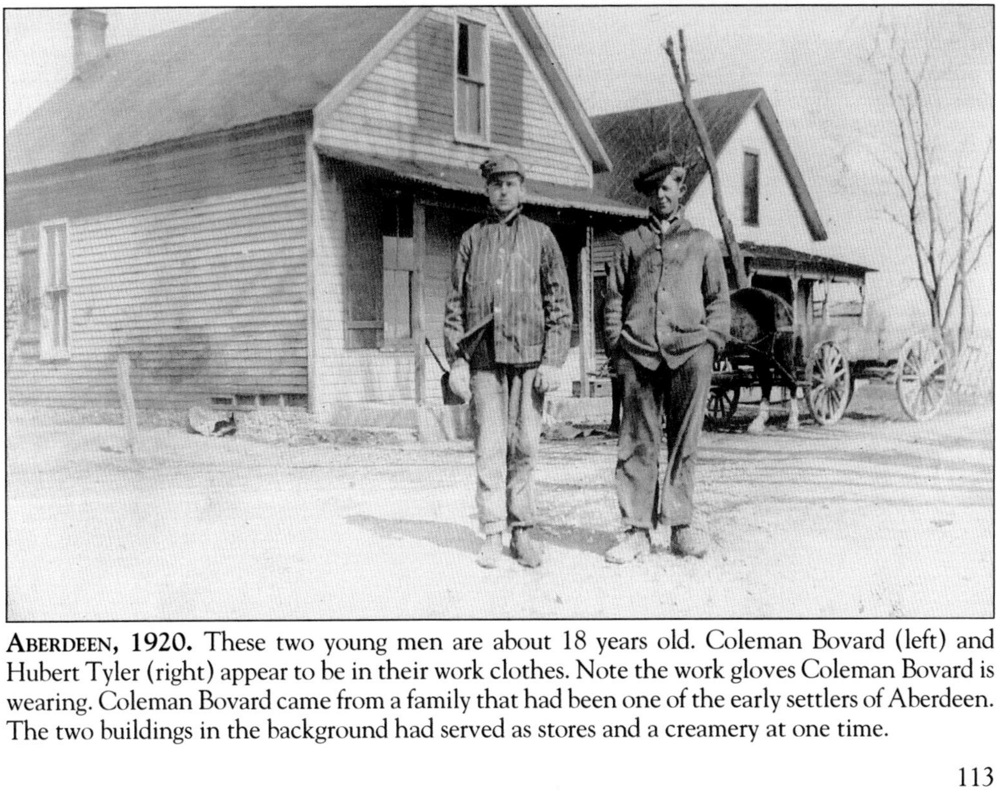

**Aberdeen, 1920.** These two young men are about 18 years old. Coleman Bovard (left) and Hubert Tyler (right) appear to be in their work clothes. Note the work gloves Coleman Bovard is wearing. Coleman Bovard came from a family that had been one of the early settlers of Aberdeen. The two buildings in the background had served as stores and a creamery at one time.

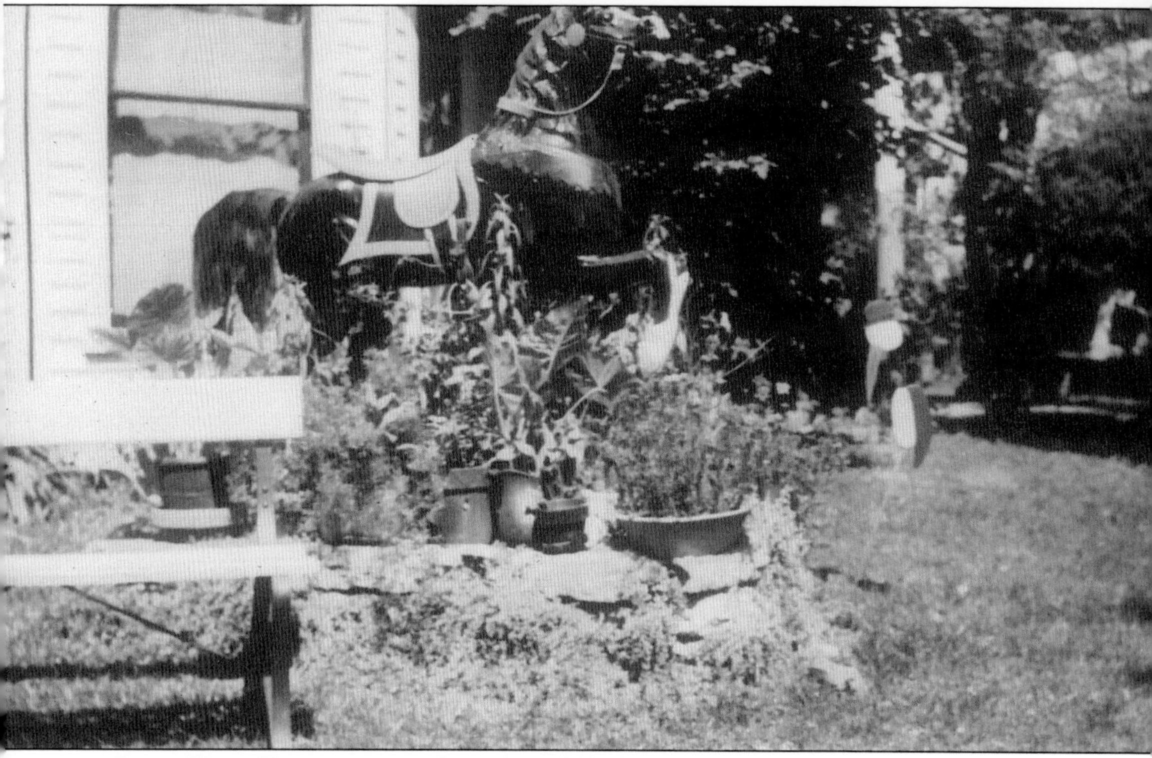

**Black Horse Tavern, 1939.** The trademark black carousel horse on the property easily identified the Black Horse Tavern located on the southeast corner of the main road through Aberdeen. During the mid-1900s, the tavern was a popular destination for travelers and local people.

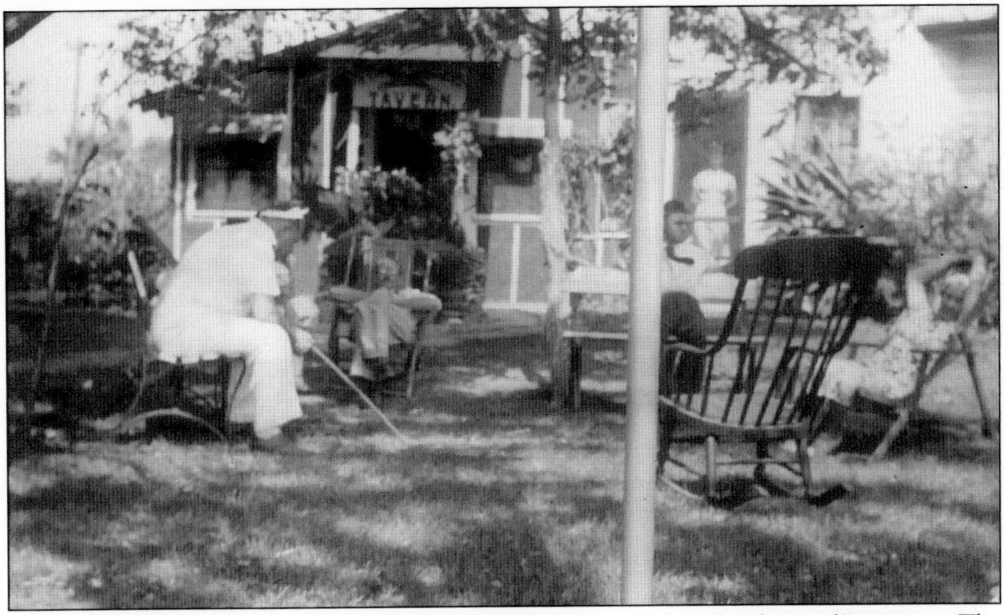

**Black Horse Tavern, 1939.** The Black Horse Tavern served sandwiches and ice cream. The ice cream was made on site and was said to be very good. It was a relaxed atmosphere where friends gathered to sit in the shade and share stories in a variety of chairs. Note the Black Horse Tavern sign over the door. The sign is in the collection of the Ohio County Historical Society.

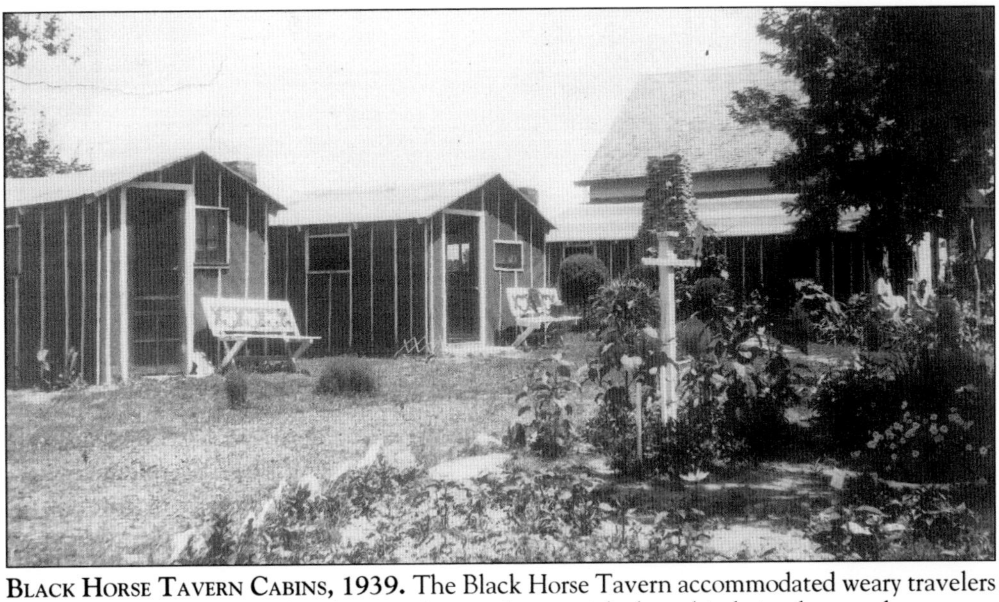

**Black Horse Tavern Cabins, 1939.** The Black Horse Tavern accommodated weary travelers with their cabins for rent. Similar to a shotgun house with the cabin being long and one room wide, each one had a bench outside for relaxing in the cool summer breeze. The cabins faced a nicely landscaped garden.

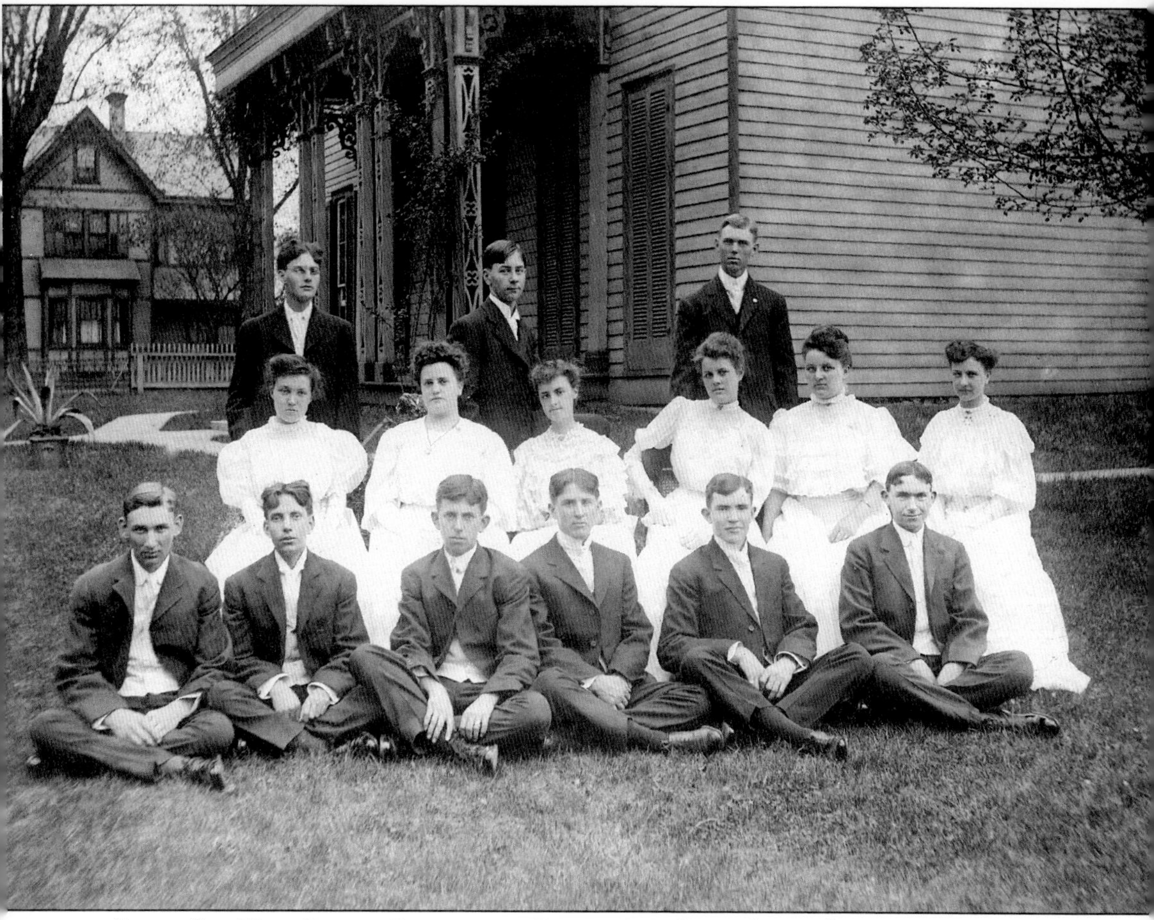

**RISING SUN HIGH SCHOOL GRADUATING CLASS, 1907.** Being the smallest county in Indiana does keep the graduating class small. In 1907, the graduating class numbered 15. From left to right are as follows: (front row) Earl Driver, Jim Harris, Loring Hartford, Charlie Voris, Shelby Cowen, and Carl Turner; (middle row), Lelah Dickey, Mary Hunter, Harriet Tumy, Emma Neal, Dorothy Humphry, and Edna Neaman; (back row) Fred Egelston, Ross Daly, and Albert Schroeder.

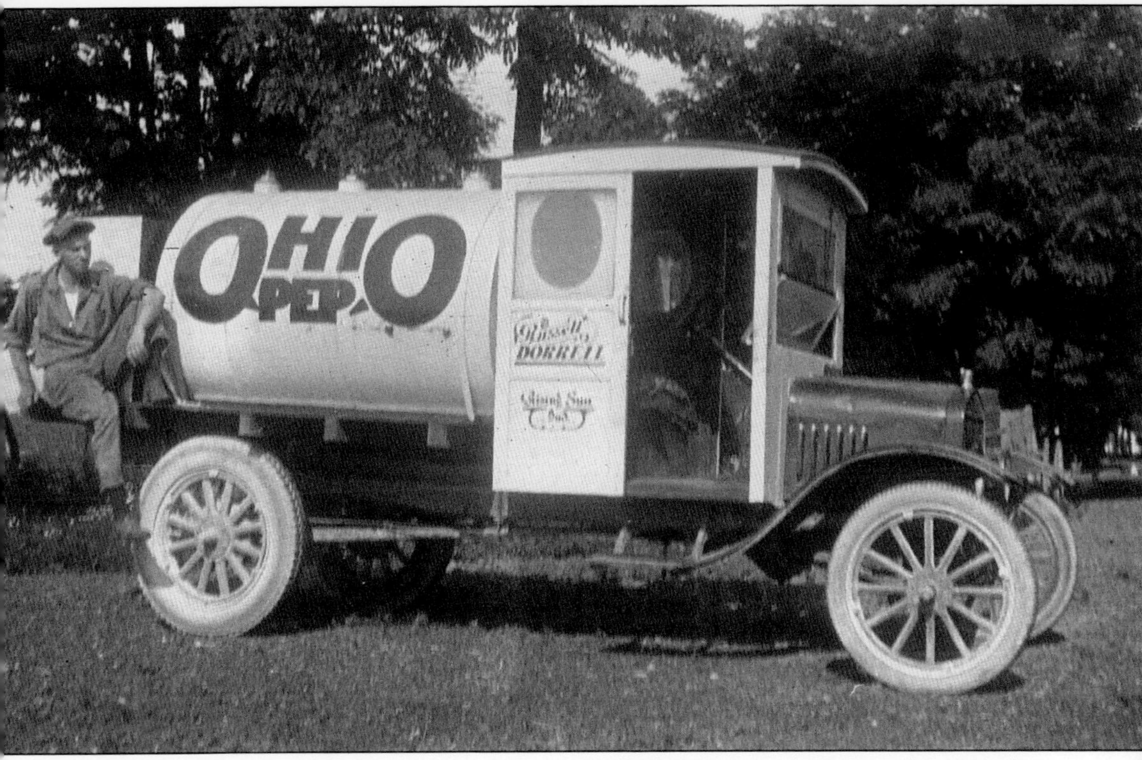


**Gas Truck, 1924.** Russell Dorrell owned this sharp looking gas truck. During the 1920s he delivered gas for the Ohio Pep Company. On the back of the tank read *Go Devil Benzol Gas "Fresh From the Still."* Denver Dorrell later on bought this business from Russell, and also had an oil delivery business in the late 1920s that he operated out of Aberdeen. He sold Ohio Pep and later United Petroleum products.

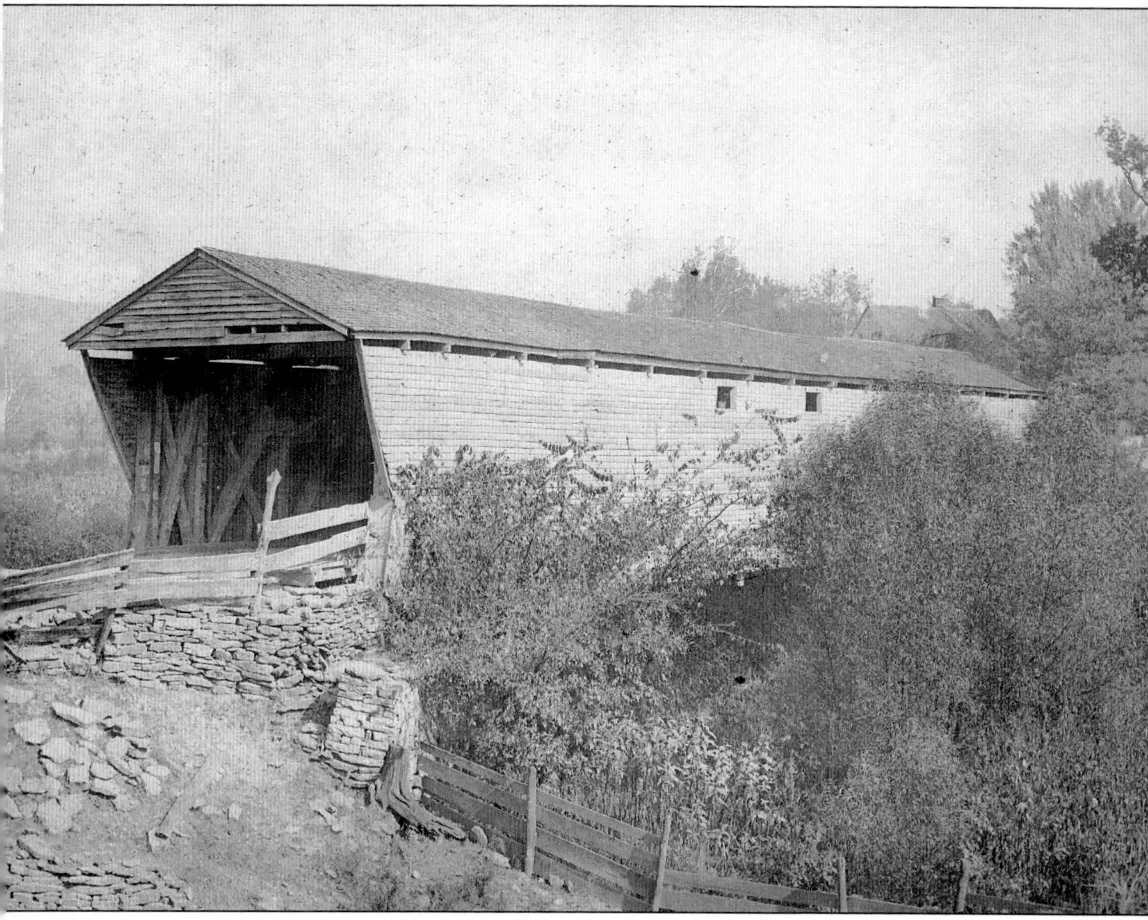

**COVERED BRIDGE, C. 1890.** In 1893, this, the last covered bridge in Ohio County, was dismantled. It was replaced by a bridge known as Neaman's Bridge at a cost of $3,400. The bridge crosses over Arnold's Creek just outside of Rising Sun on what is now State Road 262. The opening to the bridge leads away from Rising Sun. The outskirts of the town can be viewed just above the right end of the bridge with rooftops.

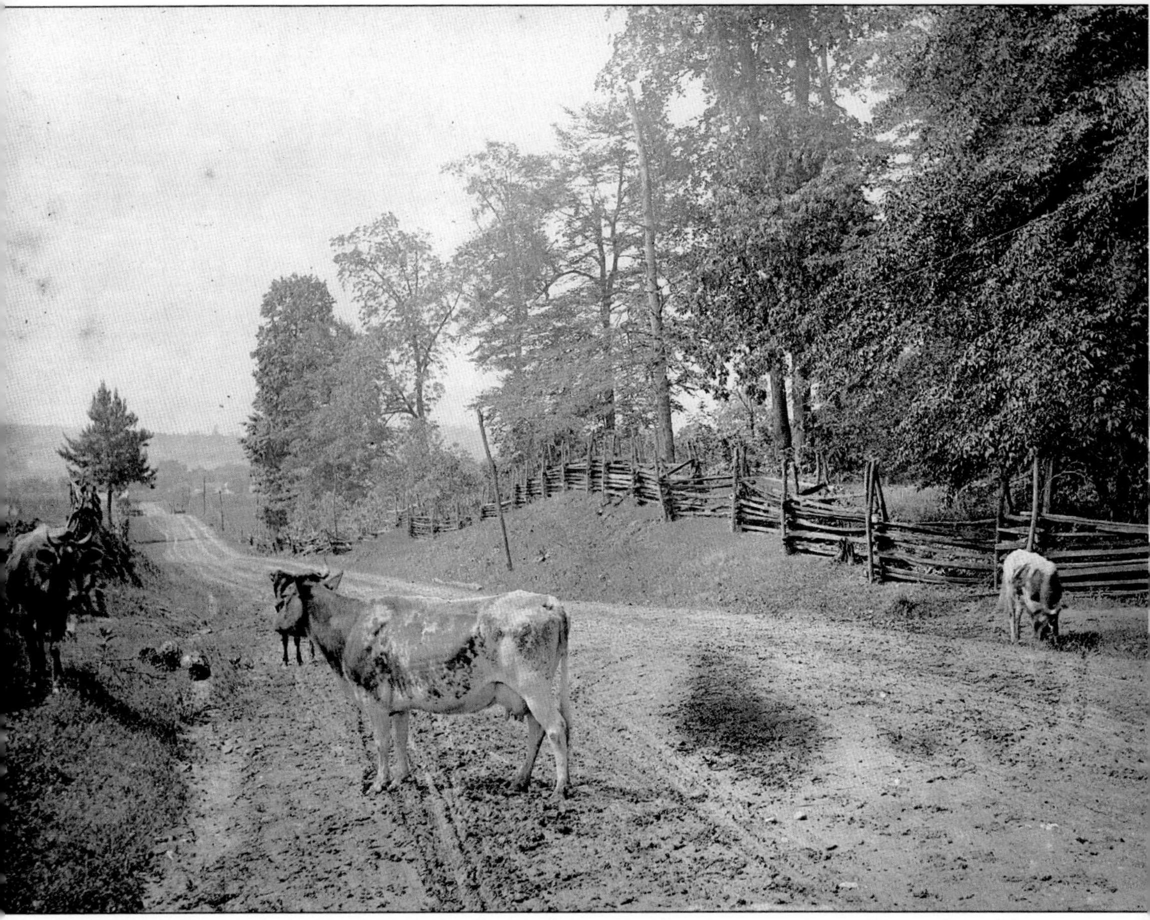

**Simms Woods, c. 1900.** A great view of a rural scene and a major road into Rising Sun. The road is the Rising Sun-Aurora Turnpike. The term "turnpike" does not usually conjure up a beautiful tree lined road with grazing cows walking along or in the road. To the right is Simms Woods with a zigzagged style fence. Originally, Col. Benjamin Chambers, who came to the area in the late 1700s to survey the land, owned the land. The land was cleared around 1904.

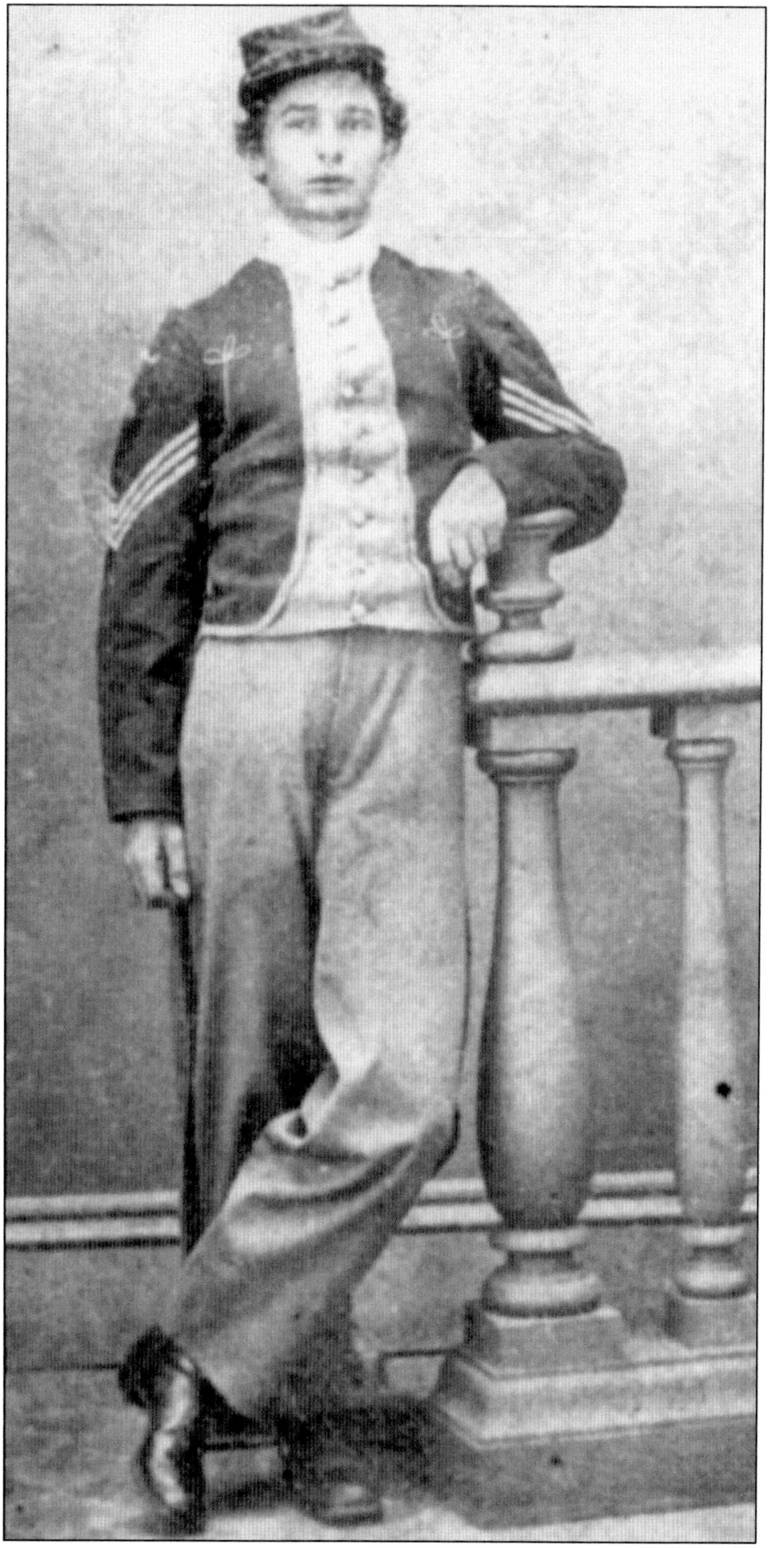

**Lucius Taylor Barbour, c. 1862.** This dignified 20-year old man, Lucius Taylor Barbour, enlisted in the Civil War with the 12th Indiana Volunteer Infantry out of Fort Wayne, Indiana. After the Battle of Missionary Ridge, Lucius was taken prisoner and sent to Andersonville Prison. He survived the ordeal though he nearly died. He met his wife, Elizabeth Loring, through his sisters who attended the seminary in Oxford, Ohio, with Elizabeth. They were married in Rising Sun in 1866. They lived in Rising Sun for a short time and then moved to Warsaw, Indiana, where Lucius was a druggist. Following the birth of their third child, they separated and Elizabeth returned to Rising Sun with the children.

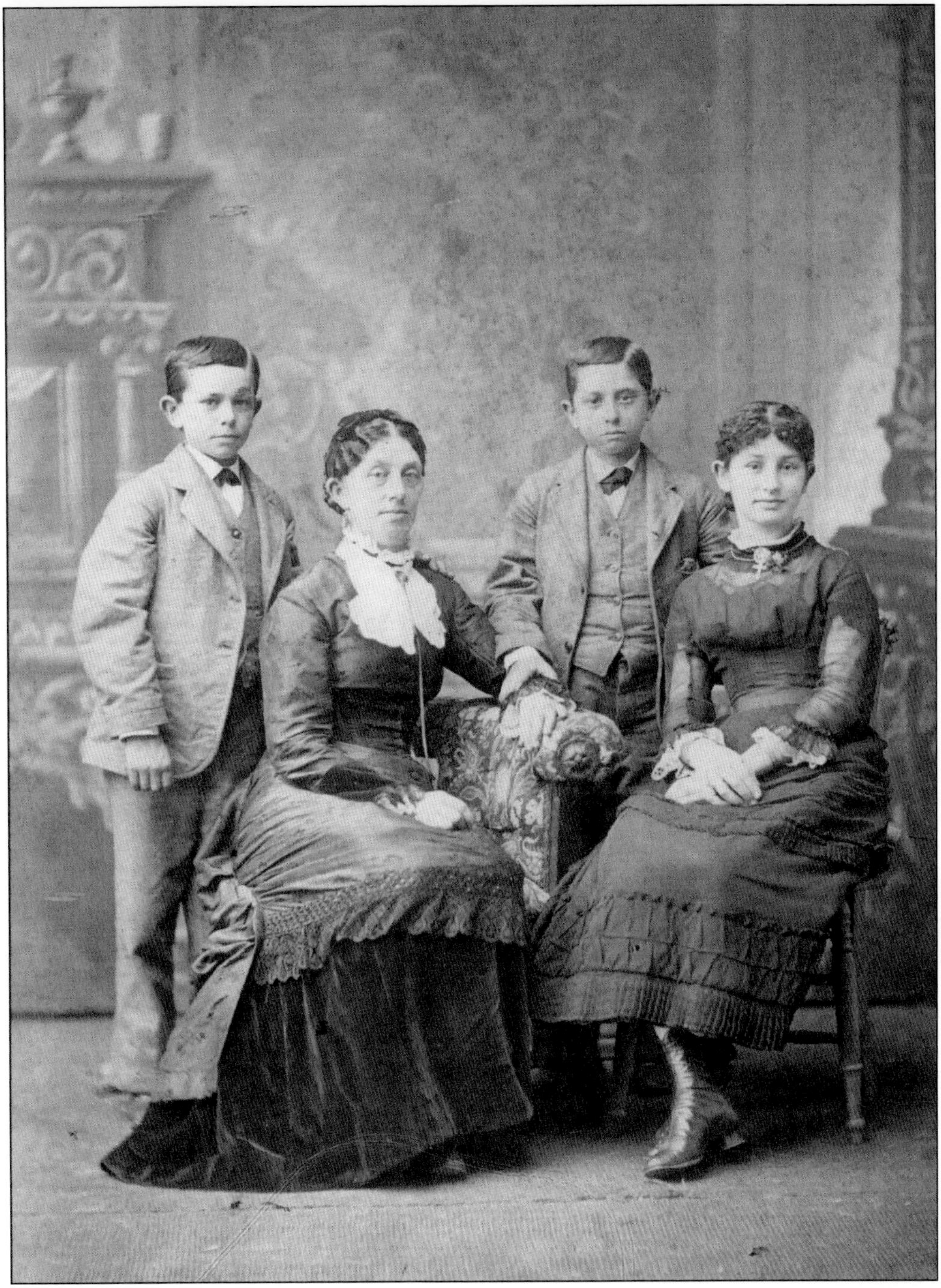

**Barbour Family, c. 1875.** Elizabeth Loring Barbour and her children are, from the left, as follows: Myron, Frank, and Jeannette. The family traveled to Aurora to have their portrait taken by Mr. Walton. A portrait of Jeannette Inslee Loring born in New York, 1818, and died in Rising Sun, 1896, hangs in the museum. She was the mother of Elizabeth Barbour. Jeannette was named after her grandmother. Frank's two oldest sons, Myron and Frank, served during World War I, Myron in the Aviation Corps and Frank with the Transportation Corps.

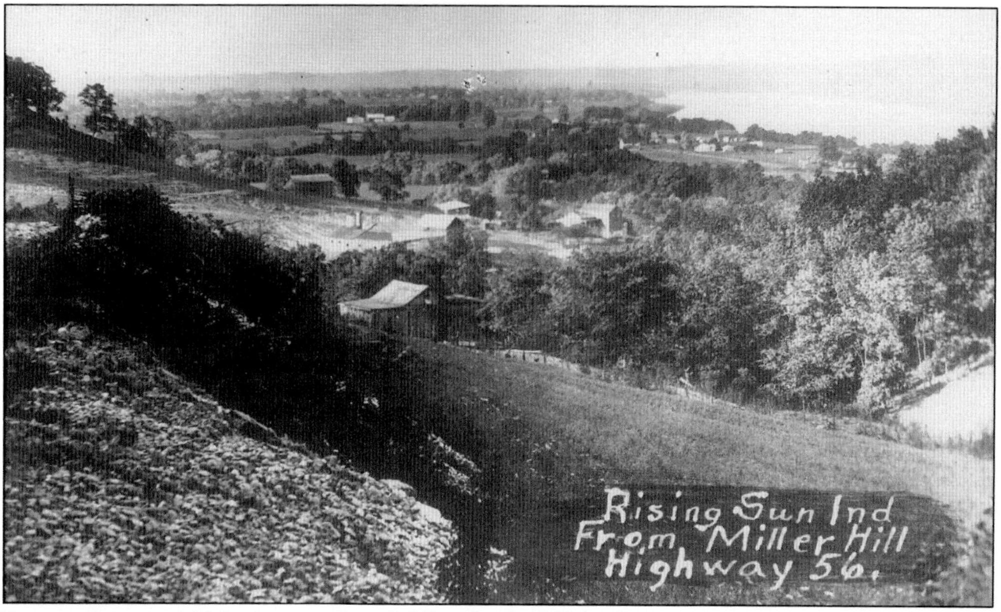


**RISING SUN, C. 1935.** A view from Miller Brick Hill looking into Rising Sun and the Ohio River. The picture was taken from Highway 56. Today Highway 56 makes a wide cut through the hill after crossing Arnold's Creek. This route takes you away from the river, while Highway 156 (Ohio River Scenic By-way) follows the river closely.

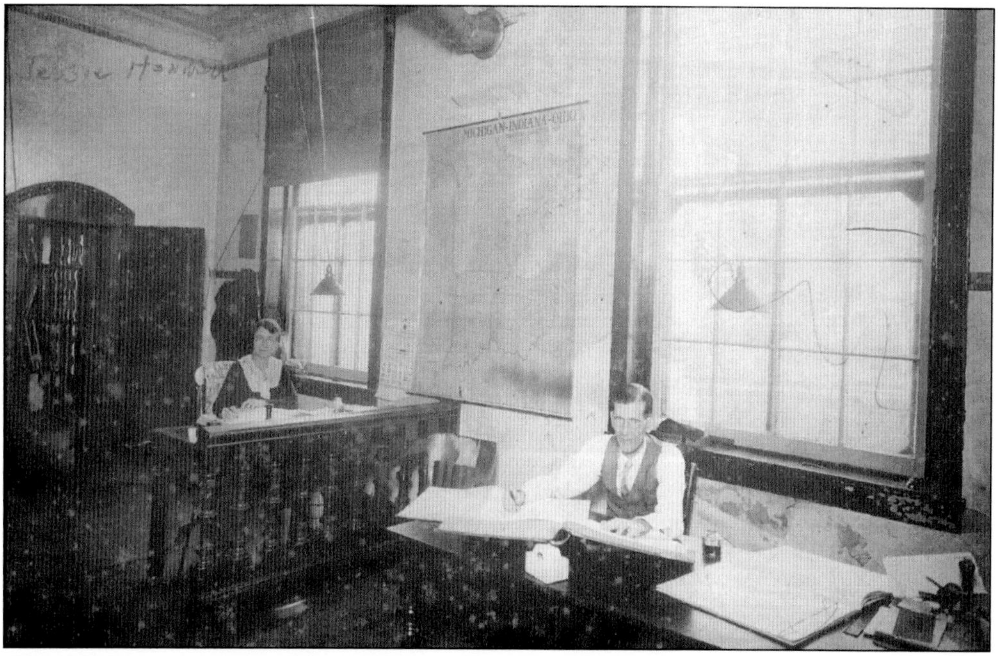

**EDGAR PENDRY, C. 1930S.** Edgar Pendry served two terms as Ohio County Auditor beginning in 1930 and was re-elected again in 1934. In the 1940s Mr. Pendry served as Clerk of the Ohio County Draft Board. After World War II began, he resigned and was replaced by Jessie Hannah, the woman in the photograph. Prior to his resignation from the Draft Board, he purchased the Ideal Restaurant from Estal Draut.

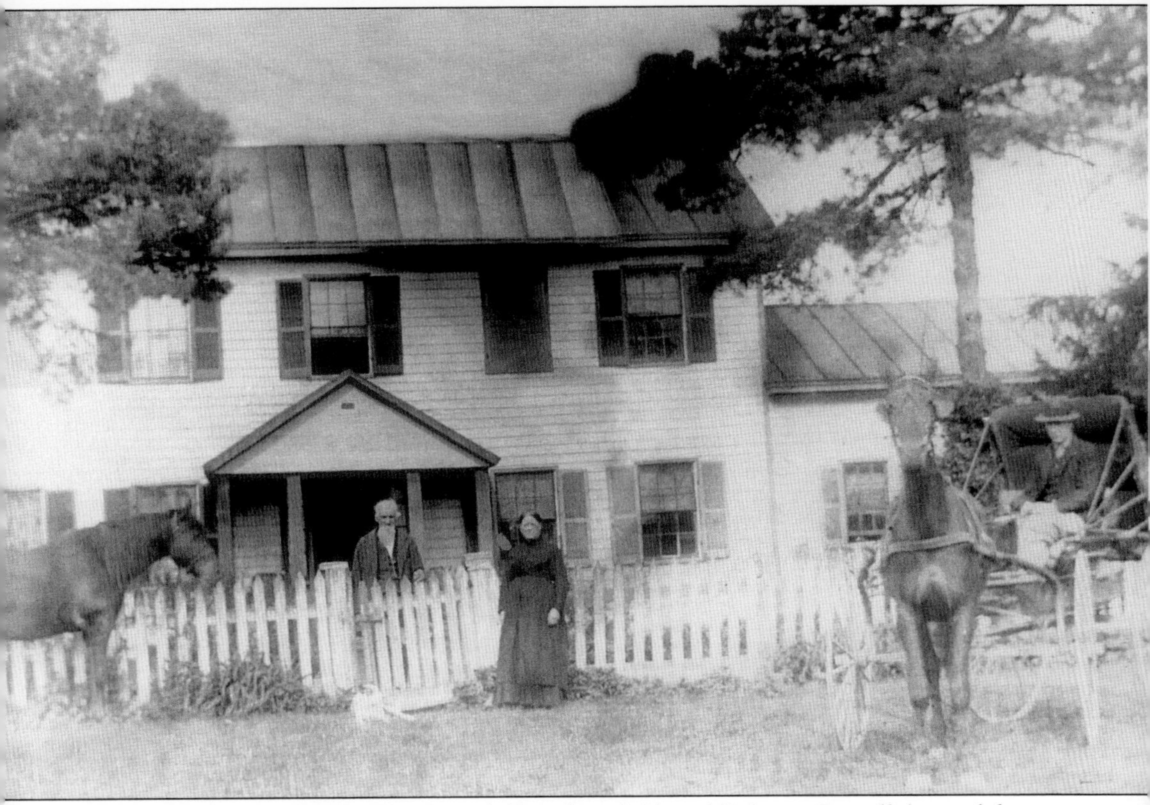

**DORRELL HOMESTEAD, 1888.** The Daniel (first from left) and Rebecca Dorrell (second from left) homestead was located at what is now 2749 Nelson Road. Daniel Dorrell, born in 1815, raised fine breeding horses and was credited with improving the stock in Ohio County. During the Civil War, Mr. Dorrell owned Wilson Blue Bull, a sorrel. This horse could run a mile in three minutes. The horse ran in races at fairs in the surrounding towns and never failed to come home the winner.

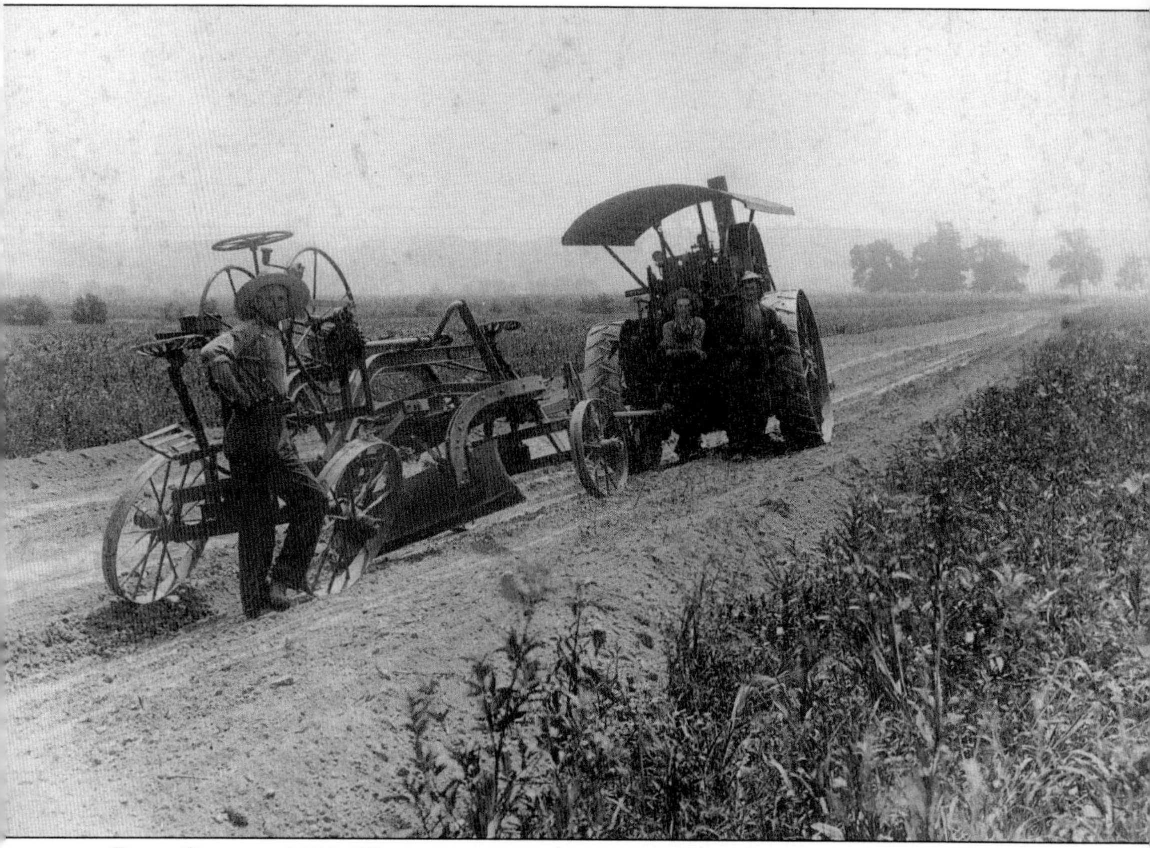

**Road Crew, c. 1910.** These men are working on an Ohio County road project. The thresher is hooked up to the road grader to pull it along the roads. The grader is obviously grading the roads to make them less bumpy. It must have been a difficult task for the grader with no power steering and no shock absorbers.

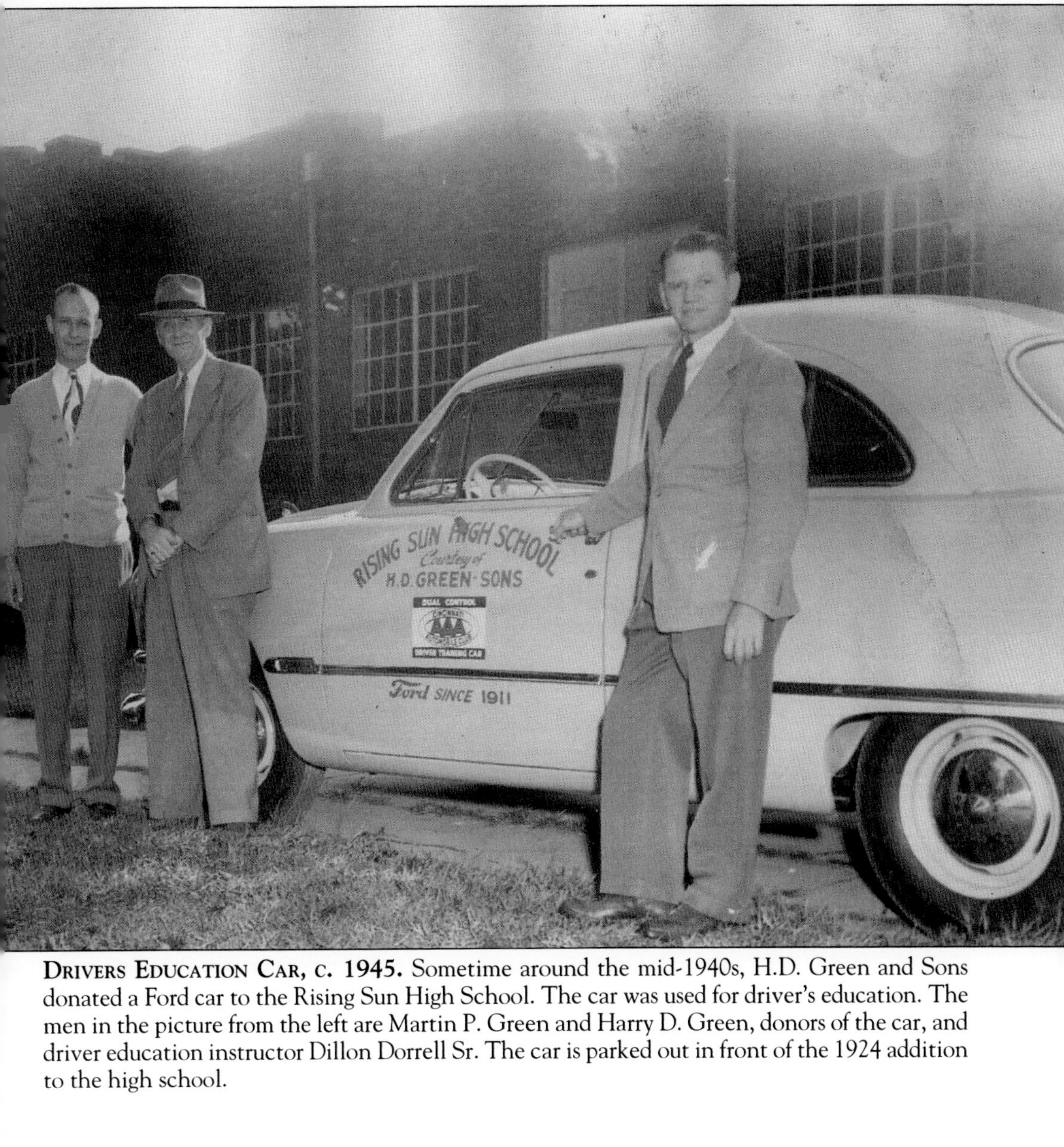


**Drivers Education Car, c. 1945.** Sometime around the mid-1940s, H.D. Green and Sons donated a Ford car to the Rising Sun High School. The car was used for driver's education. The men in the picture from the left are Martin P. Green and Harry D. Green, donors of the car, and driver education instructor Dillon Dorrell Sr. The car is parked out in front of the 1924 addition to the high school.

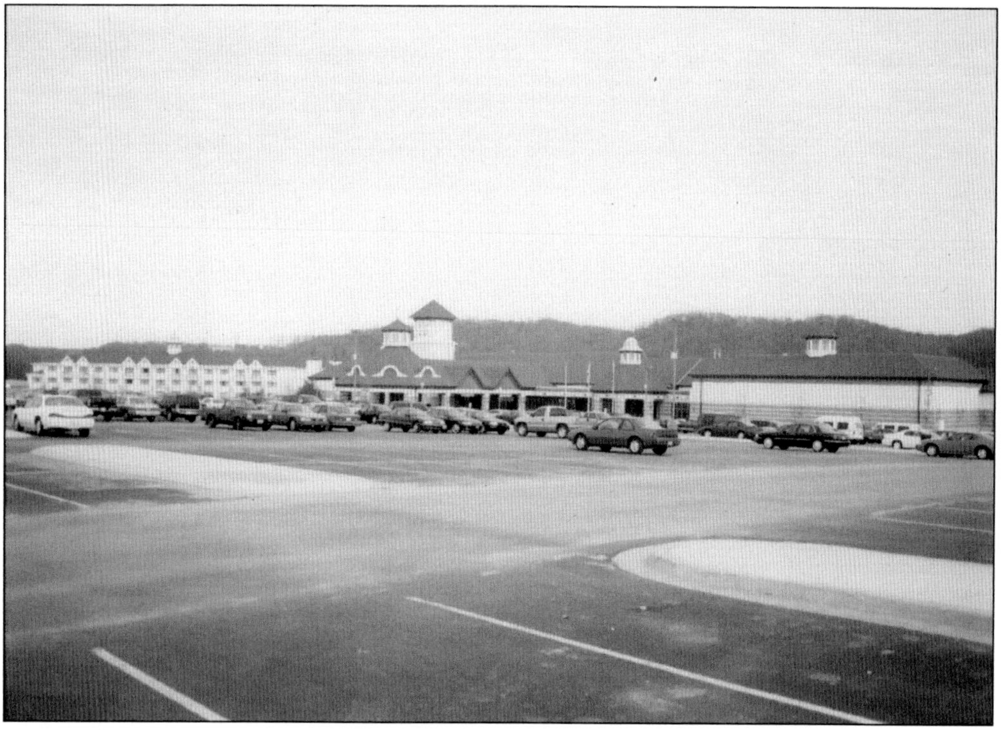

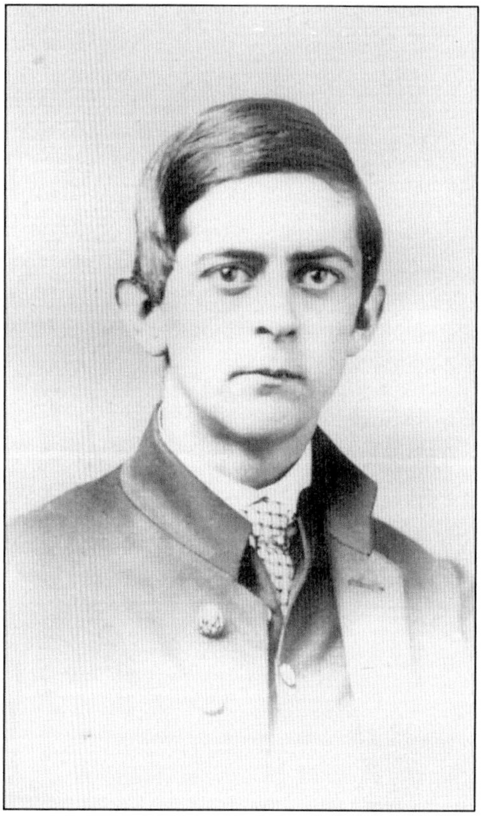

**GRAND VICTORIA CASINO & RESORT, MARCH 2001.** The Grand Victoria Casino & Resort opened in Rising Sun in 1996. The casino is the county's largest employer. Besides bringing big name entertainment such as Crystal Gayle and Englebert Humperdink to town, it has provided funding for a community pool, Main Street streetscape, a community center, and has allowed for many other improvements in the county. The casino has gaming sessions on the riverboat and offers an 18-hole golf course that opened in 2000.

**GEORGE B. COVINGTON, 1861.** At the age of 16 George B. Covington joined the 17th Indiana Volunteers under Colonel Hascal as a volunteer aid, for he was too young to enlist. Nearly three years later, he rose in rank to lieutenant and adjutant of the 17th Indiana Volunteers under Colonel Wilder. While part of Sherman's March to the Sea, George received a mortal wound near Dallas, Georgia. He died en route to Rising Sun, where he is buried. To honor him, his comrades named their camp the George B. Covington Camp, No. 69, Sons of Veterans, at Rising Sun.

**Leonard Cope Gibson, 1892.** At the age of five Leonard Gibson strikes a confident pose in Mr. Gamble's Aurora photographic studio. Leonard is the father of Roy Gibson and son of Mathias (Matt) Gibson. After receiving a degree from Purdue University, Leonard worked for the Maxwell Auto Company located in New Castle, Indiana. Upon his Uncle Harry Gibson's death, Leonard purchased his share in the G.B. Gibson's Sons Hardware store. Leonard and his son Roy sold the business in 1956.

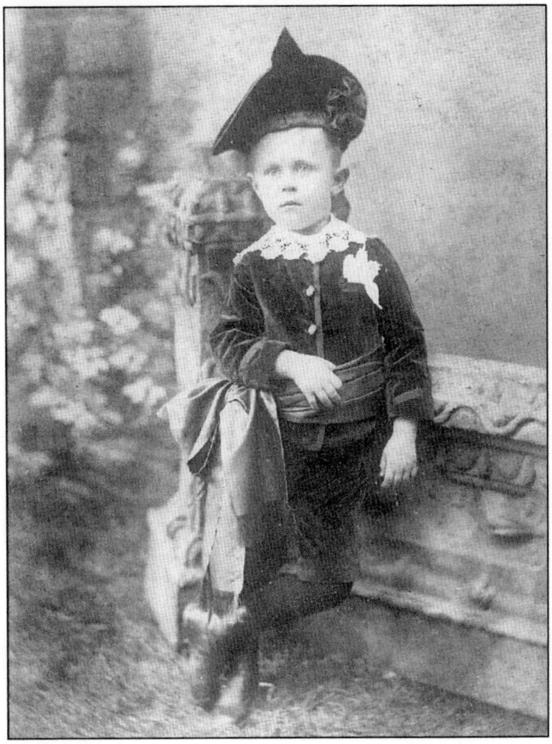

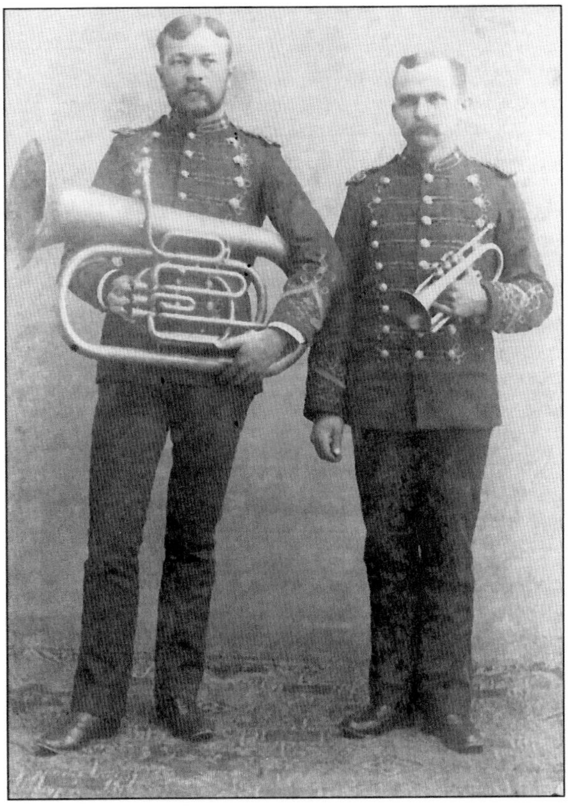

**Grant Hempill & Matt Gibson, 1890.** Matt Gibson was the son of George B. Gibson founder of the G.B. Gibson's Sons Hardware store. He was one of six brothers. The others were Will, Hugh, Harry, John, and Charles. Will was the only brother who never worked in the hardware store as he left Rising Sun. Matt died in 1922 while watching J.W. Whitlock race the *Hoosier Boy*.

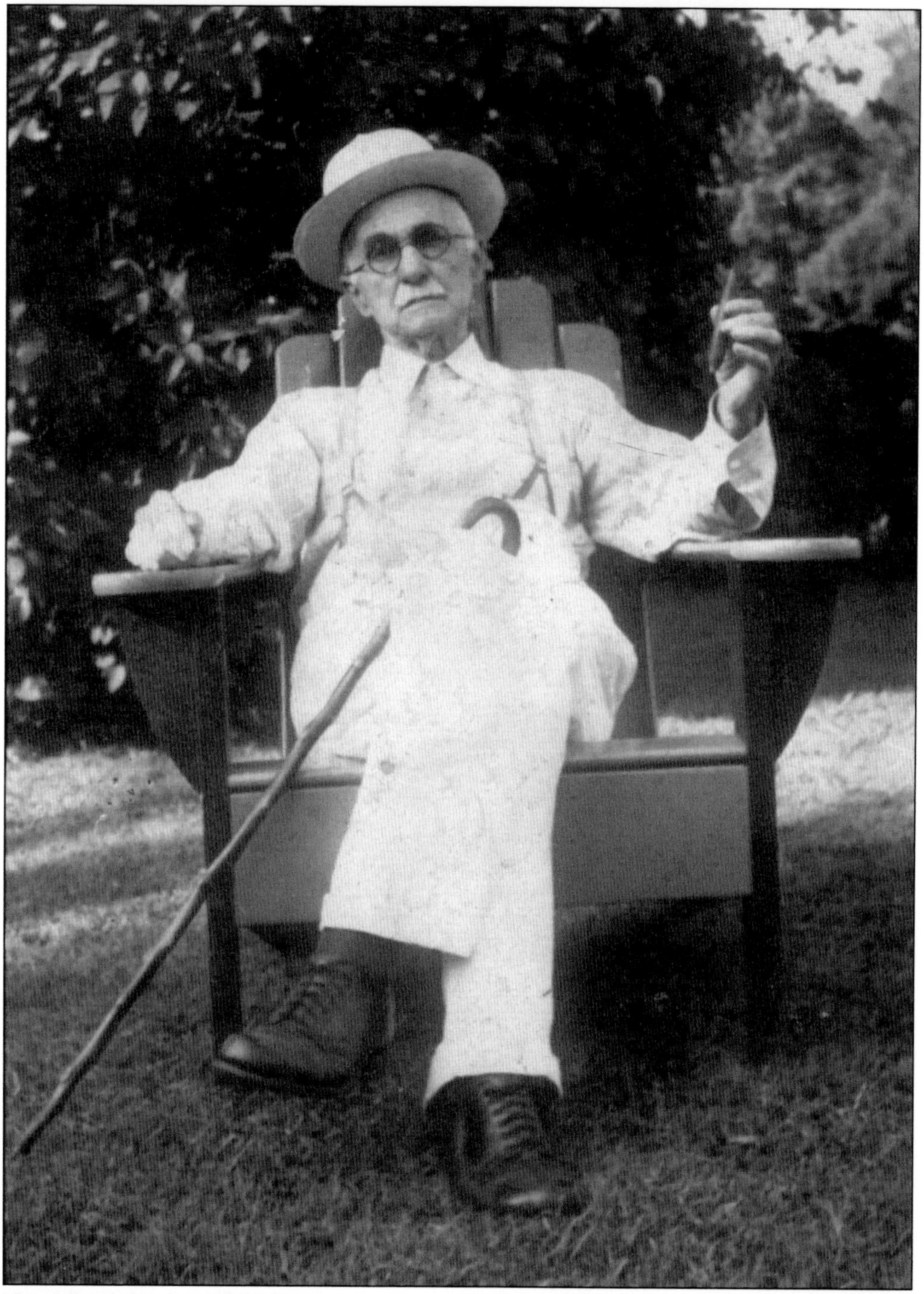

**HUGH ESPEY JR., C. 1940.** Hugh Stewert Espey Jr., born in Rising Sun in 1858, joined his father as a partner in 1879. The H.S. Espey & Son business dealt with groceries, provisions, and pork packing. Hugh Espey Jr. became known as Captain Espey due to the fact that he captained many a flatboat up and down the Ohio River loaded with provisions for the store. In the fire of 1885, Captain Espey's two-story brick house burned, as did many buildings on Main Street.